The
How-To Book of
SACRAMENTALS

The How-To Book of SACRAMENTALS

*Everything You Need to Know
But No One Ever Taught You*

Ann Ball

Our Sunday Visitor Publishing Division
Our Sunday Visitor, Inc.
Huntington, Indiana 46750

Nihil Obstat: Rev. Michael Heintz, *Censor Librorum*
Imprimatur: ✠ John M. D'Arcy
Bishop of Fort Wayne-South Bend
August 3, 2005

The *Nihil Obstat* and *Imprimatur* are official declarations that a book or pamphlet is free of doctrinal or moral error. No implication is contained therein that those who have granted the *Nihil Obstat* or *Imprimatur* agree with the contents, opinions, or statements expressed.

Our Sunday Visitor Publishing Division
Our Sunday Visitor, Inc.
200 Noll Plaza
Huntington, IN 46750

ISBN-13: 978-1-59276-096-1
ISBN-10: 1-59276-096-1 (Inventory No. T148)
LCCN: 2005930269
Cover design by Tyler Ottinger
Interior design by Sherri L. Hoffman
Unless otherwise indicated, all photos courtesy of the author. All photos used with permission.

PRINTED IN THE UNITED STATES OF AMERICA

CONTENTS

PREFACE — DEDICATION

Years ago, I was in one of our local Catholic bookstores and noticed a chaplet I had never seen before. An accompanying card explained how to pray it, but didn't give any other information as to where it came from. I asked the store owner, my friend Rocky Vaccaro, where it came from. He responded with a smile, "From a nice distributor in New York! But if you mean the history of it, I don't know. Why don't you find out and write a book about the sacramentals since we get questions about them all the time." I took his suggestion, and the result was the *Handbook of Catholic Sacramentals*.

Like Rocky, I am often asked about unusual sacramentals. This revised edition includes most of those in the previous edition, as well as others I have only learned about in the past few years.

In compiling the first edition, I was determined to write about all the sacramentals that existed. Fortunately, my friend Michael Miller, C.S.B., saved me from what would have been a fruitless quest by explaining that any bishop can declare a sacramental for his own diocese: there's no official "count" on sacramentals, so they cannot all be listed. This book, then, contains only a few of the many and varied blessings, actions, and objects of devotion known and used in the Church. I hope this text provides readers with sufficient information to display the beauty and variety of Catholic sacramentals . . . those things which, when well used, can provide for us a special touch of faith and draw us ever closer to Our Creator.

Sacramentals fascinated me even before I was Catholic. With my curious nature, they still provide me with a rich field of research. If you, the reader, have a favorite sacramental that is not mentioned in this volume, I would love to hear from you about it. Who knows, one day I may be working on yet another revision to this book.

We have made every effort to make this new edition more "user friendly." The reorganization of its contents and an extensive index will help the reader locate sacramentals included in this book, while the individual photos may help in identification of unknown sacramentals in the reader's possession.

Special thanks to my friends, Matt Bunson and Brent Devitt, for their help in writing some of the entries in this book; a special thanks also to my friends, Danielle and Robert Gonzalez, Carol and Lawrence LeLeux, and the Basilian Fathers Missions, for providing some images; and the Discalced Carmelite nuns in Colorado Springs, Colorado, for their help in securing the photo of the Sacred Hearts badge.

Finally, this book is dedicated to some friends who have been constant supporters and helpers in all my work: my sister and best friend, Julie Douglas; also, Karin Murthough, Pat Rensing, Bea Whitfill, and Jackie Lindsey.

The Author

SACRAMENTALS IN CATHOLIC THEOLOGY

Most Rev. J. Michael Miller, C.S.B.

Titular Archbishop of Vertara

Secretary of the Congregation of Catholic Education

Over a five-year period at the outset of his papal ministry, Pope John Paul II developed a "Theology of the Body" in his weekly addresses. By doing so, the Holy Father confronted head-on today's false spiritualism. Contrary to conventional wisdom as it might seem, the Church does not need a "more spiritual" Christianity, but precisely the opposite. Catholics must develop a less spiritual, but more bodily, more incarnational, and more sacramental vision in living their faith.

In this collection of popular devotions, Ann Ball develops the Pope's Theology of the Body by addressing a topic often relegated to the fringes of professional theological concern: the sacramentals. If the Holy Father was right — that the Incarnation places the body and material creation at the center of our faith[1]— then sacramentals deserve our serious attention.

The very fact of the Incarnation tells us that the material cosmos is not evil. It is the means through which God has chosen to share his life with us. Through the Eternal Son's taking flesh, "the terrible and tragic rip in the fabric of Creation is being reknit."[2] The Incarnation is an act of reversal of the Fall, bringing spirit and flesh together again. In God's redemptive hands, created realities can once more serve as instruments of grace.

Right from her beginning, the Church denounced those who held that we are saved independently of anything created. These early heretical dualists believed that God was hostile to creation. Christians answered this pessimism with a ringing affirmation of creation as "very good." Not establishing an abyss between God and humanity, the created world is a "sign" of God's presence. His plan is for *salus carnis*: salvation through the flesh of Jesus' passion and death, and salvation for our flesh through the resurrection of the body.

Because of this strongly incarnational perspective, the Catholic tradition has cultivated a sense that human beings should feel "at home in the world."[3] Likewise fundamental to this vision is the law of sacramentality: that bodily and created reality can mediate the divine. "The whole world is a sacrament," writes Peter Kreeft, "a sacred thing, a gift."[4] Since we cannot hear or see God directly, we rely on created realities to bring Him first to us, and us back to Him.

According to the Old Testament, the chosen people's access to God was always mediated — through the prophetic word, the priesthood, the Temple, the prescriptions of the Law. With the coming of Christ, God's love became palpable, humanly visible. In the Incarnate Son, the Trinity revealed Its love, mercy, faithfulness, simplicity, and openness. God's own way of saving us is, therefore, sacramental. He uses His creation to share with us His divine life, the foremost of which was the Son's human nature. By becoming brothers and sisters of the Word made flesh, humanity likewise returns to God in a similar bodily and visible way.

Since Jesus' ascension into heaven, the seven sacraments of the Church are the primary means we have of encountering God. Through these visible signs of invisible and life-giving grace, the human person encounters Christ in His Body, the Church. Instituted by Christ, who is the principal celebrant of every sacrament, each rite confers the unique grace it signifies when celebrated in the Church.

Prior to the high Middle Ages, the term "sacrament" (*sacramentum*) was also used for rites, prayer, and objects other than the seven sacraments. Not until the thirteenth century did the Church draw a clear distinction between "sacraments" and "sacramentals." Theologians then defined sacraments as those seven actions instituted by Christ that cause what they signify. Sacramentals, they maintained, resembled the sacraments, but were instituted by the Church and prepared the participants to receive grace.

These sacramentals (or "little sacraments") are as integral to an incarnational-bodily Christianity as are the seven major sacraments. Not just optional "add-ons," they are essential to experiencing the world through Catholic eyes and, even more importantly, with a Catholic heart. All creation speaks to us of God. Times and seasons will have their place in our devotion, since we are beings who live in history. Spaces, places, and special clothing are also indispensable. That's why we build beautiful cathedrals, set aside sanctuary areas, wear religious habits, and buy our children First Communion outfits.

Material objects and blessings enfold Catholic life as reminders of the mysteries of creation and redemption. "There is hardly any proper use of material things," declared Vatican II, "which cannot thus be directed toward the sanctification of men and women and the praise of God."[5] The variety of sacramentals is endless: blessing fields, walking the Way of the Cross, saying Rosaries, venerating crucifixes and statues in churches and homes.

WHAT IS A SACRAMENTAL?

After discussing the sacraments in their document on the sacred liturgy, the Fathers at Vatican II defined sacramentals as "sacred signs that bear a resemblance to the sacraments; they signify effects, particularly of a spiritual kind, which are obtained through the Church's intercession."[6] By making holy various occasions of life, the sacramentals dispose believers to receive divine life. They are "any object or prayer or action that can put us in touch with God's grace in Christ."[7] Like sacraments, sacramentals make available to us the stream of "divine grace which flows from the paschal mystery of the passion, death, and resurrection of Christ, the fountain from which all sacraments and sacramentals draw their power."[8]

From ancient times, the Church has pronounced her blessings over men and women, their activities, and the objects they use in everyday life. The minister of the sacramental action expresses the Church's faith in divine providence and prays that God grant a special grace to the person, either directly or through correct use of the object blessed.

First among the Church's sacramentals are blessings that invoke God's protection and beneficence. Praise of the God "who has blessed us in Christ with every spiritual blessing in the heavenly places" (Eph.1:3) is necessary to every sacramental blessing. Sacramentals are primarily blessings or actions using the Church's prayer. Through simple gestures and prayer, the Church implores God's blessing on persons or things — from making the Sign of the Cross on the brow of your children to wearing scapulars, honoring holy pictures, and lighting blessed candles.

An object is sacramental only because it has been so blessed by this intercessory prayer. Sacramentals are primarily prayers directed to God and, secondarily, through His response, a sanctification of persons or objects.

When a blessing sets apart a particular object exclusively for God, we commonly call it a "consecration." These blessings withdraw certain persons — or, more commonly, certain objects — from the everyday world and consecrate them totally to God and His service. The prayer offered asks that the objects be the bearers of a blessing for those who use them, occasions for encountering God.

ORIGIN OF SACRAMENTALS

In Christianity, believers sanctify their everyday lives primarily by presenting their bodies "as a living sacrifice, holy and acceptable" to God, their "spiritual worship" (Rom. 12:1). But they accompany their bodily gift with other visible signs, reminding themselves that God blesses every dimension of their lives. These sacred signs allow created realities to reveal the eternal by directing us heavenward. They saturate and sanctify human life "with divine energy."[9]

The Church has no definitive list of sacramentals; she multiplies them according to need. In medieval Europe, ecclesiastics threw a net of blessings over every dimension of life: from food to animals, from throats to vines. As the Church moves through history, we can look forward to a continual unfolding of new sacramentals that help to restore all things in Christ.

All authentic sacramentals are dependent on the seven great sacraments with which we are familiar. For example, the Eucharist, as the summit and source of Christian worship, is, the reason all food and meals are holy. Each commemorates the Eucharistic banquet. In the same way, all sacramentals that involve the sprinkling of water recall the cleansing power of Baptism. The sacramentals are "the small change, as it were, of the sacraments, the fringes (often picturesque) of sacramental life."[10] Intrinsically linked to the major sacraments, these "little sacraments" prepare us for their celebration and prolong their effects. That is their primary purpose.

Unlike the sacraments instituted by Christ, the Church herself creates sacramentals for another purpose: to sanctify everyday life. Although indirectly, even these sacramentals come from the Incarnate Word, who by his taking flesh consecrated the world, thereby making human activity a sign of his creative and redemptive presence. The Church gives us the sacramentals in service of the sacraments, of which they are imitations. As her actions, they express the Church's desire to sanctify humanity on its pilgrim journey. Through the sacramentals all created reality comes into the orbit of God's blessing, making all manner of people, situations and objects occasions of grace.

CELEBRATING SACRAMENTALS

For sacramentals closely connected to the Church's public worship, it is appropriate that her minister, whether deacon, priest, or bishop, perform the blessing. The bishop presides at the most solemn blessings, and the priest presides over the more ordinary ones in the community to which he ministers. That the 1983 Code of Canon Law allows the laity to administer certain sacramentals reflects Vatican II's recognition of the faithful's common priesthood.[11] Because of their special responsibility, parents may bless their children and catechists bless their students. In these and other situations laymen and laywomen may bless, thereby ministering certain sacramentals.

The right to establish official sacramentals belongs to the Holy See.[12] Without hesitation, however, the Pope grants requests to individual bishops and bishops' conferences to institute sacramentals appropriate to specific cultures and situations.

Whereas the seven sacraments confer sanctifying grace because they are actions of Christ himself, the sacramentals prepare us to cooperate with that grace. In traditional theological language, the sacramentals are efficacious *ex opere operantis Ecclesiae*; that is, they bring forth spiritual fruits by virtue of the Church's intercessory prayer and the recipient's willing cooperation in faith and love.

When a medal or a scapular is blessed, it does not itself become a cause of grace. What happens is that God responds to our petition to give special graces when the faithful use these things with the proper dispositions.[13] The sacramentals provide actual graces that prepare the soul to receive an increase of sanctifying grace, an intensification of friendship between God and the individual. Although sacramentals have primarily a spiritual purpose, they are directed towards the whole person, body and soul. Through them we are often aided in our temporal needs: restored health, pleasant weather and abundant harvests.[14]

The use of sacramentals obliges the participants to continue deepening their relationship with God. Without such a commitment, sacramentals become objects or practices that people manipulate to extort divine help without submitting to conversion. Sacramentals are not charms adopted to protect us from physical and spiritual harm but means by which we are to grow in faith, hope, and love.

PASTORAL CONCERNS

Contemporary society is uncomfortable with religious ritual because of its connection with the magical. Why bother to bless a person or a thing? Christian worship, they say, is essentially a spiritual matter. Sacramentals, with their embarrassing tangibility and emphasis on externals, seem far removed from Jesus' demand for worship "in spirit and in truth" (Jn. 4:23). No wonder sacramentals are marginalized, considered merely folkloric or colorful holdovers from a bygone era.

Non-Catholics — and even some Catholics — object as well that sacramentals and devotional practices contribute to a kind of "automatism" in our relationship with God. These challengers accuse us of holding that by just doing something, going somewhere, or reciting fixed prayers, we imagine ourselves to be saved. Critics think that this focus on "little sacraments" in Catholicism does not promote interior conversion of heart, but instead settles for a set of pious exercises that supposedly guarantees its users spiritual and temporal results. Everything of that nature, from lighting candles to sprinkling holy water to visiting Fátima, is frowned upon. These gestures are too easy, too external, and too worldly to be taken seriously as truly religious practices! For the critics, using sacramentals is at best superstition, and at worst idolatry.

It is perhaps true that, in earlier days, a mistaken worldview led some people to think that a blessed object contained the power of the person who blessed it. Even now, that same attitude sometimes shows up in the use of medals, Rosaries, Lourdes water, and so on. Who could deny that such things might "represent a superstitious quest of an effectiveness unconnected with faith"?[15] On the other hand, these practices more often reveal a spirit of genuine faith and trust in God's providence. Those who love and use the Church's sacramentals should never forget their real purpose: to lead us to praise and love of God. If we use them only to secure benefits, usually of a temporal kind, then, indubitably, we are abusing the sacramentals.

GUIDELINES FOR USING SACRAMENTALS WISELY

The Fathers at Vatican II expressed their hope that the Church would adapt her sacramentals to present-day needs. Accordingly, they recommended "the sacramentals are to be revised, account being taken of the primary principle of enabling the faithful to participate intelligently, actively and easily."[16]

Sacramentals feed popular piety, those forms of religious expression not part of official Catholic worship. Overemphasizing these nonliturgical practices can lead to a distortion of true religion and a sterile piety. (For example, a good Lent means much more than simply having a priest smear your forehead with ashes at its outset!) The Church must root out what is obviously superstitious or false from her use of sacramentals.

In renewing our use of sacramentals, therefore, Catholics would do well to attend to the following five guidelines.[17] By doing so, they will avoid either exaggerating or diminishing their significance to Catholic life.

- Every form of Christian devotion ought to have a *biblical imprint*. As the Bible becomes increasingly familiar to Catholics, the sacramental blessing prayers should draw their inspiration, even their wording, from the Word of God. That is why, in all her blessings, the Church encourages reading from the Sacred Scriptures. In addition, the activities or objects "sacramentalized" should be intimately related to the great events of salvation history, and not just our private, temporal needs.

- The Second Vatican Council extolled the practices of piety and devotion that have nourished Catholic life for centuries. But it also wisely advised that we use sacramentals *in harmony with the sacred liturgy.* In order to conform to the norms of Vatican II, we should make a special effort so that sacramentals "harmonize with the liturgical seasons, accord with the sacred liturgy, are in some way derived from it, and lead the people to it."[18] Ann Ball's arrangement of some sacramentals and devotional practices into those associated with the Advent-Christmas cycle and others with the Lent-Easter cycle follows this guideline. Furthermore, we ought not treat the principal acts of the liturgy as mere occasions for using sacramentals. Christ's Eucharistic Sacrifice remains the heart of all worship. Would it be true devotion to go to Mass on Palm Sunday just to get blessed palms to braid for the crucifix over the bed?

- Not all sacramentals appeal to every person, culture, or age. They must be *pertinent to the life-situation* of the believer. Blessing the fields is not likely to appeal to an urban attorney. Except for those sacramentals most intimately tied to liturgical celebrations — holy water, ashes, palms, crucifixes, candles, etc. — the Church does not favor any particular sacramentals.

Certain sacramentals, valid in themselves, may be very suitable for one period of history or culture and less suitable for another. Many of our present sacramentals will undoubtedly remain. Holy water and the Rosary are not likely to fall into disuse. Other sacramentals, such as the use of incense, may be more widely revived in the future. Yet others remain to be discovered.

- Removal of the scandal of division and the restoration of full communion among Christians is the goal of the ecumenical movement. To achieve this, we should now be more *ecumenically sensitive* than we were before Vatican II. Without in any way minimizing or discouraging use of sacramentals, the Church asks us to avoid any exaggeration in our devotional practices that could mislead other Christians about true Catholic doctrine. How others understand the sacramental blessings and practices that we celebrate must always be taken into account if we are to be responsible evangelizers.
- Sacramentals should bespeak a *noble simplicity*. The Council Fathers thought that certain practices had made "the nature and purpose" of the sacramentals "far from clear."[19] If cluttered by repetitious prayers, individualistic piety and lack of participation, they should be eliminated. Sacramentals that demand complicated formulas, odd practices or difficult duties to perform are best abandoned. As signs of the sacred, sacramentals should find a clear echo in believers' hearts and minds. They are not a trickster's guide to heaven.

Following the lead of John Paul II, parents, teachers, and pastors ought to encourage the use of appropriate sacramentals within their families, schools, and parishes. Catholic life and devotion, which takes all its energy from God's betrothal of humanity in Christ, rests on the firm foundation of the incarnation and its spillover effects. Ann Ball has unearthed for us a treasure trove of devotional and sacramental riches. From this vast Catholic storehouse the wise steward can bring out old sacramentals and dream about new possibilities.

ENDNOTES

1. See John Paul II's writings collected by the Daughters of St. Paul in *Original Unity of Man and Woman* (Boston, 1981); *Blessed Are the Pure in Heart* (Boston, 1983); *Reflections on* Humanae Vitae (Boston, 1984); *The Theology of Marriage and Celibacy* (Boston, 1986).

2. Thomas Howard, *Evangelical Is Not Enough* (San Francisco, 1984), 29.

3. Laurence F.X. Brett, *Redeemed Creation: Sacramentals Today* (Wilmington, 1984), 12.

4. Peter Kreeft, *Fundamentals of the Faith: Essays in Christian Apologetics* (San Francisco, 1988), 284.

5. *Sacrosanctum Concilium*, 61.

6. *Sacrosanctum Concilium*, 60. See also the 1983 Code of Canon Law's definition: "Somewhat in imitation of the sacraments, sacramentals are sacred signs by which spiritual effects especially are signified and are obtained by the intercession of the Church" (canon 1166).

7. Patrick Bishop, "Sacramentals," *The New Dictionary of Sacramental Worship*, ed. Peter E. Fink (Collegeville, 1991), 1115.

8. *Sacrosanctum Concilium*, 61.

9. Louis Bouyer, *Rite and Man* (Notre Dame, 1963), 67.

10. *A New Catechism* (New York, 1971), 256.

11. Code of Canon Law (1983), canon 1168; *Lumen Gentium*, 10.

12. Code of Canon Law (1983), canon 1167:1.

13. Cyprian Vagaggini, *Theological Dimensions of the Liturgy* (Collegeville, 1976), 88.

14. J.R. Quinn, "Sacramentals," *New Catholic Encyclopedia* (New York, 1967), vol. 12, 791.

15. Jean Evanou, "Blessings and Popular Religion," in *The Church at Prayer, vol. 3, The Sacraments*, ed. A.G. Martimort (Collegeville, 1987), 284.

16. *Sacrosanctum Concilium*, 79.

17. Pope Paul VI applied four of these guidelines to renewing devotion to the Blessed Virgin Mary in *Marialis Cultus* (1974) nn. 29-38. They can, however, also serve as an authentic guide for the proper devotional use of sacramentals.

18. *Sacrosanctum Concilium*, 13.

19. *Sacrosanctum Concilium*, 62.

SACRAMENTALS IN THE ORIENTAL RITES

Rev. Anselm Walker

ST. BASIL'S BYZANTINE CATHOLIC CENTER
HOUSTON, TEXAS

As Pope Pius XI said, "The Church is neither Latin, nor Greek, nor Slav, but Catholic." This undoubted fact has not penetrated the thought of many Catholic savants, let alone theologians and especially canonists, however; so it is therefore heartening to see a work such as the present one, inviting an exposition of the Oriental perspective on sacramentals alongside of that of the Latin-Western one, for the sake of comparison and contrast. By so doing, we begin to live up to our name "Catholic"— i.e., all-inclusive.

RITES

In the One Holy Catholic and Apostolic Church, in which we profess our faith Sunday after Sunday and feast after feast, there are, besides the predominant Western Latin rite, some nine Eastern or Oriental rites ("Oriental" here means the Near East, the Balkans, and Eastern Europe). The largest of these rites is the Byzantine, originating in the modern Turkish city of Istanbul, whose ancient name was Byzantion or Byzantium, a Greek fishing village established by Megarans from Megara, on the Gulf of Corinth. In A.D. 320, the Emperor Constantine I moved the capital of the Roman Empire to Byzantion, christening it "New Rome." It also became known as Constantinople very soon after its foundation. From 320 to 1453, it remained the capital of the

Roman Empire, and its liturgical rites became those of the whole Greek-speaking East.

To most of us, "rite" means a ceremony, or a complex of ceremonies, by which a community engages in the concerted action of honoring some person or event. Among Christians, these persons are the Holy Trinity and the mysteries that were wrought through the Incarnation, Life, Death, and Resurrection of Our Lord Jesus Christ. These include the Mass — the Divine Liturgy in the East — the sacraments, and the sacramentals. But "rite" also includes the theology flowing from a given liturgical tradition, its art, architecture, its spirituality and its canon law; i.e., a whole Christian culture. Each rite in the past has produced — when it was allowed to — whole Christian cultures, all of which deserve our respect, our affection, and our study. In Christ, St. Paul says, "are hid all the treasures of wisdom and knowledge" (Col. 2:3), and "He is the head of the body, the church" (1:18) — therefore, in the Church, His body and bride, the same fullness of wisdom and knowledge is found.

We must always remember that most Christians who worship according to the Oriental rites are separated juridically from the Catholic Church. Only the Maronites are totally Catholic. The East Syrian Chaldeans may soon become so, if they are allowed to continue unhindered. In this treatise we will deal principally with the Byzantine rite, followed by some ten million Catholics and some 230 million orthodox.

SACRAMENTALITY

Catholic Christianity, both Eastern and Western, is a historical religion. In other words, it takes time seriously but redeems it by celebrating at specific times and dates, thus linking the here and now — sacramentally and mystically, through celebration — with past events in God's economy visible among His people. At the same time it is linked, through eager expectation and divine promises, to the consummation of all things — i.e., the life of the world to come. All this is done by, through, and with the Holy Spirit. The key point in this process is the Incarnation of God in Christ.

Only historical Christianity takes the Incarnation in all its content, applications, and implications seriously. By contrast, Reformation Christianity — where it has not surreptitiously reclaimed parts of its heritage lost in the name of the "Salvation by Faith Alone" theory — finds most of its slanders of "paganism" in the historic understanding of the Incarnation. For example, the term "mother of God," applied to the Holy Virgin to safeguard the divinity of Christ, is reviled as pagan. In this sense, most biblical evangelicals are, in effect, "Nestorians," because they deny that a woman can give birth in the flesh to God for man's salvation, thus also denying that "God has shed His own blood" to purchase the Church.

But if Christ is the wisdom and the power of God, in whom dwells the fullness of the Godhead bodily — and in Him we are being filled unto all the fullness of God — and if the Church is the fullness of Christ whom He fills up completely, then Jesus Christ is the first, fundamental, basic, and primordial sacrament. In Him, God condescends to us and we ascend to the Father through the Son, by the Holy Spirit. In the Church, the body of Christ, we have the sacraments that communicate to us that fullness of Grace that was and is in Christ. So, too, St. Leo the Great, probably the greatest theologian ever to sit on the throne of St. Peter, tells us, "That which was present in Our Lord has now passed over into the sacraments." Besides the sacraments — the most blessed of which, the Eucharist, signifies and contains and communicates Christ's glorified body and blood substantially, really, and truly along with His soul and divinity — we have a whole complex of sacrament-like entities. These sacrament-like entities are visible things that dispose us through humility, faith, hope, and charity to receive the grace of God and to hear, assimilate, and apply the teaching of Christ to ourselves and to society.

As the brilliant Russian philosopher Vladimir Soloviev (1858-1900) said, "The faith of Catholics and Orthodox is the same, for what is holy to one is holy to the other."

THE SIGN OF THE CROSS

The most obvious and frequently used sacramental is the Sign of the Cross. In the Byzantine rite, it is made by joining the thumb and the next two fingers to represent the Holy Trinity. The last two fingers are folded down on the palm of the right hand to represent the two natures in Christ. Formerly in Russia, and still among the "Old Believers" (also known as *Raskolniki*, or "schismatics," because they split from the state church as a result of the liturgical reforms of the Patriarch Nikon in the mid 1600s), this order is reversed. The thumb and the next finger are joined while the next three fingers are held down over the palm. The symbolism is then reversed. There are over twenty million of these people in Russia today — there are several parishes of them in this country. With the fingers of the right hand so disposed, one touches the forehead, then the upper sternum, then the right shoulder and finally the left. Some believers touch their hearts instead of the left shoulder. While making the Sign of the Cross, the same invocation is made as in the West. At the beginning of the Divine Liturgy it is made while the celebrant intones, "Blessed is the Kingdom of the Father and of the Son and of the Holy Spirit." Other offices begin with "Blessed is Our God now and always . . . etc."

The Sign of the Cross is made continually in the course of Byzantine worship. As often as the Holy Trinity is invoked, which is very often, the Sign of the Cross is made. When the censer is swung in one's direction it is made, as well as when one's own devotion prompts it. The East is much more spontaneous in these matters than the West.

There are blessings by the celebrant often during the liturgy. In blessing the faithful, he disposes the fingers of his right hand in such way as to form *I. C. X. C.*, Our Lord's initials. He makes the

Sign of the Cross with the Gospel book over the faithful when he finishes singing the Gospel. He does the same with the chalice and paten at the end of the offertory procession. He makes the same gesture with the chalice over the worshipers twice after Holy Communion.

If a Bishop is celebrating, he makes the Sign of the Cross with the *Dikerion*, symbolizing the two natures in Christ, and the *Trikerion*, symbolizing the three persons of the Holy Trinity. These candelabra — the three branches in the right and the two in the left — are raised over the head of the bishop, brought down paralleling each other, then brought up and crossed before his face. Needless to say, there are lighted candles in both candelabra while this is being done. Usually this gesture is repeated toward the four points of the compass. This is done at least three times during the course of the liturgy, and may be made at least twice more depending on the occasion and the desire of the bishop. While blessing, the bishop chants, "O Lord, look down from Heaven and visit this vine, which your own right hand has planted." At the end of each of these invocations, the people sing in Greek, "Unto many years, O Master — *Eti polla eti despota.*" These candelabra are borne before the bishop by deacons or lesser clergy, who hold them with humeral veils when the bishop is not using them. Otherwise, they are placed on the back of the altar alongside the seven-branched candelabra that is always there.

One often sees bishops and priests blessing, outside of church, with both hands with their fingers disposed as are the candles on the *dikerion* and *trikerion,* three fingers on the right hand held erect and two on the left. With these they imitate the motions of a bishop when he is blessing liturgically.

Needless to say, the Sign of the Cross signifies for them — as for us — the Trinity, the Incarnation, the Redemption, and much more. Among the other Oriental rites, the Sign of the Cross is made as Latin Catholics make it, except that the Syrian Jacobites often make it with the middle finger only to emphasize their

Monophysitic belief that in Our Lord is but one person and one nature.

POSTURES

Historical Christian worship is "Catholic" not only in the sense that it teaches all the truths all the time to all men of sincerity and goodwill, but also in the sense that it engages the whole man in its worship — intellect, will, voice, and body — while it emphasizes all man's senses in the adoration process. Where this ancient Christian system and pedagogy have remained in effect, the Church has held her own; where they have disintegrated, her teaching efforts have been fragmented, dispensed, and have become ineffectual. Two modern slogans express this rather pointedly, but accurately: 1) "If it feels good, do it"; and 2) "Do whatever you are comfortable with." This is secular humanism at its most blatant.

Man worships God for God's glory, not for man's comfort. In Oriental Christian worship, the predominant posture is standing. This is because standing recalls the resurrection of Christ into which the Christian has been initiated by Baptism and continues to participate in by Holy Communion and other liturgical acts. In Byzantine-rite churches, when they are arranged according to tradition, there are no pews. Chairs are available for the elderly and the infirm and one stands every Sunday continuously from Easter to Pentecost to express the resurrection. During Lent, prostrations are in order, especially when the beautiful prayer of St. Ephraim for humility is recited. Kneeling is in order at the kneeling prayers for the vespers of Pentecost. The Orthodox now begin to kneel during the Invocation to the Holy Spirit during the Anaphora of the Divine Liturgy to emphasize their rather recently introduced belief that the invocation *Epiklesis* effects the consecration, not the actual words of consecration as Catholics believe. The layperson in the nave of the church may prostrate or kneel, as his or her devotion prompts.

Prostration before the holy chalice, just before receiving Holy Communion, is a common practice. The especially devout may even prostrate every time the Holy Trinity is invoked at the several *ekphoneses* of the Divine Liturgy. Bows from the shoulders and from the waist are also made at such times by all present.

KISSING

Kissing objects of devotion is used much more in the Byzantine rite than in the West. On entering the church, one kisses the ikon and/or ikons on the *Anatogion* to salute the saints in their holy images. One may also touch the ikons with one's forehead as a gesture of reverence and of trying to acquire the mind of Christ from his saints. The Kiss of Peace has long since disappeared for the laity in the Byzantine rite, but it is given by the clergy in the *sitar* (sanctuary) at a pontifical liturgy, or when two or more priests concelebrate. It is a pious custom for those who communicate to kiss the base of the chalice and the hand of the priest after communicating; they go immediately to kiss the ikon of the Savior to express their Chalcedonian orthodoxy, as well as to honor the teaching of the seventh general council on the veneration of the Holy Ikons. At the end of Orthos, as the great Doxology is being sung, the celebrant brings the book of the Gospels down into the nave of the church, where all present venerate Christ present in his Word by bowing, crossing themselves, and kissing the holy volume. During the entrances of the liturgy with the Gospel book (little) and the chalice and paten (great), the faithful who are within reach often kiss the hem of the priest's *philon* (chasuble) as he passes them in procession. During Lent, on weekdays when the liturgy is celebrated, the great entrance is made with the presanctified gifts (body and blood); the devout laity often lay down in the path of the processing clergy, so that these have to step over them.

Something of this has been carried over into the regular Sunday and festal liturgies when the faithful kneel down in the entrances, even though at the great entrance the gifts are not yet consecrated. At the end of the liturgy, all come forward to receive the *antidoron* (blessed bread) and to kiss the cross and the hand of the celebrant. It is also a pious custom for those members of the family who have not communicated to kiss the lips of the one who has done so, and thus to participate in Holy Communion. At Byzantine funerals, as the beautiful canon of St. John Damascene is being sung, all present file by the casket and give a farewell kiss to the departed. (Now this is done by placing a small ikon on the chest of the departed, and that is kissed instead of the lips.)

HOLY WATER

Epiphany (Theophany) — feast of the Jordan and the feast of Holy Lights, January 6 — is devoted to the Baptism of Our Lord. On this day water is blessed, preferably at streams, lakes, bays, and gulfs, to honor the occasion. Thus on this day the Greeks bless the Aegean, the Adriatic, the Mediterranean, the Gulf of Mexico, and holy-water fonts. In Russia, holes in the form of 27 are cut in the frozen rivers, and the blessing is performed over these. The service is rather lengthy and includes the ceremony of tossing the cross into the blessed body of water, to be retrieved by swimmers who receive a prize for their efforts. This ceremony supplies holy water for the coming year. The faithful use holy water in much the same way that it is used in the West.

All homes in the parish are blessed after this feast, and again after Easter. In Byzantine areas, the clergy go in procession to perform these blessings. In some places, this blessing in its "lesser" form is also repeated on the sixth of every month.

HOLY OIL

As in the West, chrisms are of various kinds and grades. The highest is the *Holy Myron,* consisting of almost 100 ingredients, which is blessed on various occasions by the various patriarchs of the different Byzantine jurisdictions. Receiving Myron from the prelate acknowledges that one recognizes his jurisdiction.

Another kind of holy oil is *prayer oil,* blessed each time the anointing of the sick is celebrated by the chief celebrant. When the liturgical books are followed, it requires seven priests, though one can suffice. At vespers on all great feasts, Lytia is celebrated, which includes the blessing of wheat, wine, and oil as food to be consumed at the all-night vigil service. The oil is used to anoint all those present, either after the Lytia or after the Divine Liturgy the next day. On some feasts, the faithful may be blessed with oil from the lamp burning before the ikon of the feast. A small mixture of oil and fragrances is poured over the departed just before burial.

HOLY FOODS

At every liturgy, the portion of the *Prosphora* (loaf) not placed in the *diskos* (paten) is sliced up and blessed during the Liturgy when the Holy Father and the hierarchs are commemorated. This is the *antidoron,* as mentioned above. It is passed out to all comers at the end of the liturgy. On Easter Night, a large *Prosphora* is blessed and remains on display during Bright Week (Easter Week). On Thomas Sunday (Sunday in White), it is sliced and passed out. On Easter night after the Matins and the Liturgy of the Resurrection, a family brings a basket with bread, meat, cheese, and special Easter sweets (*kulich* and *postka*), and these are blessed for the Easter breakfast that follows the liturgical services. On the feast of the Transfiguration, grapes are blessed and eaten, and on the feast of Our Lady's Falling Asleep (Assumption), sweet basil and other herbs are blessed and used in seasoning various dishes.

OTHER SACRAMENTALS

Every Byzantine-rite Christian should receive a blessed cross at Baptism, which is to be worn for the rest of his life. Medals are made of the small copies of ikons and blessed and worn. Prayer ropes, *chatkies,* or *konvoskinous* are made and blessed to be a part of the monastic habit, "swords of the spirit." On those, the Jesus prayer is recited. Flowers from the *Plachnitza Epitaphios* — Holy Shroud, for the lamentations at the tomb of Christ — or from before the ikon of Our Lady, for the chanting of the *Akathistos* Hymn on the last Saturday of Lent, are taken by those worshipers, as well as candles from those services and the resurrection procession on Easter morning, and kept as sacramentals in their homes. Palms blessed on Palm Sunday are placed over the Holy Ikons. Among the Ukrainians, beautiful towels of linen are hand-embroidered and draped around the tops of ikons both at home and in the churches. Ikons of Our Lord, Our Lady, and the Holy Mysteries of the Liturgical Year are painted (literally, "written"). The boards and brushes, paints, and painters of these are blessed before the ikon is begun. Every Byzantine house should have an ikon corner, which holds the family ikons with their towels, a hand censer, holy water, the prayer book, the family Bible, etc., and before it the family conducts its prayers. Ikons are the wedding presents, and on their backs are recorded births, baptisms, and the wedding of the family being founded. Parents bless their children on the first day of school with the family ikon; brides are so blessed, as are young men upon entering the armed services and on similar occasions. When entering Byzantine homes, one first salutes the holy ikons and then greets one's hosts. When entering a church, one should venerate the ikons before beginning one's own devotions.

In Byzantine areas, small wayside shrines containing ikons often dot the countryside, and one is expected to salute them as one passes. Ikons are literally everywhere to remind the Byzantine faithful that they are always surrounded by a "cloud of witnesses," Our Lord, Our Lady, and the saints.

Among our Byzantine Orthodox Brethren, our seven sacraments are known as the "seven holy mysteries," but many are loath to limit sacramentality to those seven alone. There are those who include the instruction of monastics, the consecrations of churches, funerals, and other ecclesiastical rites that can be occasions of grace for the recipients. In the Oriental understanding, sacramental mysteries are events in which God does something to us and for us while we are passive under His efforts. It is God who works in us both to will and to accomplish — in all church ceremonies, it is Christ the Incarnate Wisdom who gives us the power to become the sons and daughters of God.

Corresponding to the Roman Ritual, Byzantines have the *Euchologion/Trebnik* or "Book of Needs," which contains the prayers and ceremonies ranging from the "Blessing of Expectant Mothers" all the way to the *Prastos/Panicheda* service for the faithful departed. By this means the Byzantine Christian is encapsulated by the intercessory power of the Church from conception to corruption, thus making him a participant in the kingdom of God and a partaker in the divine nature.

BLESSINGS AND GESTURES

Blessing means placing a thing or person under the care of God. A liturgical blessing is one that uses a prescribed formula or ceremony, given by a priest (although some blessings are reserved to the Pope or to the bishops). The simplest blessings are made with the Sign of the Cross, sometimes accompanied by the sprinkling of holy water. The official blessings of the Church are contained in the Roman Ritual. The visible signs and the formula of words of blessings invoke God's benediction invoked on persons, places, and things.

In the Old Testament, we read of God's blessing our first parents, of Noah blessing his two sons, of Isaac blessing Jacob, and of Jacob blessing his twelve sons. We read of Moses blessing the tribes of Israel. The Jewish priests blessed the people every day. In the New Testament, Our Lord blessed the loaves and fishes, the young children, and the Apostles before the Ascension

The sacramentals, including the blessings, derive their efficacy chiefly from the intercessory power of the Church. The faithful's cooperation has a very large part to play if blessings are to attain their full promise, raising human thoughts and aspirations out of the realm of the profane and up to the realm of the sacred.

From the Church, the sacramentals widen out to embrace the totality of the Christian life. At one time, there were special blessings for all facets of life. To be certain, abuse and superstition eventually crept in, especially in the later Middle Ages. In order to end the misuse, Pope Paul V finally stepped in and, by a Bull of June 16, 1614, published the official Roman Ritual, to which model all diocesan rituals were thenceforth to conform. Unfortu-

In the ordination service, the Church, through the bishop, anoints and blesses the hands of the new priest, saying, "May it please you, O Lord, to consecrate and sanctify these hands . . . that whatever they bless may be blessed, and whatever they consecrate may be consecrated in the name of our Lord Jesus Christ." One of the main tasks of the priest is the duty of dispensing blessings. As mediator between God and men, the priest is the dispenser of God's mysteries. For a priest, all else must be kept subordinate to his sacramental ministry. In the first age of the Church, the Apostles began to ordain deacons and assistants to help with their work, but the priest cannot turn over his sacramental powers, including that of bestowing blessings.

nately, in the seventeenth and eighteenth centuries, the abuse was revived, particularly through the religious orders that printed private collections of blessings, and especially exorcisms, with prayers and formulas of such a nature as to outdo even the superstitions of the late Middle Ages.

The Roman Ritual contains the approved rites of the Catholic Church. Many beautiful blessings are found in this book which, when used fruitfully, may turn all parts of Christian life toward the Creator. Two examples of the variety and beauty of these blessings follow.

Many things are blessed and designated for ordinary use — items such as bread, cheese, and butter, medicine, fire, automobiles, etc. In the solemn blessing for a fishing boat, the priest asks God to "send Your holy angel from on high to watch over it and all on board, to ward off any threat of disaster, and to guide its course through calm waters to the desired port."

Perhaps it is a conscientious fear of reviving superstition that makes us so hesitant today about restoring the sacramentals to their onetime place of honor. Admittedly, some of the older pious customs can seem foolish. Yet many of these sacramentals can and should be used to considerable profit, even today.

THE *BOOK OF BLESSINGS*

The *Book of Blessings,* confirmed by the Apostolic See in 1989, provides a great variety of blessings for persons, places, and things that are sacramentals by definition. According to the Bishops' Committee on the Liturgy of the National Conference of Catholic Bishops, there are over 40 new blessings for the United States, in addition to the ones in the Roman Ritual. Under blessings of persons, we find blessings for families, married couples, children, engaged couples, elderly people confined to their homes, the sick, missionaries, organizations, and travelers, among others. Under the section for blessings related to buildings and various forms of human activity, we find blessings for new building sites, homes, seminaries and religious houses, schools, libraries, hospitals, shops, offices and factories, athletic fields, various means of transportation, technical equipment, tools and other equipment for work, animals, fields and flocks, and prayers of thanksgiving for a good harvest, as well as the blessings before and after meals. One section contains blessings of objects designed for use in churches, in the liturgy, and in popular devotions. There are special blessings of articles meant to foster the devotion of the people and blessings for various other needs and occasions.

SIGN OF THE CROSS

Many wordless gestures, or those accompanied with nonverbal prayer, also call to mind the sacred. The making of the Sign of the Cross, professing faith both in the redemption of Christ and in the Trinity, was practiced from the earliest centuries. St. Augustine (d. 430) mentioned and described it many times in his sermons and letters. In those days, Christians made the Sign of the Cross (Redemption) with three fingers (Trinity) on their foreheads. The words "In the name of the Father and the Son and the Holy Ghost"

Lilies are blessed on the feast of St. Anthony of Padua. As part of the ritual blessing, the priest prays: "You [God] in your great kindness have given them to man, and endowed them with a sweet fragrance to lighten the burden of the sick. Therefore, let them be filled with such power that, whether they are used by the sick, or kept in homes or other places, or devoutly carried on one's person, they may serve to drive out evil spirits, safeguard holy chastity, and turn away illness — all this through the prayers of St. Anthony — and finally impart to your servants grace and peace; through Christ our Lord."

were added later. In the third century, Tertullian had already reported this touching and beautiful early Christian practice:

> In all our undertakings — when we enter a place or leave it; before we dress; before we bathe; when we take our meals; when we light the lamps in the evening; before we retire at night; when we sit down to read; before each new task — we trace the Sign of the Cross on our foreheads.

In many places, it is customary to make the Sign of the Cross when passing a church. Some people make the Sign of the Cross on seeing an ambulance or fire truck, accompanying the sign with a brief prayer for the safety of those involved in the calamity as well as the helpers going to them.

One Hispanic custom uses two Signs of the Cross together, one following the other. The thumb and forefingers are crossed to form a cross. First, the *persignarse*, or "signing yourself," is made by making the Sign of the Cross on the forehead, the mouth, and the breast, while praying the words "By the sign of the Holy Cross, deliver us, Lord, from our enemies." Then the *santiguarse*, or "blessing yourself" is made — the traditional Sign of the Cross. At the conclusion, with thumb and forefingers still forming a cross, the person puts his hands to his lips and kisses the cross thus formed.

Genuflecting is the act of bending the right knee to the floor and rising back up as an act of reverence before the Blessed Sacrament. Bowing, where the person inclines his head or his whole body from the waist, gives reverence to a sacred object or to a person such as a bishop or the celebrant of a liturgical service. In Japan, bowing has replaced genuflection to show reverence for the Blessed Sacrament.

Striking the breast has been a gesture of repentance since the early days of the Church. This custom is still practiced by some at Mass during the Confiteor and Lamb of God.

THINGS DESIGNATED FOR SACRED PURPOSES

Numerous sacramentals are commonly used inside churches. Each object used has a history and a specific purpose.

THE ALTAR, SACRED VESSELS, ALTAR LINENS

The sacrifice of the Mass is offered on a consecrated *altar*. Placing the gift on the altar signifies its handing over to God. In

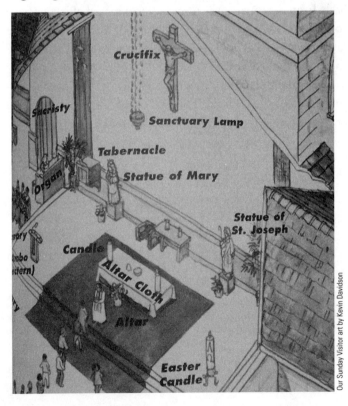

the Christian religion, the altar symbolizes Christ, for He was the altar as well as the priest and the victim of the sacrifice.

In the early centuries, when the threat of persecution was always present, Christians met to worship in private homes, where a table was used for an altar. It was on just such a table that Christ instituted the Mass for the Church.

Beginning about the fourth century, Mass was often celebrated over or under the tombs of the martyrs; from this arose the custom of having a saint's relics under or in every altar. By the sixth century, Mass was celebrated in churches, and the Holy Sacrifice was offered on altars of stone. In those days the altar was built so that the priest offering Mass faced the people. Later, altars were built in the apse of the church so that the people were behind the priest. In an instruction prepared by a special liturgical commission established by Pope Paul VI for the implementation of the decrees of the Constitution on the Sacred Liturgy of Vatican Council II, the document declared, "It is proper that the main altar be constructed separately from the wall, so that one may go around it with ease and so that celebration may take place facing the people."

Today's altar is consecrated by a bishop with special ceremonies. For the celebration of Mass, a crucifix is placed near the altar and candles are lit. The Byzantine altar is square and has a wooden top.

Credence tables are small tables or shelves at the side of the sanctuary where the chalice, ciborium, cruets, basin, and towel, etc., may be placed.

The *tabernacle* is a kind of safe, usually made of metal with a locking door, in which the Blessed Sacrament is reserved. Some early tabernacles took various forms, such as that of a dove, and were sometimes suspended over the altar. In the Old Testament, the tabernacle was the tent that sheltered the Ark of the Covenant. It was a wooden frame covered with cloth and ram skins, and it was portable. The tabernacle for the Holy Eucharist developed over the centuries, and by the sixteenth century its present form was in common use.

A *sanctuary lamp* is kept burning day and night whenever the Blessed Sacrament is in the tabernacle.

The *Missal* is the book containing the prayers and ceremonies of the Mass.

Cruets are the vessels from which the acolyte or sacristan pours water and wine into the chalice held by the celebrant.

SACRED VESSELS

The main sacred vessels used for the altar are the *chalice, paten, ciborium,* and *monstrance (ostensorium).* These vessels, once consecrated, should be handled with reverence.

The most sacred of all the vessels are the chalice, the cup that holds the wine for consecration, and the paten. After consecration, the chalice contains the precious blood of Christ. It represents the chalice in which Our Lord first offered His blood at the Last Supper. It also symbolizes the cup of the Passion, and lastly, it stands for the Heart of Jesus, from which flowed His blood for our redemption. The paten is the small plate on which the Host is laid. In Holy Communion, our hearts become living chalices, our tongues and our hands other patens, on which lies Our Lord.

The ciborium resembles the chalice and is used to hold the small Hosts distributed for the communion of the faithful. A *pyx* is a small vessel, sometimes watch-shaped, in which the Blessed Sacrament is kept and carried to the sick.

The monstrance, or ostensorium, is the large metal container used for exposition and benediction of the Blessed Sacrament. Often the monstrance is made of gold and other precious metals, and it is sometimes decorated lavishly with jewels. The sacred Host used for Benediction is reserved in a *luna* or *lunette,* placed in the glassed portion of the monstrance.

Incense is a perfume burned on certain occasions such as solemn Mass and Benediction. Incense is symbolic of prayer. The incense is scooped from an incense boat and burned in a censer. The incense used liturgically is a mixture that is based on frankincense. It is the distinctive odor of that resin that lets you know that you are in a Catholic church, wherever in the world you are. In the Oriental countries, joss sticks, another form of incense, are also used, often burned near the photos of the dead and in the crypts.

Other sacramentals commonly used in or near the altar are *reliquaries,* a *holy water font* and *sprinkler,* a *Missal stand, candlesticks,* and *bells.*

Bells were not often used in a Christian context until the sixth century. In the Celtic tradition, bells were treated with particular reverence, and by the eighth century bell towers began to be built on churches and blessings were instituted for them. Beginning in medieval times, bells began to be pealed at the Angelus. The ringing of a bell during the canon of the Mass seems to have begun when the elevation became part of the ritual in the early thirteenth century.

An *antependium,* or decorated covering, usually of cloth, covers the front of altars that are not richly ornamented or carved in front. Some of these cloths are made elaborate with embroidery or other decorations, and are usually in the color designated for the liturgy.

CLOTHS

A number of linen cloths are used for the Holy Sacrifice of the Mass. The *corporal, purificator,* and *pall* have been called "holy cloths." All are made of white linen. The priest uses a finger towel after washing his fingers before the consecration. This towel has no special significance.

The corporal is a square of fine linen, with a small cross worked in the center, and sometimes bordered with lace. The priest spreads the corporal on the altar; on it he places the chalice and the Host after consecration. The purificator is an oblong piece of linen, used to wipe the inside of the chalice before putting in the wine, the rim of the cup after reception by the priest and communicants, and after the Ablution. The priest also wipes his mouth with it after the Ablution.

The pall is a small square of linen used to cover the chalice. Originally, the corporal was larger and was folded back to cover the chalice. When its size was reduced in about the year 1000, the pall was introduced. (This is no longer, or rarely, used.)

PRIESTLY VESTMENTS

In the Old Testament, God Himself gave directions about the vestments of the priests. The main vestments worn by Catholic priests today have come down to us from the time of the Apostles. There are symbolic significances attached to the various vestments, and the prayers said by the priest as he vests — or puts on each piece of attire — show the meaning attached by the Church.

Putting on the *alb*, a white linen tunic that envelops his whole body, the priest prays, "Purify me, O Lord, from all stain and cleanse my heart, that, washed in the Blood of the Lamb, I may enjoy eternal delights." The alb is a survival of the long inner tunic worn in Roman times.

Fastening the alb at the waist with the *cincture* (or *girdle*), he prays, "Gird me, O Lord, with the cincture of purity, and quench in my heart the fire of concupiscence, that the virtue of continence and chastity may remain in me."

At one time, the priest laid a short narrow strip of cloth, the *maniple*, to hang from his left arm as he prayed, "Let me deserve, O Lord, to bear the maniple of tears and sorrow, so that one day I may come with joy into the reward of my labors." Originally a handkerchief carried by a Roman official, the maniple was used for the "Tridentine" Mass of Pope St. Pius V.

The *stole* is the symbol of ordained priesthood. The origin of the stole is not known with certainty, although it is believed to be descended from the official scarf, or *lorum*, of the Roman magistrate.

The outermost vestment worn by the celebrant at Mass is the *chasuble*. It hangs from the shoulders in front and in back, down almost to the knees. As the priest robes in the chasuble, he prays, "O Lord, Who says, 'My yoke is sweet and my burden light,' grant that I may carry it so as to obtain Thy grace." The general shape of the chasuble is the same as those worn in Rome in the seventeenth century. It was originally the ordinary mantle, or *paenula*, worn by men in the Roman Empire, becoming proper to the clergy in the sixth century. Its size was gradually reduced between the thirteenth and eighteenth centuries.

The chasuble, stole, formerly the maniple, and the veil for the chalice were made as a set of vestments. They are of the same material, color proper to the day, and design.

Outside of Mass, there are a number of other vestments that the priest uses. The *cassock*, or *soutane*, is the main vestment used by ecclesiastics. This is a robe reaching down to the feet and buttoned in front. For priests, this is black; bishops wear violet, cardinals wear red, and the Pope wears white. In some countries ecclesiastics go everywhere in their cassocks; this is also the custom among some religious orders. In the United States in modern times, however, this is more the exception than the rule. Today's priests and bishops generally wear a conservative black suit with a Roman collar.

When a priest is preaching or joins a procession he wears a *surplice*, a short alb. The *cope* is a mantle worn at benediction, at processions and for some other occasions. The origin of the cope is the same as that of the chasuble, except that it was worn outside in wet weather. Its Latin name, *pluvial*, is the equivalent of the English "raincoat."

The *humeral veil* is the long silk cloth used by the priest when carrying the Blessed Sacrament and giving benediction. Some of the vestments, such as the *amice, alb, surplice,* and *benediction veil,* are always white. The stole for hearing confessions is always purple.

THE PALLIUM

The *pallium* is a white woolen circular band two inches wide, ornamented with six small crosses, and which has a weighted pendant in the front and in the back. It slips over the head and hangs down in front and back in the shape of a "Y." It is worn ceremonially by the Pope, metropolitan archbishops, and patriarchs. The

LITURGICAL COLORS

Various liturgical colors are used at Mass, according to the season and the event being commemorated. In the early days of the Church, the vestments were all white, although black was used for mourning. Today, the priest's vestments are in the prescribed color.

White, symbolic of purity and joy, is worn during Christmastide and Eastertide, and on the feasts of Our Lord, Our Lady, the angels, confessors, and virgins, as well as for funerals.

Red, the color of fire and blood, is used at Pentecost in commemoration of the descent of the Holy Spirit in the form of tongues of fire. Additionally, it is used on the feasts of the Apostles and martyrs, feasts commemorating the Passion of Our Lord, and those commemorating the Sacred Relics, on Palm Sunday, and on Good Friday.

Green, a symbol of hope and growth, is used for the greater part of the year. From early in January (the Monday following the feast of the Baptism of Jesus) to the beginning of Lent, and from Monday after Trinity Sunday till the eve of the First Sunday of Advent, the priest dresses in green except when Masses are offered in honor of saints, martyrs, or the dead.

Purple vestments are worn during Advent and Lent. (Formerly they were worn on Rogation Days, on Ember days — except those on Pentecost octave — and on the five vigils of the feasts of the Ascension, Assumption, St. John the Baptist, St. Peter and St. Paul, and St. Lawrence.) This color is a penitential color.

Black vestments are rarely used in today's liturgy.

pallium is a symbol of the fullness of the episcopal power enjoyed by the Pope and shared in by the archbishops, and of union with the Holy See. Until an archbishop receives a pallium, he may not exercise metropolitan jurisdiction; if he should be transferred to a new archdiocese, he must ask for a new pallium. The archbishops are buried with their pallia.

The investiture of the Pope with the pallium at his coronation is the most solemn part of the ceremony, and it is a symbol older than the wearing of the papal tiara. The pallia are made by the Oblates of St. Frances of Rome, from the wool of two lambs blessed in the church of St. Agnes on her feast, January 21. Since the fourth century, the lambs have been presented at solemn Mass in the basilica and are carefully cared for until the time of shearing. When completed, the pallia are blessed by the Pope on the feast of Sts. Peter and Paul, and they are stored in a casket in the crypt of St. Peter.

VESSELS, VESTMENTS, AND OTHER LITURGICAL APPURTENANCES OF THE BYZANTINE RITE

Just as a pleasant garden has varied and beautiful flowers combining their fragrances for our delight, so, too, Mother Church blossoms with different rites exhaling the fragrance of their prayers and hymns, virtues and sacrifices, as an incense of perpetual adoration to the Creator.

In many large cities in the United States today are churches of Eastern Catholic rites. Members of the Western rite may visit these churches and receive Holy Communion. There, the priest will use a golden spoon to drop upon their tongue a small piece of bread, which has been dipped into the Precious Blood in the chalice. Such a visit will help us to realize in full the meaning of the word "catholic" — that the Church is not tied to a single language, or a single set of ceremonies and customs.

A number of the sacramentals used in the Mass of the Byzantine rite are described below.

The *antimension* takes the place of the altar stone used in the Western rite. This is a silk or linen cloth laid upon the altar at Mass. The antimension bears the picture of the burial of Christ and the instruments of His Passion. Relics of martyrs are sewn into the center of the front border. Latin-rite military chaplains have used this in time of war.

The *elleton* corresponds to the corporal used in the Western rite. The *poterion* (chalice) is the cup used to hold the Precious Blood. The *diskos*, a shallow plate sometimes elevated on a low stand, corresponds to the paten.

The *asteriskos* is placed over the *diskos* and covered with a veil. This is made of two curved bands of gold or silver that cross each other to form a double arch; a star depends from the junction, which forms a cross. Three veils are used. The smallest of these covers the *poterion,* the next covers the *diskos,* and the largest covers both. The spoon, peculiar to the Byzantine rite, is used in giving Holy Communion to the faithful. A *lance* is a metal knife used in cutting up the bread to be consecrated.

The *sticharion* is a long white garment made of linen with wide sleeves and decorated with embroidery. Originally used as the vestment for the clerics of minor orders, it signifies the purity of the priest.

The *epitrachelion* is a stole with ends sewn together; it has a loop through which the head is passed. Several crosses on it signify the priestly duties.

A narrow clasped belt of the same material as the *epitrachelion* is called a *zone.* This signifies the wisdom of the priest, his strength against the enemies of the Church, and his willingness to fulfill his holy duties.

Ornamental cuffs called *epimanikia* symbolize (right) strength and (left) patience and goodwill.

The *phelonion* is an ample cape-like vestment that is long at the back and sides and cut away in front. It signifies the higher gifts of the Holy Spirit.

THE HOLY BIBLE

The Bible, together with Tradition, constitutes revelation, the supreme rule of faith. Inspired by God and committed once and for all to writing, this revelation imparts the word of God Himself without change, and makes the voice of the Holy Spirit resound in the words of the prophets and Apostles.

The Bible is the guide for all preaching in the Church, and its constant source of nourishment. The first part of the Mass is called the liturgy of the word because here the priest reads, with the people, the word of God, explaining that word to them.

The Bible is the basis for theology in the Church. The sacred Scriptures contain the word of God — since they are inspired, they truly are the "words" of God.

The Bible was written originally in three main languages: Hebrew, Aramaic, and Greek. The earliest Church used the Bible in the Greek translation. When Latin became the common spoken language, it was translated into Latin. St. Jerome made one of the better Latin translations, called the Vulgate. Throughout the centuries, as Christianity spread, the Church provided translations of the Latin Vulgate into many of the languages of the people. Today, scholars have better facilities to study the ancient languages, and new translations are being made from the original languages. Thus, the translations are closer to what was really written by the inspired authors. Today's Bible scholars use all the scientific means possible to interpret the meaning of the Scriptures. The Church encourages all the people of God to read the Scriptures diligently and to study them carefully.

Since the Council of Ephesus (431), the Gospels have been enthroned at the ecumenical councils. An elaborate stand was put in a prominent place, usually near the altar where Mass was celebrated for the Council Fathers. Enthroned in this manner, the Gospels were to symbolize the presence of Christ Himself at the council.

The Bible is the story of God's revelation in history, written by men under the inspiration of the Holy Spirit and contained in the

Old and New Testaments. Depending on the manner in which the sacred books are divided, their number will differ. Catholics have generally divided the Bible into 72 books. The books of the Bible were composed by many different writers and were written over a period of approximately 1300 years, from Moses to St. John the Evangelist. The authors of the Bible were free instruments of God and brought their own personalities with them in what they wrote. Therefore, we find various kinds of literary forms, styles, and degrees of grammatical accuracy in their writing.

The Bible is divided into two parts, the Old and the New Testaments. Catholic scholars generally divide the Old Testament into 45 books, containing the story of why man needs salvation and what God did to prepare for the final act of salvation.

The New Testament consists of those books written about Jesus Christ and the fullness of revelation brought by Him. The four Gospels (Matthew, Mark, Luke, and John) are the apostolic witness to, and interpretation of, the words and deeds of Jesus Christ. They were written in the latter part of the first century, in order to teach the Christian community what it should know about the Savior.

The Acts of the Apostles, written by St. Luke, contains an account of the missionary activity and growth of the early Church. It also contains an account of the missionary journeys of St. Paul. The epistles, or letters, of St. Paul and others were written to some of the early Christian churches or individuals, in response to some particular problem or situation. They give us a good insight into the gradual development of much of the theology of the New Testament. The "catholic" epistles are called by this name because of their more universal destination, since for the most part they were not sent to any particular community or church.

The Book of Revelation, or Apocalypse of St. John, was written to console early Christians at a time of persecution. It is filled with much symbolism that they would have understood. Revelation records the ultimate victory of the kingdom of God.

SACRED PLACES

In addition to those places we normally think of as sacred — churches, chapels, or shrines — there are other physical places that call to mind the Divine. The sites in the Holy Land, Palestine, and modern Israel associated with the life and ministry of Our Lord are known as Holy Places.

Holy wells are wells or springs that are associated with devotion to Our Lord, the Virgin Mary, or a saint. Some well known examples of these are the wells at Ladyewell in England, the well at the shrine of *Santo Niño de Atocha* in Chimayo, New Mexico, and the well associated with the devotion to the Holy Child of Good Luck in Tacubayo, near Mexico City, Mexico.

The Hill of Crosses is a site in Siauliai, Lithuania, on which pilgrims place handmade crosses symbolic of the completion of their pilgrimage to the spot and of the tribulations that country has faced, along with their prayers for an end to them. Pope John Paul II visited the hill in 1993 and placed a cross there.

Wayside shrines are found worldwide. A longstanding tradition in many countries, these small shrines and chapels are often constructed as an *ex voto,* or in fulfillment of a *manda,* or vow. (This custom is not limited to Christianity; the Orient is replete with examples from Buddhism and Shinto.)

In the Middle Ages, chapels were built for private devotion, to commemorate some special event, or to enshrine a treasured relic. Some became famous places of pilgrimage. Wayside and bridge chapels, intended for the use of travelers, were often found on the way to important shrines. Although the Church has special regulations for private chapels where Mass is to be said, there are no restrictions on the construction of a small building, or in setting aside a portion of a home to be used for private prayer and devotion.

The countryside in the Bavaria region of Germany is covered with small wayside stopping places or shrines. These range from elaborate chapels to simple religious images, pictures, or statues in small shelters on poles across the roadside.

A yard shrine

A roadside shrine

In Mexico, street corners often have a glass-fronted box enclosing a picture or statue of the Virgin. Small chapels are scattered along the roadsides as well.

Simple crosses or small shrines along the wayside in Mexico and the American Southwest, known as *descansos* (resting places), are a death-related aspect of folk art.

In former times, the distance between a church and the cemetery meant that the pallbearers would often have to stop and rest. As the procession entered the *camposanto*, or graveyard, the

Descanso

Gruta (Blessed Miguel Pro)

group would stop at the entrance and each of the four corners of the cemetery, where prayers were recited. Later, this custom and the custom of the raising of the cross (see p. 66) extended to marking the place of death, where the soul left the body. Usually, families place a simple wooden cross at the scene of the accident, which may be replaced soon afterward by a more permanent marker. The markers are made of many materials, some even incorporating parts of the automobiles involved in a fatal accident to warn travelers of a dangerous spot in the road. Some of the shrines have a *boveda*, or small replica of a tomb, complete with a glass door at the front. Photographs and votive candles, as well as flowers, are placed inside.

Grutas, or small grotto-type shrines, are common in Mexico and the American Southwest. These are found not only along the roadside, but also in people's yards. Unlike the *descansos*, which commemorate a death, the *grutas* (*traileros* in Mexico) are built in payment of a promise of thanks to a favorite saint, or to the Virgin for favors received.

Nichos are small boxes, often attached near the doors of houses, which hold the image of a favorite Virgin or saint. *Nichos* can also be found inside houses on interior walls.

Cemeteries, too, can be sacred places. Until the middle of the seventeenth century, the cemetery corresponded to the Roman forum and the idea of a public square or mall. They were protected by the privilege of sanctuary, and it was here the people conducted their spiritual and temporal business. During Carolingian times, judicial assemblies, both Church and civil, were held in the cemetery; Joan of Arc's trial was held at the cemetery of Rouen in the fifteenth century. Commerce gradually moved outside the cemetery when the Church forbade certain practices inside it. Today, visiting a cemetery and devoutly praying for the dead is a way to gain indulgences for the souls in purgatory. An indulgence is also granted for visiting a catacomb or cemetery of the early Christians.

Inside our own homes, too, there are sacred places.

In the homes of the Eastern Catholics, there will be an *ikon corner* where the family gathers for prayers and blessings. (See section "Sacramentals in the Eastern rites.")

Home altars, also called *altercites* (little altars), are the custom of setting aside a shelf or small table for sacramentals, which are used as a focal point for family prayer. The traditions of such domestic shrines vary from country to country. In Slovak homes, there may be an elaborately carved and painted wooden altar containing images of favorite saints and pictures of loved ones who have died. A Hispanic home altar would typically include candles and a number of statues. The home altars in Oriental Catholic homes may include incense and tablets on which are written the names of the family dead, as well as images and other blessed items.

NICHOS

The building of *nichos* is a Mexican-American custom popular throughout the American Southwest. *Nichos* are small shrines built on the outside of a home, on the wall, in the garden, or in the yard.

A *nicho* (Spanish for "niche") is often built as the result of a promise made to a favorite saint, although some simply make a statement that the home is a Catholic one. When the *nicho* or *gruta* (grotto) is made in gratitude, the petitioner asks the saint for some form of intervention during a life crisis such as a debilitating illness or dangerous military service. He or she promises

Nicho

to dedicate a shrine to the saint if prayers are answered. The completion of this vow, or *manda*, is seen as a serious and binding one.

Nichos are made in different sizes using a variety of material and generally have a border. The boundary, often made of bricks, rocks, or plants, sets off the sacred area. *Milagros*, small metal *ex votos* in the shape of people, animals, or hearts, are sometimes attached to the hands of the statue. Other *ex votos* — such as photographs of the loved one who was helped — are sometimes incorporated in the *nicho.*

Nicho of Our Lady of Guadalupe

Although *nichos* feature many favorite saints, the most popular saint is Our Lady of Guadalupe. A shrine in her honor may also contain the figure of St. Juan Diego. While the majority of the images depicted in *nichos* are those canonized by the Catholic Church, so-called "folk saints" (such as the famous *curandero* ["holy one" and faith healer] Don Pedrito Jaramillo) are also honored in this way. Even the process of acquiring an image can be part of the vow, and families often travel together to a famous shrine to acquire a replica of the image there.

Small *nichos* in the form of glass-fronted boxes are often placed near the door of the home. Folk artists also make small *nichos* as decorative holders for religious icons to be hung inside on the walls of the home.

RELICS

Relics, honored in the Catholic Church, are the bodies of the saints or objects connected with them or with Our Lord. God has often shown His approval of the use of relics as sacramentals by working miracles through them. Relics deserve to be venerated. The bodies of the saints were temples of the Holy Spirit and instruments through which God worked. However, no Catholic is required to believe in miracles (such as that of the blood of St. Januarius, which is kept in a vial at Naples and liquefies several times a year for certain periods), any more than one is obliged to believe in private revelations such as those of Lourdes and

Various relics

A *theca* is a sheath or cloth covering in which relics are kept. The term also refers to the metal holder in which first class relics are customarily distributed. These are often displayed in elaborate cases, or holders, known as reliquaries.

Theca with relic of St. John Bosco

Fátima. We honor relics by preserving them with reverence, visiting the places were they are enshrined, and praying before them.

The word *relic* comes from the Latin *reliquiae*, or "remains." Relics are classified in three categories. First-class relics are parts of the bodies of saints, or instruments of the Passion (like fragments of the True Cross). Second-class relics are objects that have been in close contact with the saints, such as articles of clothing or personal items. In the case of a martyr, the instruments of martyrdom are also considered to be in this category. Third-class relics are objects such as Rosaries or cloths that have been touched to the body of the saint, or to either first- or second-class relics.

Brandea is the term for a paper or cloth that has been touched to the bodies of saints or persons with a reputation for holiness and is then kept as a relic. The term is also used for a piece of the tomb or dust from it or other objects that have come in contact with the body of a saint.

Veneration of relics is not limited to Catholics; its origins predate Christianity. Relics of Buddha, who died nearly half a century before Christ, are still venerated today throughout the Buddhist world. The Chinese have venerated those of Confucius since 195 B.C. Those of Mohammed (d. A.D. 632) are kept with reverence in Jerusalem, in a building called the Dome of the Rock. Other famous leaders whose relics were venerated in early ages were the Persian Zoroaster (Zarathushtra) and the Greek

Oedipus. And, according to Shakespeare, the Romans dipped cloths in the spilled blood of Julius Caesar.

In Victorian times, locks of hair were given to lovers, and family members often treasured the tresses of their departed loved ones. In the United States, hair from family members was made into elaborate floral pictures. The piano virtuoso Pachmann used to hold aloft a couple of pieces of unlaundered clothing just before he began to play. Emotionally, he would sniffle and announce, "*Les chaussettes de Chopin!* (Chopin's socks!)" He would then proceed to reduce the audience to tears with his rendition of the master's works.

In the Old Testament, the miraculous relics of the prophet Elisha are mentioned in 2 Kings 13:20-21. In the New Testament (Acts 19:11-12), mention is made of second-class relics, cloths being touched to the hands of the Apostle Paul. The inhabitants of Smyrna wrote one of the earliest mentions of honor paid to relics, about A.D. 156. These described the death of St. Polycarp, who was burned at the stake. His faithful disciples gathered his ashes and bones and enshrined them. When St. Ignatius, Bishop of Antioch, was thrown to the lions (c. 107), two of his companions came and gathered up his bones for veneration. St. Cyril of Jerusalem (d. 386) wrote that relics of the Cross were already distributed throughout the world.

RELICS OF CHRIST

Most prized of all relics are the relics of Christ's passion, particularly of the cross on which He died. Some scoff at the relics of the cross and say that there are too many to be genuine. In reality, however, even if all known pieces were put together, they would make a block smaller than half a cubic foot.

Today, the twelve most famous portions of the True Cross range from 6.33 cubic inches to 33 cubic inches. The largest of these are found in Jerusalem, Brussels, Ghent, and Rome. The particles venerated are very small.

The True Cross was found by St. Helena, mother of the emperor Constantine the Great, in the year 326. Her workmen, digging on Mount Calvary in search of the True Cross of Christ, found three crosses. Two of the crosses were applied without result to a very sick woman. As soon as the third cross touched her, she was instantly cured.

The emperor Charlemagne (d. 814) instigated a search for relics at Rome, Constantinople, and Jerusalem, and when found shared them with his friends. He hoped to find relics of Our Lord's Passion that had gone undiscovered by St. Helena when she searched for the Cross.

Adoration of the Cross on Good Friday is part of the Holy Week devotions, while the Feast of the Exaltation of the Cross is kept on September 14.

RELICS OF MARTYRS

After the death of Christ, the persecutions of Christians resulted in the death of countless martyrs. They were buried in the secrecy of the catacombs, which later became a veritable treasury of relics. A rivalry soon sprang up for possession of these precious mementos, and the remains were divided; although some shrank from the thought of disturbing the dead, the relics were divided for the sake of veneration, not desecration. As the Christians increased and spread forth throughout the world, they took with them the honored relics.

After the persecutions finally ended in A.D. 313, and during the reign of Constantine, the graves of the martyrs were turned into magnificent sanctuaries and basilicas. When churches were built apart from the tombs, relics were transferred and enshrined, often within the altars. Even today, relics of saints are enclosed in the altars of modern churches.

No one knows when the practice of venerating minute fragments of the bodies of saints first became popular, but by the fourth century the practice was widespread. The relics were so greatly esteemed by their owners that the cases in which they were preserved were often decorated with priceless jewels and fine metalwork. Pilgrims often traveled great distances to pray and make vows at the shrines of these relics. During the Middle Ages, when the cult of relics was at its pinnacle, many great churches owed their renown simply to the presence of important relics.

ABUSES

It was during the Middle Ages that possessing relics became so popular that abuses became a problem; sometimes, important relics were stolen outright, or fraudulent relics were distributed — because a town without its own saint, and appropriate relics, was considered a poor town. Indeed, the greatest festivals of those times were the "translations" of the relics of a saint from the tomb to a newly built church or shrine in his or her honor. These were celebrated with great pomp, commemorated annually and, in the earlier centuries, amounted to canonization.

So great was the popularity of such occasions that often, when a body was discovered buried in an ancient church, it would be readily assumed to be that of a holy person, and a new shrine would be built for the glory of the saint and the renown of the hometown as a place of pilgrimage. Soon, rivalries sprang up between the larger towns, and this led to the veneration of such historically questionable objects as the crib of Bethlehem and the pillar of Our Lord's scourging. Questionable or not, if no scandalous money-making took place at such shrines, the Church seldom questioned the authenticity of relics which had been venerated for centuries, so as not to upset genuinely pious people. Unfortunately, the faking of relics, the sale of relics, and other scandalous abuses of the Church doctrine on relics became widespread.

One problem with many of the oldest relics is that it is nearly impossible to prove their authenticity scientifically. In earlier days, it was as difficult to disprove the authenticity of a relic as it was to substantiate it. It is reasonable to assume that some famous relics, such as the nails of the crucifixion, are false, but not necessarily deliberate fraud. In the case of the nails, copies that had touched the authentic ones were first venerated as second-class relics from having touched the originals. As time passed and written records were misplaced, eventually many of the copies were regarded as the originals. Even a false relic, however, which has been honored through the centuries does not dishonor God or the saint in question; in truth, we venerate the person from whom the relic came, not the piece of bone or cloth called the relic.

St. Augustine, in the fourth century, denounced imposters who wandered about clothed as monks and profited by selling fake relics. St. Gregory of Tours (d. 593) and St. Gregory the Great (d. 604) mention the trade in fraudulent relics by unscrupulous persons. Church authority did what it could, but the number of relics made the task difficult. The Councils of Lyons in 1245 and 1275 prohibited the veneration of recently found relics unless the Roman Pontiff first approved them. The Council of Trent (1545-1563) ordered bishops to take special pains with regard to the distribution of relics and established the norm that all relics be subject to the control of the Vatican. It is not known when it became customary for a relic to be accompanied by a

---

CURRENT REGULATIONS

Currently the Relic Office in the Vatican receives, keeps, and distributes relics of saints and blesseds. Instructions from the vicar general of the Diocese of Rome read, "Relics should be handled intelligently, without abuses. They are signs that can be useful to spread devotion to holy men and women all over the world. When major relics are requested for private and public veneration they must be accompanied by official papers warranting their validity and authenticity. In no way may they be sold. A contribution may be requested merely to cover expenses such as for the relic case and mailing charges."

document of authentication. Both the Council of Trent and the Code of Canon Law, promulgated in 1918 set penalties for the abuses connected with relics.

Relics of various martyrs

Joan Carroll Cruz has written one of the most complete books about relics available (*Relics,* Our Sunday Visitor, 1984). The reader who wishes more information than the scope of this text allows can consult Mrs. Cruz's book for a complete discussion of all the major relics venerated in the Church today. In addition, the International Crusade for Holy Relics maintains a web site with a great deal of information on this subject.

Because of their very nature, major relics are scarce and difficult to obtain. It is a common custom, however, for the postulators of causes for beatification and for religious orders to distribute second- and third-class relics, often on cards with prayers for the cause.

Although the Church today neither encourages nor discourages the cult of relics, their use as sacramentals is actually on the increase. Unfortunately, many people treat holy relics as "collector's items," and a booming trade in the sale of relics goes on through the Internet. Catholics should be aware that this is against canon law: trading in relics, known as simony, is prohibited to the faithful. In addition, a number of the relics sold in this manner are false or are misidentified. In recent years there has been at least one

An elaborate casket reliquary in the Baroque style

Altar reliquary of an unknown Christian martyr

major scandal of a man selling counterfeit relics. Some pious Catholics buy relics with the intention of "rescuing" them. Unfortunately, this only increases the market and encourages their sale. It's far better to contact the postulator, promoter, or headquarters of the cause for beatification or canonization to obtain these sacramentals.

While the honor and veneration of relics is commendable — provided superstitious practices do not accompany it — Our Lord Himself, in an apparition to St. Gertrude the Great, mentioned a non-materialistic relic that all Christians would do well to consider. The saint had desired to have some relics of the wood of the cross. Our Lord said to her, "If you desire to have some relics which will draw My Heart into yours, read My Passion, and meditate attentively on every word contained therein; and it will be to you a true relic which will merit more graces for you than any other . . . thence you may know and be assured that the words which I uttered when on earth are the most precious relics which you can possess."

CRUCIFIXES AND CROSSES

The cross is the most widespread and venerated sacramental of the church. This symbol of mankind's redemption has been used since the early days of the Church, and today it is present in all Catholic and most Christian churches.

During the earliest days of the Church, in the time of the persecutions of the Christians, the cross was often disguised as a part of other symbols. It was often disguised as an anchor or hidden in a monogram. Crosses of various types were found carved on the stone slabs in the oldest sections of the Roman catacombs.

In 326, St. Helena searched for and found the true cross. Later it fell into the hands of the Persians, but it was recovered by King Heraclius of Judea in 629. Relics of the cross made their way to many parts of the world, and many of them still exist. A relic of the True Cross is the only relic that can be carried under a canopy in procession, and it is the only relic that receives a genuflection when exposed.

Helena's son, Constantine the Great, made a remarkable impact on the history of the world by ending the persecutions of the Christians. During a battle at the Milvian Bridge, an apparition of the cross appeared in the heavens with the words, "In this sign, conquer." Constantine had the sign placed on his banner and did indeed defeat the enemy.

Until the end of the sixth century, crosses were shown without the figure of the Redeemer. The usual crucifix today represents Our Lord suffering, but this began about the thirteenth century and became most popular during the Counter-Reformation. Other traditional crucifixes, particularly those of Spanish influence, depicted Christ as crowned, robed, and reigning from the cross.

The crucifix is placed on or above all altars where Mass is offered except in the Nestorian and Coptic churches. In the Eastern Churches, because of the prohibition against rounded repre-

Various Kinds of Crosses — *top row from left*: Latin Cross, Greek Cross, Cross of Constantine; *second row*: Cross of St. Andrew, Celtic Cross, Anchor Cross; *third row*: Patriarchal Cross, Papal Cross, Orthodox Cross; *last row*: Jerusalem Cross, Cross of Caravaca, Pectoral Cross.

sentations, the crucifix is usually painted, or a cross with a painted figure is used.

Crosses have been made worldwide and celebrated with artworks in many distinct forms.

Crucifixes and crosses adorn vestments and religious habits, other sacramental items, altars, tombs, and buildings. Some sacramental uses of the cross are found below.

Crosses on vestments are a comparatively modern development. The cross on most modern chasubles does not seem to have been adopted with any symbolic purpose; it was probably originally used to conceal the seams.

The *papal cross,* carried before a pope, is a cross with three transverse bars of varying length, the smallest at the top. The *patriarchal cross,* or *archiepiscopal cross,* is a cross with two crossbars, of which the upper is shorter than the lower. This is usually carried before an archbishop in processions in his own province. A pectoral cross is a cross worn on the breast by a bishop. It is suspended from a cord or chain and worn outside the clothing. Usually, this is of gold, ornamented with precious stones, and contains relics.

The *pectoral cross* can be worn by others who are not bishops — such as a prefect apostolic — when they have the privilege of pontificating.

Processional crosses are crucifixes mounted on long shafts of metal or wood and carried aloft at the head of processions. The figure is turned forward, and the processional cross is accompanied on either side by an acolyte with candle.

The *Russian cross* is a three-barred cross used by the Russian Church. The upper bar represents the title of the cross, the second the arms, and the lowest, always inclined at an angle, the footrest. This last is angled because Christ is said to have pushed it down in a moment of extreme pain.

St. Andrew's cross (cross saltire) is shaped like the Greek letter *chi* (X). This is also known as *crux decussata,* so called from its resemblance to the Greek symbol for the numeral ten. St. Andrew is said to have suffered martyrdom on such a cross, his hands and feet bound to its four arms.

The *altar cross* is the crucifix placed behind or above the tabernacle on the old baroque altars, usually visible to all in the body of the church and with the tabernacle the center of the altar. It is usually suspended above or behind the table altars recommended by Vatican Council II.

A small cross, held in the hand, is a sacramental used in giving blessings, both liturgical and nonliturgical. This *hand cross* is commonly employed by priests of the Armenian, Maronite, and Syrian rites, and by bishops of all Eastern rites.

The crucifix has been the inspiration and comfort of millions. A number of saints have received mystical graces, visions, and communications through the cross of Our Lord. The cross figures prominently in art and literature worldwide.

THE PARDON CRUCIFIX

In the early days of the twentieth century, the Pious Union of the Pardon Crucifix came into being in France. The aim of this union was to obtain pardon of God and inculcate in the wearer of the crucifix the desire to pardon his neighbor. The headquarters for this pious union was in Lyons, France.

Pardon Crucifix

The faithful were recommended to carry or wear the crucifix on their person, and to devoutly kiss it with the following intentions: To testify love for Our Lord and the Blessed Virgin, and gratitude toward the Holy Father, the Pope; to beg for the remission of our sins, the deliverance of souls in purgatory, the return of the nations to the Faith, forgiveness among Christians, and reconciliation among the members of the Catholic Church.

Two invocations which were to be said before the crucifix are: "Our Father, who art in heaven, forgive us our trespasses as we forgive those who trespass against us," and "I beg the Blessed Virgin Mary to pray to the Lord our God for me."

The front of the crucifix is ornately chased metal. The obverse is plain and is centered with a design of the Sacred Heart. Along the length are found the words, "Behold this heart which has so loved men." On the crossbar are found the words, "Father, forgive them."

THE CRUCIFIX THAT SPOKE TO ST. FRANCIS

Francis Bernardone, the son of a wealthy cloth merchant, had been sent to Foligno to sell a bolt of velvet. On the way, he passed the little half-ruined church of San Damiano. Something made Francis stop his horse and enter. Inside, among the ruins, it was dark and quiet. Only a single light shone before a Byzantine cross with a painted image of the crucifix. The eyes of the painting seemed to look lovingly at him.

For some time, Francis had been disturbed about his carefree way of life. He had determined to follow God's will for him, but

The Crucifix That Spoke to St. Francis, a twelfth-century Umbrian cross painted in egg tempera, now preserved in the Church of St. Clare in Assisi, Italy

was uncertain how to proceed. In front of this beautiful crucifix, in the little deserted church, Francis prayed, "Great God, and You, my Savior Jesus Christ, dispel the darkness of my soul, give me pure faith, lasting hope, and perfect charity. Let Thy will, O God, be my will; make me and keep me Thine, now and forever."

Suddenly, the lips of the crucifix appeared to move. A silverly voice that Francis seemed to have been hearing in his heart in the past few weeks said, "Francis, my son. Do you not see that my church is failing into ruins? Go quickly and build up its walls." Three times the injunction was repeated.

Francis joyfully raced to the market, sold the cloth, and returned to the church. He attempted to give the money to the resident priest to rebuild the church.

Francis' father, learning of his son's actions, became furious. He appealed to the bishop of Assisi to return the funds. Through the intercession of the bishop, Francis returned his father's money. Peter Bernardone subsequently disinherited his son. Francis then embraced "Lady Poverty" and begged for the funds to restore the church.

Thus, Francis of Assisi went out into the world to preach. He had built up the walls of the little chapel of San Damiano; now he started forth to repair his Father's Church — men's faith in God.

Francis banded together with some companions, and they became mendicant friars and the seed of the Franciscan Order. Copies of the crucifix that spoke to St. Francis, like the brothers and sisters of the Franciscan family, have spread throughout the world. The crucifix, an Umbrian twelfth-century egg tempera, is preserved in the Church of St. Clare in Assisi.

THE CRUCIFIX OF CHRIST OF THE AGONY OF LIMPIAS

In Limpias, a town on the northern coast of Spain, the parish church contains a life-size wooden crucifix known as the "Christ of the Agony." The crucifix is the work of a seventeenth century artist, Pedro de Mena. It was brought from southern Spain and donated to the church by a parishioner about the year 1776.

In the first part of the twentieth century, many of the inhabitants of the small town had moved, and the Limpias church was being visited by only a handful of the faithful, even on Sundays. The parish priest asked two Capuchins, Fathers Jalon and Agatangelo, to conduct a parochial mission, which they did from March 22 to 30, 1919.

On the final Sunday of the mission, while Father Agatangelo was preaching and Father Jalon was hearing confessions, a young girl came up to Father Jalon and excitedly said, "Father Jalon, come and see! Christ has closed his eyes!" The priest, thinking the child was playing a joke, sent her back to her seat, but soon other girls came to him ready to swear that they, too, had witnessed the phenomenon. After the sermon, the two priests went up to the altar, but could see nothing unusual.

Soon, however, the strange phenomenon was seen again by a number of adults. Father Jalon, at the request of the faithful, had a ladder brought. He climbed up and touched the corpus, then noticed that his fingers were covered with what seemed to be perspiration that

Replica of the Limpias Crucifix

was running down from the neck and chest of the figure. Not all of the people in the church saw the phenomenon, but all were moved by the faith of the witnesses. The news spread rapidly, and the manifestations continued.

In April of 1919, the eyes of the figure were seen to move, and on Easter Sunday the lips were also seen to move. The manifestations continued for over a year, with some 15,000 persons declared to have benefited from them. Fifteen hundred persons gave sworn testimonies in the years 1919 and 1920 alone. Different witnesses testified to seeing different things; for some, the eyes appeared to move; for others, the expression on the face of the Christ changed. For some, the crucifix appeared to be alive, and suffering in agony.

One doctor who came to ridicule the believers became terrified and ran out of the church after witnessing a metamorphosis of the corpus. First, he saw the body turn into a skeleton, then into a mummy; then it appeared to grow back the flesh. After this experience, his disbelief changed to belief, and he gave a sworn testimony of what he had seen.

The testimony of a Dr. Penamaría was published in a Fonsagrada newspaper in May 1920. He stated that he had neither expected nor desired to see a miracle, but that a sense of curiosity rather than piety led him to go to the church and look attentively at the *Santo Cristo de la Agonía*. Surprisingly, he was an immediate witness of the miracle. First, the eyes of the crucifix appeared to open and close. Thinking that he was seeing an optical illusion, the doctor moved to various spots in the sanctuary. The eyes of the Christ, however, followed him and appeared to be looking at him in a way that moved the doctor to state, "The *Cristo* then looked at me in a way that was so deep, so expressive, that it felt as if He wanted to heal me of my disbelief."

Dr. Penamaría, fearing that he was hallucinating, attempted to pray for more proof, upon which he seemed to see the complete agony of the crucifixion. The statue moved and went through the motions of suffocation and death that, as a medical doctor, Dr. Penamaría was familiar with. For over two hours, Dr. Penamaría witnessed the agony of the miraculous crucifix of Limpias. He concluded his testimony thus: "While the death of a beloved one leaves in one's heart a deep bleeding, incurable wound, the sight of Christ's death leaves way down in one's soul a feeling of bliss, inner peace, deep calm, a feeling of happy release, similar to what one feels when awakening from a nightmare."

The crucifix of Limpias is only one of many representations of Christ that have, throughout the years, been surrounded by supernatural phenomena. In January and February of 1986, a copy of the head of the Limpias crucifix belonging to Mrs. M. Linden of Maasmechelen, Belgium, was seen to shed tears of blood.

THE CRUCIFIX OF *EL CRISTO NEGRO DE ESQUIPULAS*

From the late sixteenth century, a beautiful crucifix has been venerated by the faithful in Guatemala under the title "The Black Christ of Esquipulas."

In 1525, the Chorti Indians of the Mayan group were conquered by the Spanish and branded as slaves. Thus began a long period of suffering for the Indians. In 1595, one of the Indians experienced a vision of a giant host with the image of Christ crucified on it. The Indian community then banded together and embraced Christianity. The provisor of the bishop of Guatemala, Fray Cristobal Morales, ordered an image made for the faithful of the town of Esquipulas.

The sculptor, Quirio Catano, was a mystic as well as an artist. Originally from Portugal, he was living in Antigua, Guatemala. Through his art, he was able to project the pain and the compassion of Our Lord dying on the cross. The expression on the face of the corpus — along with the dark color of the skin — appealed greatly to the Indians. The Chortis were dark and had also suffered, and the image seemed to reflect their own race and feelings.

Devotion to the image began from the day of its delivery, March 9, 1595. Bishop Gómez Fernéndez de Córdova led the image in procession from Antigua to Esquipulas. Throughout the journey, people went to meet the procession, and a number of cures were reported. The fame of the image began to spread because of the miracles, and soon pilgrimages to Esquipulas began. These pilgrimages still occur today.

The crucifix, carved of orange wood, was first displayed in the parish church, Santiago de Esquipulas. Because of the ever-increasing number of pilgrims, a larger church was needed. In 1737, Archbishop Pedro Pardo de Figueroa, miraculously cured through prayers before the crucifix, ordered the building of a new shrine in gratitude.

By 1953, devotion to the Black Christ of Esquipulas had spread throughout Central America. A copy of the crucifix was blessed before the original and taken to the cathedral in Guatemala City. In 1957, a prelature of Esquipulas was created and a bishop named for it. In 1961, the shrine was elevated to the status of a minor basilica.

Black Christ of Esquipulas

Today, Esquipulas is considered one of the holiest places of Central America. Thousands of miracles have been claimed. Crutches, *retablos,* and other thanksgiving offerings testify to the gratitude of the petitioners of *Señor Cristo Negro.* In 1984, a group one thousand strong went on foot from Tiquisate to Esquipulas — a 17-day journey — asking for peace for Central America and for Guatemala. When the Central American presidents met to work out a peace plan, they were lodged at the Benedictine convent charged with the pastoral care of the basilica.

In 1988, another replica of the Black Christ of Esquipulas was blessed and was brought to San Antonio, Texas, to San Fernando Cathedral. In 2003, a beautiful copy carved from ebony was brought to St. Raphael Catholic Church in Los Angeles.

An unusual feature of this crucifix is that the cross is covered with leaves. For this reason, it is sometimes referred to as the Cross of Life.

THE MIRACULOUS CRUCIFIX OF BUGA

In Buga, Colombia, a miraculous crucifix has inspired love and devotion for nearly 400 years. The story of this crucifix contains both pious legend and historical fact. Pilgrims come from all over the world to pay homage to Our Lord here under the title of Christ of Miracles.

The crucifix itself is by no means a work of art, as it suffers from a lack of proper proportion. The corpus, if extended, would be approximately one and a half meters in length. It is made of wood and depicts Our Lord in death. Disregarding its lack of artistic value, the crucifix inspires a tender devotion, and records testify to numerous miracles obtained by its devotees.

The legend of the origin of the devotion was written in the chronicles of the convent of the Redemptorist Fathers, who arrived in Buga to be in charge of the devotion in 1884. In these chronicles, the writer states that the source and origin of the sacred image is not found in authentic documents but rather in ancient tradition.

About 1580, there was a small village in the dense jungle with only a few houses, a parochial church, and a town hall. The Buga River then ran where the Church of the Hermitage is today. On the left bank of the river was a small hut that belonged to an old Indian washerwoman. For a long time, this faithful woman had been saving her money to purchase a small image of Christ to keep in her home. Eventually, she had saved about 70 *reales* (coins), enough to buy a small crucifix.

On the day she was going to travel to Quito to make her purchase, however, an old friend of hers passed by her house crying. When she asked him what was wrong, the man, father of a family, told her that he was going to be sent to jail because of debt. He owed precisely 70 *reales*.

Moved by the plight of her neighbor, the woman gave him the money she had saved. With much gratitude, the man blessed her. The woman determined to begin again to save in order to buy an image of Christ.

Miraculous Crucifix of Buga

Some days later, as she was washing clothes in the river, a wooden crucifix floated up and landed by her feet. As no one lived upriver, the happy woman knew she could take the image home with a clear conscience. She set up a little altar and put the crucifix in a small wooden box for safekeeping.

One night, she heard a knocking sound from the area where she kept the crucifix. When she went to investigate the noise, she saw that the crucifix had grown in size. At first she thought she was imagining it but, several days later, she realized that the crucifix had grown to the size of a small child.

Surprised by this miracle, the old woman contacted the parish priest. Along with other town notables, they visited her home to see the image. All agreed that the old woman had no resources or money to obtain such a large crucifix. Its existence could not be explained as anything but a miracle. The woman's home became a place of worship, and a number of other miracles occurred. The crucifix became famous as the Lord of Miracles.

After the old woman's death, the people wanted to erect a temple to the honored image. They discussed whether to build it where her hut was or in the main plaza of the town. While they were still deciding, a great flood occurred and the river moved to the south, about three blocks from where the crucifix had appeared. Accepting this as the will of God, and another miracle, the people erected a chapel where the crucifix first appeared. The chapel was called the Hermitage, named after the woman's home.

From historical records, more information is given about the history of the devotion to the Lord of Miracles of Buga. Between the years of 1573 and 1576, a small hermitage was constructed in Buga on land donated by Rodrigo Diez de Fuenmayor. An image of Christ was honored here. With the passing of the years, the chapel began to deteriorate. In the first years of the seventeenth century, an ecclesiastical visitor from Popayán ordered the chapel burned. The flames did not destroy the crucifix; instead, it began to sweat abundantly, and the townspeople saved the sweat with cotton. Historical records in the church in Buga contain a description of this phenomenon, which was witnessed by a number of persons that were present. In 1665, Doña Luisa de la Espada gave testimony before a notary. She testified that the image sweated for two days, and the community took cotton and wiped it off. From that time a great devotion began.

In 1783, Dr. D. José Matias García, rector of the college-seminary of Popayán and chaplain of Christ the Miraculous of Buga, wrote to the Holy See to obtain indulgences and privileges in favor of the hermitage and the pilgrims of Buga. His request was approved by the Bishop of Popayán. He wrote, "Through the image, the Almighty works stupendous miracles, not only to the faithful of Buga but to those in America and Europe. These miracles have been repeated for more than two centuries — blind are able to see, mutes can again speak, lame and lepers have gotten well immediately. There is no illness that hasn't been cured, even when the doctors had abandoned the case and the persons were close to death."

In 1884, when the Redemptorists arrived to take charge of the devotion, they realized that the temple had to be enlarged. In 1891, with the approval of the Bishop of Popayán, the task was begun. Construction was not completed until 1907. The church was named a minor basilica by Pius XI in 1937.

THE CROSS OF CARAVACA

Through papal documents, the medieval Church gave special recognition to the Cross of Caravaca, referring to it as the True Cross.

According to tradition, the relic arrived in Spain during the time of the Moorish conquest. Pious legend says that in 1232, Muslim leader El sayid Abu Ceit asked a prisoner-priest to demonstrate the celebration of Mass. The cleric began the liturgy, then halted, lacking a symbol of the Cross on the altar. At that moment, two angels transported the *lignun cruces* (literally "wood of the cross") through the window and placed it on the altar, so the Mass could continue. After witnessing the miracle, El sayid Abu-Ceit and his court converted. It was later discovered that the relic was from Patriarch Robert of Jerusalem. This tradition is recorded in the oldest historical books of the area, dating to the seventeenth century.

Cross of Caravaca

In 1241, Ferdinand III of Castile conquered the region, and the relic was placed in the custody of the Knights Templar.

Over the next 250 years, during the struggles between the Moors and the Christians, many miracles were attributed to the relic as a symbol of protection.

After the dispersion of the Knights Templar, the city and the relic passed into the custody of the Knights of Santiago. The fame of the cross spread throughout Spain. After the disappearance of that military order of knights, custody of the relic passed to the chaplains of the castle. Today, the custodians are a small band of Claretian Fathers.

Through the centuries, a number of reliquaries have been fashioned to hold the precious wood. The one used now is made of gold and was a gift of the duke of Alba in 1777.

The Cross of Caravaca is known worldwide. (In some instances, its image has attracted superstitious belief as a "good luck" amulet.) In 1996, Pope John Paul II declared a Jubilee year for the Cross of Caravaca, and a new chapel to house the relic was dedicated.

ST. BRIGID'S CROSS

The legend of St. Brigid's Cross is that Brigid, renowned for her charity, once acted as nurse to a pagan chieftain. As he slept, she made a cross with some rushes from the floor. On waking, the chieftain asked why she had formed the cross, and the saint told him the story of Calvary. He was deeply impressed and his subsequent conversion, combined with a return to health, was attributed to her prayers.

St. Brigid's Cross

In rural Ireland, a couple just taking possession of a farm or homestead will nail a St. Brigid's cross under the barn eaves. In some places, it is placed in dwellings and on farm buildings on the eve of the Feast of St. Brigid, February 1.

MISSION CROSS

A mission cross is a small cross or crucifix presented ceremonially by some religious orders to their members when they leave for mission territory. This term also denotes a permanent cross that is erected in the place where a mission has been preached. Various types of the latter are made of durable and appealing material, fastened in a definite place or sustained by a firm base, blessed by the priest who preached the mission, and erected with the permission of the local bishop.

RAISING OF THE CROSS

An old Mexican custom called *Levantamiento de la Cruz* (the raising of the cross) involves the faithful taking a cross made of wood or iron to the church, having it blessed, and then taking it the cemetery to conclude the rites and prayers that accompany the death of a loved one. This is a reminder that death is provisional and that Christ has conquered death.

WATER

Our pre-Christian ancestors knew nothing of chemistry or physics, but from constant observation they knew the effects of rain, or the lack of it, on vegetation and life. To them, water possessed a magical property, producing fertility and new growth. This became the basis for many pre-Christian water rites.

The Church, acknowledging the life-giving properties of water and its significance in Christian history, provided a Christian version of the ancient water rites, thus elevating the pre-Christian symbolism of nature into a Christian sacramental.

Water is used in many ways liturgically. The mingling of a few drops of water with the wine to be consecrated at Mass was observed from the beginning, possibly by Our Lord Himself, for the Jews took water with their wine. It symbolizes the union of two natures in Christ, the unity of Christ and His people, and the water that came out with blood from His side. Water is used in the sacrament of baptism, blessing of bells, consecrating a church, and in the myriad blessings and other uses for holy water.

The ceremony of blessing originated in the eighth century in the Carolinian Empire, as did most of the other liturgical blessings. The words of St. Paul that through baptism we rise with Christ into the newness of life (Rom. 6:4-6) point to a special relation between the weekly memorial of the Resurrection and our own baptism. In the ninth century, this thought seems to have prompted some bishops of the Frankish realm to introduce the custom of sprinkling holy water upon the faithful before Mass, to remind them of the grace of baptism. A century later, the same practice was prescribed at Verona, Italy, and soon afterward it was accepted by Rome. Thus, the rite of the *Asperges* became a part of the solemn service on Sunday. During the Middle Ages, in many places, processions were held around the church, and holy water was sprinkled upon the graves of the faithful.

Holy water is simply ordinary water sanctified by the blessing of the Church. The blessing once consisted of exorcisms of water and salt; the salt was added to the water in the form of a cross to signify that the water was preserved from corruption. The practice of putting salt into the water came from the incident of the miraculous cure of the poisoned water, when the prophet Elisha used salt to purify water from a spring (2 Kings 2:19-22).

In the Roman Ritual, the priest prays, "May this creature of yours, when used in your mysteries and endowed with your grace, serve to cast out demons and to banish disease. May everything that this water sprinkles in the homes and gatherings of the faithful be delivered from all that is unclean and hurtful; let no breath of contagion hover there, no taint of corruption; let all the wiles of the lurking enemy come to nothing. By the sprinkling of this water may everything opposed to the safety and peace of the occupants of these homes be banished, so that in calling on your holy name they may know the well-being they desire, and be protected from every peril; through Christ our Lord. Amen."

Christ's faithful are permitted to take holy water home with them to sprinkle the sick, their homes, fields, etc. It is recommended that they put it in fonts in the rooms of their homes and use it to bless themselves daily and frequently.

SEASONAL WATER

Water blessed during the Easter Vigil is known as Easter Water. It is customary for millions the world over to obtain this Easter water for their homes, after it is blessed on Easter Saturday.

A special blessing of water on the Eve of the Epiphany was approved for the Roman Ritual in 1890. This blessing comes from the Orient, where the church has long emphasized the mystery of our Lord's baptism in her celebration of Epiphany. Years before the Latin Rite officially adopted the blessing of Epiphany water, diocesan rituals in lower Italy had contained such a blessing.

WATER AND THE SAINTS

Water is specially blessed and is a part of the cultus of a number of the saints.

- A papal brief of 1628 authorizes the blessing of water for the sick, in honor of the Blessed Virgin Mary and St. Torellus. This water is drunk by the sick.
- Water is blessed in the name of St. Peter the Martyr, asking through his intercession that all who drink it or are sprinkled with it may be delivered from evil spirits, illness, and suffering of both body and spirit.
- The blessing for the water in honor of St. Vincent Ferrer asks that in the name of God the Father and of St. Vincent, the water may "heal the sick, strengthen the infirm, cheer the downcast, purify the unclean and give full well-being to those who seek it." This water is blessed with a relic or image of the saint.
- The blessing for water in the name of St. Raymond Nonnatus asks that "all who suffer from fever may be delivered from every infirmity of body and soul when they bathe in this water, or drink it, or are sprinkled with it, and so deserve to be restored unharmed to your church where they will always offer their prayers of gratitude." This water is then sprinkled with holy water.
- In the blessing of the water in honor of St. Albert, Confessor, the exposed relics of the saint are immersed in the water. The prayer for this blessing asks that through the prayers of blessed Albert, the faithful who reverently drink this water may regain health of body and soul and so persevere in God's holy service. The same is true of water blessed in

honor of St. Ignatius, Confessor, and St. Vincent de Paul, except the relics are left in the reliquary and a medal may be substituted for the actual relics.

- In some churches, the people bring water, wine, bread, and fruit to church on St. Blaise's feast day to be blessed. The blessing of these items, which are sprinkled with holy water, asks that all those "who eat and drink these gifts be fully healed of all ailments of the throat and of all maladies of body and soul, through the merits of St. Blaise, bishop and martyr."

LOURDES WATER

In 1858, Bernadette Soubirous, a young, poor, uneducated French girl, was favored with a number of visions of Our Lady. Messages given to the world by Our Lady through this humble seer called for penance and confirmed the dogma of the Immaculate Conception that had been recently proclaimed by Pope Pius IX.

At first, people thought the visions were the foolish dreams of a sickly child. Because she looked so beautiful while in ecstasy, more and more people came to see for themselves. At the ninth apparition on February 25, 1858, the crowd — who could neither see the beautiful lady Bernadette spoke of nor hear her words — noticed Bernadette do a strange thing. In the midst of praying at the grotto called Massabielle, she turned and started toward the nearby river, then came back to the grotto and appeared to be digging in the earth. From the hole she had scraped out, muddy ooze began to seep, which Bernadette attempted to drink and put on her face. The crowd, who had not heard the directions to Bernadette to drink from and wash with the water from the spring as Our Lady indicated, simply thought she had gone crazy.

Soon, however, clear water began to trickle from this spot toward the river. People began to imitate Bernadette, and drink and wash with the water. The sick got well; the injured were cured, and the people began to call the water miraculous.

Although by 1981 only 65 of the cases examined at Lourdes had been declared miraculous by competent Church authorities, millions of people worldwide claim they were cured or helped by the water of this spring, or through the intercession of Our Lady of Lourdes. Today, water still flows from this spring at the rate of over 30,000 gallons a day, and Lourdes is a popular place of pilgrimage. Water from the spring has been piped to taps and to baths at the grotto, and shipped all over the world.

Lourdes Water

Lourdes Water is not holy water; it is water from the miraculous spring at Lourdes, France, but it has received no special blessing and may be drunk or used externally. The Lourdes Center in Boston, Massachusetts was founded by the Archbishop of Boston and the Bishop of Lourdes and entrusted to the Marist Fathers; its purpose is to promote devotion to Our Lady of Lourdes in America, distribute Lourdes Water, organize pilgrimages to Lourdes, and to serve as a center of information on Lourdes. Lourdes Water is free, but a donation to cover the cost of shipping and mailing is requested.

ST. ODILIA WATER

Authentic particulars about the life of St. Odilia are almost wholly lacking, although she is widely venerated in both Europe and America. Popular tradition has her the daughter of a nobleman, born blind, and hated by her father on that account. At length she recovered her sight, and he was reconciled with her. Later, she and a group of virgins (of which she was abbess) were martyred at Cologne.

In 1287, she appeared to John Novelan, a lay brother of the Crosier Order in Paris, informing him she had been appointed to be patroness of his order. She begged him to obtain permission to travel to Cologne to get her relics and told him where they were to be found, in an orchard near the city. After a third apparition, he was given leave to go with a priest of the order to search for the relics. The two had little trouble finding the relics, and they joyfully informed the archbishop, who came personally to witness the discovery. The relics were taken from Cologne to the motherhouse of the Order at Huy, Belgium; on the way, a number of miraculous cures took place.

During the French Revolution, however, the monastery at Huy was destroyed. Although the relics were saved, they were lost to the Order for over a century and a half.

At last, in 1949, the relics were returned to the Crosier Order and, in 1952, a major relic of the saint was brought to the seminary in Onamia, Minnesota, where a shrine in her honor was established.

St. Odilia is a patroness of the blind and of those afflicted with eye disease. For centuries it has been the practice in the Crosier Order to bless water in honor of St. Odilia, dipping her relic in it and asking God to give it a "power against all diseases and bodily infirmities." Many cures, especially of diseases of the eyes, are credited to her intercession.

FÁTIMA WATER

In 1917, when Our Lady appeared at Fátima, the nature of the soil at the Cova da Iria was so porous that it lacked any pockets of water. As this greatly inconvenienced pilgrims to the site, the Bishop of Leiria decided to build a concrete cistern to hold rainwater for the pilgrims' use. As ground was broken for this event in 1921, a pure spring of drinking water bubbled up in a crystalline stream. The water flows by the monument of the Sacred Heart in the Sanctuary of Fátima at the very spot where Our Lady deigned to appear to the three seers.

Father Cacella, the American "Apostle of Fátima," obtained a supply of this water by contacting the Bishop of Fátima. Monthly, ten to fifteen five-gallon demijohns of the water arrived in New York. Each was tightly sealed in wax, and each seal bore the imprint "SF" — Sanctuary of Fátima. In America, the water was transferred to sterilized vials and packed in boxes for distribution.

To this day, many miracles have been claimed as a result of the use of this water.

GREGORIAN WATER

A mixture of water, ash, salt, and wine, based on a prescription of Pope St. Gregory the Great (r. 590-604), Gregorian Water is blessed by the bishop at the consecration of a church and is used for sprinkling parts of the building.

TRINITY RAIN

Trinity Rain — rainwater collected on Trinity Sunday — is credited with special powers, health, and fertility, and the superstitious save it for drinking and bathing. Under the power of this special rain, ghosts and witches are prevented from doing harm, and magic flowers blossom at midnight; their finders receive all types of miraculous benefits. On the other hand, in popular fantasy, the neglect or desecration of this great Sunday is punished with dire misfortune. This superstition derives from the ancient lore of death demons roaming the earth at this season of the year.

PENTECOST DEW

A pious superstition in rural northern Europe ascribes special healing powers to dew that falls during Pentecost night. The custom was for people to walk barefoot through the grass in the early morning of the feast. The moisture was collected on bread that was then fed to livestock as a protection against disease and accidents.

BREAD

As a sacramental, bread has been used in a number of pious customs that involve blessing it and then eating it for a specific purpose or keeping it in honor of a saint. For example, the legend of St. Nicholas of Tolentino (1245-1305) includes his healing by giving people pieces of bread over which he had invoked the blessing of the Virgin Mary. The custom developed that bread blessed on his September 10 feast was given to the sick, to pregnant women, and even to animals. In central European and the Latin countries, *bendijo pan* (blessed bread), known as St. Blaise Sticks, is given to people on that saint's February 3 feast as a cure for sore throats. It is an Italian custom to save bread blessed on the feast of St. Joseph, called St. Joseph's Bread, as a sacramental to be used to avoid storms and sudden death.

In many Catholic countries, new loaves of bread are served on Sunday morning, and the Sign of the Cross is made three times over each. In Germany and Central Europe, a new loaf of bread is not cut until the Sign of the Cross is made over it. If a piece of bread falls from the table, the Sign of the Cross is made over it again before it is eaten.

PERPEQ

Perpeq is a traditional Albanian Easter cake, usually prepared on Holy Saturday morning and taken that afternoon to the church to be blessed. It is the first food eaten after attending the Easter Vigil. Even during the communist persecution, the tradition was continued. The sturdy Albanian Catholics made their *perpeq*, even under threat of imprisonment if they were found out. After the churches were destroyed in 1967, the people secretly brought the cakes to priests in hiding for the traditional blessing.

ANNUNCIATION BREAD

In Russia, priests bless large wafers of wheat flour and give them to the faithful on the Feast of the Annunciation. In the home, a father would hand a small piece of the wafer to each member of the family and to the servants who received it with a bow and ate it in silence. Later, they would take the crumbs of the Annunciation bread into the field and with pious superstition bury them in the ground as a protection against blight, hail, frost and drought. In a similar tradition in Central Europe, farmers put a picture of the Assumption in the seed grain while asking Our Lady's help with the crop.

PAIN BÉNIT

This is the name of the bread blessed and given to the faithful as a sign of belief in and love for Christ and as a symbol of the unity of Christ's Body, the Church. It is a sacramental and not to be confused with the consecrated Host, the true body of Christ.

PRETZEL

An interesting survival of early Christian Lenten fare is familiar today. The Christians in the Roman Empire made a special dough with flour, salt, and water only, as fat, eggs, and milk were forbidden. This was shaped in the form of two arms crossed in prayer. The little breads were called "little arms." Germans changed the Latin word to the term *brezel* or *prezel*, which became, in English, the word *pretzel*.

The oldest known picture of a pretzel is found in a fifth-century manuscript, but from medieval times to the present, these breads remained an item of Lenten food in many parts of Europe, and in some cities were distributed to the poor during Lent.

OPLATKY (OPLATEK, OBLATKY, OPLATKI)

Oplatky is a thin wafer of unleavened bread used in Polish and Eastern European Christmas customs. Similar to a host, the bread is stamped with sacred figures and blessed by the priest. The wafer is broken and eaten by all at the family table on Christmas Eve, as they exchange good wishes and honor their family members who are away from home.

HOT CROSS BUNS

Hot Cross Buns — bread rolls with a cross sliced into or frosted on the top — were a Good Friday tradition in medieval England and Ireland. The custom is said to have originated in St. Alban's Abbey in the mid-fourteenth century, when monks began distributing the marked buns to the poor on Good Friday in place of ordinary bread. Pious legend held these buns did not mold as regular bread did, and that eating them on Good Friday would protect the home from fire. They were kept through the year to be used as medicine or to ward off disease, lightning, and shipwreck.

ST. ANTHONY'S BREAD

St. Anthony's Bread is not a sacramental, but rather a pious

St. Anthony's Bread

custom of those devoted to St. Anthony of Padua. Charity is a wide avenue to the favors of heaven, and St. Anthony loves the poor now, just as he did in life.

Often, those who appeal to the "Wonder Worker" accompany their request with a promise that if the saint grants the favor they request within a certain length of time, they will donate a sum of money in his honor to the needy. The alms may be given to any charity or for the education of a poor seminarian who aspires to the priesthood.

BREAD OF THE DEAD

In many parts of the world, special breads are baked as part of the celebration of All Souls' Day, November 2. Called *Pan de los Muertos* (Bread of the Dead) in Mexico, *Ossi Dei Morti* (Bones of the Dead) in Italy, *Seelen Brot* (Soul bread) in Germany, and "dirge cakes" in Central Europe, all are made and eaten in honor of the souls of the faithful departed.

ST. AGATHA'S BREAD

Legend says St. Agatha's breasts were cut off during her martyrdom, around 250. The legend has led to her veneration today as a patroness in cases of breast cancer.

This story is honored on her feast, February 5, by baking bread in round loaves. In the region near her birthplace of Catania in Sicily, Catanese nuns make little rounded marzipan confections (meant to symbolize breasts) called *minne de vergine*, which are eaten on her feast day.

According to another legend, Agatha also miraculously freed her native city from starvation and stopped an eruption of Mount Etna, so she is additionally venerated as a "bread" saint and a patron of protection against fire. "Agatha loaves" are baked on her feast day, to which the faithful attach little pieces of paper with her picture and handwritten prayers against fire. The loaves are taken to the church to be blessed, then kept in the home as a sacramental.

OTHER FOOD

Throughout the history of the Church, food has played a sacramental part of the life of Christians. No fact of the Gospel history attests to this better than the account of Jesus' farewell supper with His disciples. The incident is narrated in all three Synoptic Gospels, plus 1 Cor. 11:23-26, where Paul explicitly says he has received the account from the church before him. It seems to have been Jesus' custom to close the day with a meal in company with His followers. After His death, they continued the practice which recalled Him to them vividly, and the new Christians observed the meal with a special memory of His last supper. Thus, the "breaking of bread" was a custom of the church from the earliest days.

THE *AGAPE* MEAL

The *agape* was a fraternal banquet celebrated by the early Christians as a symbol of their mutual charity and union in one family. The practice of holding such common meals, or "love feasts," seems to have been borrowed from pagan custom. A sacramental meal was a familiar feature of many ancient religions. At first, the *agape* preceded the Eucharistic celebration, and the interval was filled with readings from Scripture, prayers, and the singing of psalms. Toward the beginning of the second century, the *agape* was separated from the Mass, which was normally celebrated in the morning, while the *agape* took place in the evening and was seldom celebrated on Sunday.

The *agape* was held in private homes or in churches, with a bishop, presbyter, or deacon presiding. According to Hippolytus, the host provided the meal, invited the guests — including the poor and needy — and expected the guests to pray for him in return. From Tertullian, we learn the meal was begun and ended with prayer. After eating, each one present sang a hymn or psalm and, possibly, prophesied.

The *agape* was supposed to promote Christian fellowship and love and to unite those participating in closer relationship with Christ, considered to be the unseen Head of the table. Increasingly the meal became a charity supper or a memorial to the departed. When the faithful began to multiply, it became increasingly difficult to arrange these affairs, and abuses such as drunkenness and gluttony crept in (such abuses as Paul condemns in 1 Cor. 11:20-22). Consequently, by the eighth century, these "love feasts" had practically disappeared.

In modern times, the Moravians, Mennonites, Dunkards, Methodists, and some other sects revived the *agape* in one form or another. A remnant of the *agape* is found in the Cursillo movement and in the dinners hosted by the Magnificat organization.

We do not know exactly what these early Christians ate at their *agape* meals, although some biblical texts refer to wine having been served (and consumed in excess; cf. 1 Cor. 11:17-34; Jude 12). Through archeological research, we do know the foods grown and available to the early Christians, as well as the shapes of some of the cooking utensils and methods of cooking used.

KUCIOS

Kucios, also known as the Twelve Apostles Dinner, is a sumptuous and usually meatless family dinner which ends the traditional Christmas Eve fast still observed in many countries (especially in Eastern Europe). The *kucios* has a number of symbolic dishes pertaining to certain regions (for example, a bowl of porridge with fruit and honey represents the Holy Crib, or apples represent Adam and Eve). In some homes, the head of the household breaks a traditional Christmas wafer, and all who are there share it. Another custom is setting a place at the table for any family member unable to attend, or for those who have died during the previous year.

SOUL FOOD

The custom of soul food stems from the pre-Christian traditions of placing food on graves in November, when the spirits of the dead were believed to roam the earth. The Christian tradition developed of baking special breads and "soul food." At the family meal in many places on All Souls Day, an extra place is set in remembrance of the departed and the extra food is later given to the poor. An ancient belief held that the dead came back to earth on this day; therefore, many central Europeans kept their windows open so the souls in purgatory could hear the prayers said on their behalf. The Hispanic celebrations of All Souls, known as *Dia de los Muertos*, feature a number of traditional foods such as *mole* and special breads. In the orient, too, special foods accompany the ceremonies honoring the dead.

SIEBENKRAUTERSUPPE

Called the Friday of Sorrows in Central Europe, the feast of the Seven Sorrows was commemorated with a special soup consisting of seven bitter herbs called *Siebenkrautersuppe*. Traditional herbs used in making the soup are watercress, parsley, leek, nettle, sour clover, primrose, and spinach.

The liturgical seasons of Lent and Easter are filled with traditional foods served both as traditions and in a sacramental manner. (Please see separate section.)

SALT

Prior to reforms in the liturgy, salt had a more prominent sacramental usage. It was used during the scrutinies of catechumens and at the baptisms of infants. It was also used in the blessing of holy water, as well as in the rite of consecration of a church and an altar.

In the liturgies now in use, salt is no longer part of Christian initiation but has other sacramental functions. It can be blessed and kept in the home as a sacramental. Salt may also be mixed with newly blessed holy water, recalling the salt scattered over the water by the prophet Elisha.

Salt, in the Scriptures, represents wisdom and integrity of life.

ADVENT, CHRISTMAS, LENT, AND EASTER SACRAMENTALS

ADVENT AND CHRISTMAS SEASONS

No other season of the year is celebrated as festively as Christmas, the birthday of Our Lord. Throughout the centuries, worldwide, beautiful customs and sacramentals have increased the devotion of the season. Unfortunately, in our own times, the commercial value of Christmas has often been emphasized to the point where the religious significance of the holiday seems overlooked. Few people seem to be aware that nearly all popular Christmas customs have a religious background.

The variety of customs worldwide has brought forward a number of sacramentals unique to the area where they originated. The most popular, such as the Christmas tree, have found their way to other countries.

DECEMBER 25

The celebration of Christ's nativity as a special feast on December 25 was introduced in Rome about the middle of the fourth century. In the Roman Empire, it was a custom to celebrate the birthdays of rulers and other important persons. Often the celebrations continued after the death of the individual. Soon after the end of the last great persecution about the year 330, the Church in Rome definitely assigned December 25 for the celebration of the birth of Christ. The date varied in the Eastern Churches, but by the end of the fourth century, the Roman custom became universal. The most probable reason for the choice of the date is that the Romans, from the time of Emperor Aurelian in 275, had celebrated the feast of the sun god on that day; it was called the "Birthday of the Sun." Thus, it was natural for the Christians to celebrate the birth of Him who was "The Light of the World" and the "Sun of Justice."

By the fifth century, Christmas had become a feast of such importance that it marked the beginning of the ecclesiastical year. After the tenth century, the season of Advent had become an integral part of the Christmas cycle and the ecclesiastical year began on the first Sunday of Advent. In 529, Emperor Justinian prohibited work and public business on Christmas and declared the day a civic holiday. The Council of Agde (506) urged Christians to receive Holy Communion on the feast. The Council of Tours (567) established a sacred and festive season over the twelve days from Christmas to Epiphany.

As the great missionaries brought Christianity to the pagan tribes of Europe, they brought the celebration of Christmas with them. Most of these missionaries were the first bishops of the countries they converted, and thus they established and regulated the feast. By 1100, all the nations of Europe had accepted Christianity, and Christmas was celebrated everywhere with great devotion and joy. This was a time of colorful and inspiring religious services; Christmas music and plays were written, and this was the time most of the delightful Christmas customs of each country began. Some of these customs have died out; some, because of improper and scandalous actions, were suppressed; but many have survived to our day.

CHRISTMAS FORBIDDEN

In the sixteenth century, the Reformation brought sharp changes to Christmas celebrations for many countries in Europe. The Mass was suppressed, and in many countries, all that remained was a sermon and a prayer service on Christmas Day. In England, the Puritans condemned even the reduced religious celebration held in the Anglican Church after the separation from Rome, and became determined to abolish Christmas altogether. They contended that no feast of human institution should ever outrank the Sabbath. In Scotland, the celebration of Christmas was forbidden in 1583, and persons observing it were to be punished. When the Puritans finally came to political power in England, they promptly proceeded to outlaw Christmas; and, in 1647, Parliament set punishments for anyone observing Christmas and other holidays.

Even the lowly mincemeat pie was banned as being a "Papist concoction." The pie, with its rich spices, was symbolic of the three wise men's gifts; it was baked in a rectangle to symbolize the manger and often had a small dough cutout of the Christ child at its center. Each year, town criers went through the streets a few days before Christmas reminding the citizens that "Christmas day and all other superstitious festivals" should not be observed. During the year 1647, however, riots broke out in various places against the suppression laws, and the government had to break up Christmas celebrations by force of arms. With the restoration of the monarchy in 1660, Christmas celebrations were restored, but the religious aspect of the feast was left mostly to the ministers in the church service on Christmas day; celebrations at home were mere nonreligious amusements and general reveling, although a spirit of goodwill to all and of charity to the poor did remain a part of the celebration.

CHRISTMAS IN AMERICA

Christmas came to America with the missionaries and settlers from the various European countries. Thus, where the Spaniards and French settled, the feast was celebrated with liturgical solemnity and traditional customs. In the New England colonies, however, the Puritans' zeal against Christmas persisted into the middle of the nineteenth century. It was when immigrants from Ireland and continental Europe arrived in large numbers toward the middle of the last century that Christmas in America began to flourish.

THE CHRISTMAS CRIB

Various representations of the Christmas story, including the Child in the manger, have been used in church services from the first centuries. The oldest known picture is a Nativity scene dating from about 380 that served as a wall decoration in a Christian family's burial chamber, discovered in the Roman catacombs of St. Sebastian in 1877.

The use of the crib in its present form and its use outside the church is credited to St. Francis of Assisi. Three years before his death, the saint went to his friend Giovanni Velitta, a native of Greccio, and told him to "prepare what I tell you, for I want to enact the memory of the Infant who was born at Bethlehem, and how He was deprived of all the comforts babies enjoy; how He was bedded in the manger on hay between an ass and an ox. For once I want to see all this with my own eyes."

Thus on Christmas Eve, 1223, that good man prepared — in the place Francis requested — all the saint had told him. Franciscan friars were called from many communities. The people of the neighborhood prepared torches to light the night. Finally, the saint arrived, and the crib was made ready.

That night, Greccio became a new Bethlehem. The crowds rejoiced in the novelty of the celebration and sang in praise of God. A solemn Mass was sung at the crib. St. Francis sang the Gospel and preached a delightful sermon about the Nativity of the poor King and the humble town of Bethlehem.

Since the time of St. Francis, the Christmas crib has become a familiar sight in churches and homes all over the world. In central Europe, the beautiful family cribs are sometimes made up of hundreds of figures and fill an entire room of the house. The Moravian Germans were among the sects that kept the tradition of the Christmas crib even after the Reformation, and it was they who brought the custom to the United States. They called it *Putz*, from the German word for "decorate," and their scenes include not only the figures of the Nativity but dozens of figures, fanciful landscaping, waterfalls, houses, villages, and much more.

THE CHRISTMAS CANDLE

Since the early days of Christianity, it has been a religious practice to represent Christ by a burning candle, and the faithful readily adopted this symbolism from the liturgy. At Christmas, a large candle, representing the Lord, used to be set up in homes on Christmas Eve and kept burning through that Holy Night. The candle was lit every night during the holy season.

Different countries have different customs regarding the Christmas candle. In the Slavic nations, the candle is put on the table after being blessed by the priest in Church. The Ukrainians stick their Christmas candle into a loaf of bread. In parts of South America, the candle is put in a paper lantern with symbols and pictures of the Nativity on its sides. In France and England, the candle was often made of three candles twisted together in honor of the Holy Trinity. In Germany, the candle was put on top of a wooden pole decorated with evergreens, or many small candles were distributed on the shelves of a wooden structure made in the form of a pyramid, adorned with fir twigs or laurel and draped with tinsel. This pyramid was gradually replaced with the Christmas tree, although the Christmas pyramid has remained a traditional custom in some parts of Germany. In Ireland, a large holly-bedecked candle is lit on Christmas Eve, and the entire family prays for all its dear ones, living and dead. The Irish also place candles in the windows.

THE CHRISTMAS TREE

The use of Christmas trees is a fairly recent custom in countries outside of Germany, and even there it attained its immense popularity as recently as the end of the last century. The tree has its origin in a combination of two medieval religious symbols: the Paradise tree, and the Christmas light, or candle.

Beginning in the eleventh century, religious plays used to be performed in or near churches. One of the most popular of these "mystery plays" was the Paradise play. The play told the story of the creation and of the expulsion of Adam and Eve from Paradise after their sin. The ending of the play was a consoling promise of the coming Savior. This play was a favorite at Advent.

To indicate the Garden of Eden, a fir tree was hung with apples. This "Paradise tree" was the only prop on the stage, and attracted much attention, especially on the part of the children.

Because abuses had crept into their production, mystery plays were gradually forbidden in the fifteenth century. The people were so fond of their Paradise tree, however, that when they could no longer see it in church, they began putting it up in their homes in honor of the feast day of Adam and Eve, December 24. Although the Latin Church has never officially celebrated Adam and Eve as saints, the Eastern Churches do so; thus the custom of keeping their feast spread into Europe. In medieval religious "mystery" pictures, the Paradise tree stood for the Tree of Life as well as the Tree of Sin. In addition to the red apples — the fruit of sin — the trees bore wafers representing the Holy Eucharist, the fruit of life. Later, the wafers were replaced by candy and pastry representing the sweet fruit of Christ's redemption.

During the sixteenth century, people in western Germany began to combine the two symbols they had in their homes on December 24 — the Paradise tree and the Christmas pyramid. They began to transfer the decorations from the Christmas pyramid (see entry "Christmas Candle") to the tree. The Paradise tree already bore apples and sweets; the Germans added glass balls, tinsel, and topped the tree with the Star of Bethlehem. During the seventeenth century, lights were also transferred to the tree.

The first mention of the tree as it is now known dates from 1521 in German Alsace. Another description is found in a manuscript from Strasbourg in 1605. The tree slowly became popular, first in southern Germany, then throughout Europe. It was

ADVENT WREATHS, CALENDARS, AND PLAYS

The Advent wreath is a Lutheran custom that originated in eastern Germany a few hundred years ago. It probably was suggested by one of the light symbols used in folklore at the end of November and beginning of December. Our pre-Christian forefathers celebrated the month of Yule (December) with the burning of fires. Medieval Christians kept many of the light and fire symbols alive as popular customs; in the sixteenth century, these lights became a religious symbol of Advent in the homes of Christians.

The Advent wreath is made of evergreens and may be suspended from the ceiling or placed on a table, usually in front of a family shrine. Four candles are fastened to the wreath to represent the four weeks of Advent.

Every day during Advent, at a certain time, the family gathers for a short religious observance. Each Sunday another candle is lit, until all four candles announce the approaching birthday of the Lord. The initial darkness of

the candles can remind the faithful of the Old Testament centuries, when humanity was in darkness awaiting the Light of the Redeemer. The wreath, an ancient symbol of victory, symbolizes the fulfillment of time in the coming of Christ and the glory of His birth.

Our Sunday Visitor photo

Advent calendars originated in Germany and have recently spread worldwide. A colored scene printed on cardboard is put up at the beginning of December. Every day a "window" is opened by the children, revealing a picture or symbol that points to the coming feast of Christmas. On December 24, the door is opened, showing the Nativity scene.

An Advent play called *Herbergsuchen* originated in Germany. The play, whose title means "search for an inn," is a dramatic rendition of the Holy Family's fruitless efforts to find an inn in Bethlehem. A similar custom is the Spanish *Posadas,* traditional in Latin American countries, especially Mexico. A procession led by actors portraying Mary and Joseph wends its way through the *ciudad* (town), stopping and knocking at the doors of homes along the way. Shelter for the holy family is requested but refused by the homeowners until, at last, the procession arrives at a pre-designated home where they are welcomed. In this home, a traditional crib is set up with an empty manger. After prayers and blessing by the priest, adults and children alike enjoy a festive party. The children especially love the *piñata,* a papier-mâché figure hung from the ceiling. Blindfolded, the children attempt to hit the swinging *piñata* with a stick, breaking it so the contents, candy and sweetmeats, will shower on all.

introduced into France in 1837, when Princess Helen brought it to Paris after her marriage to the Duke of Orleans. Prince Albert of Saxony, the husband of Queen Victoria, had a tree set up at Windsor Castle in 1841; in 1850, Charles Dickens called the Christmas tree "a new German toy."

The Christmas tree arrived in America with the first wave of German immigrants, in about 1700. Through the second wave of German immigration, about 1830, the Christmas tree was brought to the attention of their neighbors, and soon became a much admired and familiar sight. The custom of setting up lighted Christmas trees in public places began in Boston in 1912. This custom spread rapidly over the United States and found its way to Europe shortly before World War II.

There are a number of legends regarding the origin of the Christmas tree, but all merely give a fictional explanation for the origin of an already-existing custom. The origin of the tree in legend has been ascribed variously to the Christ Child Himself, to St. Boniface, to St. Ansgar, and to Martin Luther.

CHRISTMAS CAROLS

The word *carol* comes from the Greek word *choraulein*, originally a term for a dance accompanied by the playing of flutes. Such dancing, usually done in a circle, was very popular in ancient Greece and Rome. The Romans took the custom and the name to Britain.

In medieval England, "caroling" referred to a ring or circle dance, accompanied by singing. Gradually, the meaning of the word changed and was applied to the song.

The first Christmas hymns were written in Latin, in the fifth century. Early Latin hymns, from about A.D. 400 to 1200, were profound and solemn; the origin of the modern Christmas carol was Italy. There, St. Francis and the early Franciscans introduced the joyful spirit to Christmas song, a spirit that soon spread throughout Europe.

St. Francis himself wrote a beautiful Christmas hymn called *Psalmus in Nativitate*. From Italy, the carol spread quickly to other parts of Europe; a large number of popular Christmas carols were written in Germany in the fourteenth century, under the inspiration of the Dominicans.

The earliest known English Christmas carol was written about the beginning of the fifteenth century. After the Reformation, most of the old hymns and carols were no longer sung, and were forgotten in many countries until their revival in the nineteenth century. Carols in general were discouraged by the Calvinists and suppressed altogether by the Puritans. Thus, after the restoration of Christmas in England, there were numerous festive songs, but few were religious carols. The Methodist revival in the eighteenth century inspired a number of modern hymns, first used only in Methodist churches but gradually welcomed by all English-speaking people. The best known of these is "Hark, the Herald Angels Sing," written by Charles Wesley. The Lutherans wrote new hymns for their own use. Some of those written by Martin Luther are still treasured in many churches today.

A Jesuit missionary, St. John de Brébeuf, wrote the first American carol to the Huron Indians. He adapted a sixteenth-century French folk song into the Christmas hymn *Jesous Ahatonnia* ("Jesus is Born") in the Huron language.

A great number of beautiful American carols have been introduced since the widespread revival of Christmas customs in America. A number of these were inspired by the Methodist revival, but carols have come from most of the religious sects in America. Those American carols differed from the average English Christmas songs of the past centuries because they reflected a religious spirit, whereas the English songs praised the external pleasures of feasting, reveling, and general goodwill without direct reference to the Nativity.

LENT AND EASTER SEASONS

In the liturgy of the Church, Lent is the season of penitential and prayerful preparation for the great feast of Easter. Penance was practiced from earliest times by fasting, additional prayer services, and other exercises for public sinners, in which the faithful joined in token of humble, voluntary penance.

From Ash Wednesday to Easter, solemn weddings and other joyous celebrations are prohibited in church. In the ancient Church, Lent was also the season of preparation for baptism.

From the time of the Apostles, Sunday, which replaced the ancient Sabbath as the new "Day of the Lord," and Friday, in memory of His death, have been singled out for special observation in honor of Christ's Resurrection. Eventually a longer period of fasting was observed.

ASH WEDNESDAY

The first day of Lent is called Ash Wednesday, from the ceremony of imposing blessed ashes in the form of a cross on the foreheads of all the faithful while the priest pronounces the words, "Remember, man, that you are dust, and to dust you shall return" (Gen 3:19). Pope Urban II officially introduced the name of the day itself in 1099; previously it was called "Beginning of the Fast."

The ashes used are made from burning the blessed palms of the previous Palm Sunday. They are given a special blessing before being distributed on Ash Wednesday, and the prayers in the Roman Missal for this ceremony date back to the eighth century.

Ashes have been used as a token of penance and sorrow from the time of the Old Testament. The Church accepted the custom from Jewish tradition and kept its original meaning. Originally, the imposition of ashes applied only to public sinners. By the end of the eleventh century, many devout people voluntarily submitted to it, and it has become a general practice worldwide. In medieval times, the Popes walked barefoot on Ash Wednesday, accompanied by their cardinals, to the church of Santa Sabina, where the Pope received the ashes from the oldest cardinal-bishop and distributed them to all the cardinals.

The imposition of ashes was discontinued in most Protestant churches after the Reformation, but was kept alive for a time in the Church of England. In recent times, some Protestant churches have returned to this ancient practice.

Ash Wednesday is not observed in the Oriental Churches. Their Lent begins on the Monday before Ash Wednesday, which they call "Clean Monday" because the faithful cleanse their souls in penance, and also wash and scrub all cooking utensils to remove all traces of meat and fat for the penitential season.

LAETARE SUNDAY

The fourth Sunday in Lent, formerly called *Laetare* Sunday, is a day of joy within the mourning season. The altars may be decorated with flowers, and rose-colored vestments may be worn instead of purple ones. The historical background for this sudden joyful note in the middle of the penitential season comes from the ancient practice of the *traditio symboli*, or handing over of the Apostolic Creed to the catechumens. After their period of trial, this was the last and decisive step toward baptism for those who had successfully stood the test, and Mother Church exulted over the approaching increase of her children through baptism. Hence, the liturgical expression of joy.

In later centuries, when the practice of the *traditio* in Mid-Lent was discontinued and combined with the baptismal ceremony, the reason for the Sunday's liturgical joy was forgotten. In 1216, Pope Innocent III mentioned in one of his sermons that the day marked "a measure of consoling relaxation . . . so that the faithful may not break down under the severe strain of Lenten fast but may continue to bear the restrictions with a refreshed and easier heart."

As a symbol of joy on *Laetare* Sunday, the Pope used to carry a golden rose in his right hand when returning from the celebration of Mass. This was originally a natural rose until the eleventh century, when it became customary to use one made of gold. Since the fifteenth century, this golden rose consists of a cluster or branch of roses made of pure gold and set with precious stones. The Popes bless the branch annually and sometimes confer it on churches, shrines, cities, or distinguished persons as a token of esteem and paternal affection. If the rose is bestowed, a new rose is made during the next year. In the prayer of blessing, the symbolism is expressed. The rose represents Christ in the shining splendor of His majesty, the "flower sprung from the root of Jesse."

PASSION SUNDAY

The fifth Sunday in Lent, before Vatican II reforms, was called Passion Sunday and from the ninth century occurred two weeks before Easter and inaugurated Passiontide, the final and particularly solemn preparation for the great feast. Formerly, thus, the last fourteen days of Lent were devoted entirely to the meditation of Christ's Passion. On the eve of Passion Sunday, the crucifixes, statues and pictures in the churches were draped in purple cloth as a sign of mourning. This custom originated in Rome in ancient times with the shrouding of the images in the papal chapel in the Vatican. Since Vatican II, Passion Sunday and Palm Sunday (see below) are combined.

THE STATIONS OF THE CROSS

The prevailing popular devotion of Lent, in both the Western and Eastern Catholic churches, is the Stations of the Cross.

The Stations of the Cross are fourteen tableaux depicting important events in the Passion and death of Our Lord. The stations are the prevailing popular devotion in Lent. Both the Eastern and Western Church practice this touching devotion, which originated in the time of the Crusades when the knights and pilgrims began to follow the route of Christ's way to Calvary in prayerful meditation, according to the ancient practice of pilgrims. The devotion spread throughout Europe and developed into its present form through the zealous efforts of the Franciscan friars in the fourteenth and fifteenth centuries.

The Second Station

Devotion to the Passion actually began with the Crucifixion. It is a constant tradition that the Blessed Mother walked over and over the narrow streets that led from the Praetorium of Pilate to the gate of the Holy City. From time to time, along the road sanctified by His suffering and consecrated by His Blood, the Sorrowful Mother knelt and prayed. The Blessed Virgin herself revealed to the mystic St. Bridget of Sweden that she had daily walked the way of Christ's sorrows, and visited the stations of His bitter Passion and death.

Likewise, the Apostles, disciples, and friends of Jesus who lived in Jerusalem and the surrounding areas walked this hallowed way of memories, meditating anew on the sufferings of their Master and Redeemer. From as far back as the fifth century, we know by the writings of St. Jerome that pilgrims who came to visit the Holy City always made their pilgrimage along the Way of the Cross.

Therefore, the devotion was in existence from apostolic times, although it did not attain a high form of development until the sixteenth or seventeenth century. Up to that time, the devotion remained a private exercise of piety that sprang spontaneously from faith and love. Only a limited number of faithful were actually able to make the trip to Jerusalem and walk in the footsteps of Christ on the Way of Sorrows, from the ruined court of Pilate to the basilica on the hill of Calvary. From the fifth century, Stations of the Cross were erected in a few places in Europe, but the devotion was not a general practice. These European stations were probably replicas of those along the true Way of the Cross, and their number varied.

The first stations of which there are authentic and documented records were erected in the Church of San Stefano in Bologna in the fifth century and were called *Hierosolyma* (Jerusalem). The Franciscans erected a set of stations in their cemetery in Antwerp sometime during the early years of the fifteenth century.

In the early thirteenth century, St. Francis of Assisi traveled to the Holy Land in an attempt to convert the Saracens and infidels who dwelt there. As he conceived it, his effort was in vain. However, the Franciscans did become the custodians of many of the sacred places in the Holy Land. The friars determined to bring the sacred places of Palestine to the world. In the year 1686, the Franciscans applied to Pope Innocent XI, who granted the same indulgences that pilgrims to the Holy Land obtained to all who made the Stations of the Cross in any Franciscan church. Then the Franciscans began promoting the devotion worldwide. Franciscan preachers, writers, and workers publicized the spiritual richness of the devotion. In particular, St. Leonard of Port Maurice became the great preacher of this devotion. Soon the Stations of the Cross were erected in every city, town, and hamlet of Europe.

The devotion has been called by various names: Way of the Cross, *Via Dolorosa*, Stations of the Cross, and Way of Christ's Sorrows. An Englishman named Wey was the first to use the word "stations" to describe the fourteen halts in the procession following along the Way of the Cross. These halts were made for meditation and prayer, and each commemorated some specific incident on the road to Christ's sacrifice. The number of incidents commemorated varied; Bologna had five stations, Antwerp had seven. Andrichomius, in the sixteenth century, enumerated twelve stations in the Way of the Cross in Jerusalem. At Vienne at the beginning of the nineteenth century there were eleven stations, with the first being the agony in the garden.

The stations were originally made in inverse order, beginning at the garden of the tomb and finishing in the judgment hall of the Praetorium. St. Leonard systematized and arranged the stations according to the actual sequence of the occurrence. From this time forward we find there were fourteen stations commemorated.

The Stations of the Cross, when erected in churches, may begin at either side of the church. During Lent or other times when the devotion is public, the priest moves from station to station; when the devotion is being made privately, the person making the devotion goes from one to another while meditating on the Passion of Christ.

Many beautiful meditations have been written for this devotion. There are meditations written using scriptures, those written especially for children, those which reflect modern problems in conjunction with the traditional commemorations. Short meditations have been written for use in the missions and for daily use.

Stations of the Cross

STATIONS OF THE CROSS

After an introductory prayer, each station usually begins with:

V. We adore you, O Christ, and we praise you.

R. *Because by your holy Cross you have redeemed the world.*

At each station, a meditation is made and a prayer may be added. In public devotions, a verse of the Stabat Mater *is often sung after each station.*

The First Station: Jesus is condemned to death. (Mt. 27:26; Mk. 15:15; Lk. 23:23-25; Jn. 19:16)

The Second Station: Jesus is made to carry the Cross. (Jn. 19:17)

The Third Station: Jesus falls the first time. (Mt. 27:31)

The Fourth Station: Jesus meets his Blessed Mother. (Jn. 19:25-27)

The Fifth Station: Simon helps Jesus carry his Cross. (Mt. 27:32; Mk. 15:21; Lk. 23:26)

The Sixth Station: Veronica wipes the face of Jesus. (Lk. 23:27)

The Seventh Station: Jesus falls the second time. (Lk. 23:26)

The Eighth Station: Jesus speaks to the women of Jerusalem. (Lk. 23:28-31)

The Ninth Station: Jesus falls the third time. (Jn. 19:17)

The Tenth Station: Jesus is stripped of his garments. (Lk. 23:34)

The Eleventh Station: Jesus is nailed to the Cross. (Mt. 27:33-38; Mk.15:22-27; Lk. 23:33-34; Jn. 19:18)

The Twelfth Station: Jesus dies on the Cross. (Mt. 27:46-50; Mk. 15:34-37; Lk.23:46; Jn. 19:28-30)

The Thirteenth Station: Jesus is taken down from the Cross. (Mt. 27:57-58; Mk. 15:42-45; Lk. 28:50-52; Jn. 19:38)

The Fourteenth Station: Jesus is placed in the tomb. (Mt. 27:59-61; Mk. 15:46-47; Lk. 23:53-56; Jn. 19:39-42)

The Fifteenth Station (optional): The Resurrection. (Mt. 28; Mk. 16; Lk. 24; Jn. 20)

The Stations are usually conducted with prayers for the intentions of the Holy Father, e.g., an Our Father, Hail Mary and Glory Be.

Many of today's meditations add a fifteenth station in honor of the Resurrection.

Christ said, "If any man would come after me, let him deny himself and take up his cross daily and follow me" (Lk. 9:23). The Franciscan Apostolate of the Way of the Cross promotes worldwide daily devotion to the Way of the Cross. They consider the devotion consoling and comforting to the elderly, the sick, or shut-ins, and helpful for all in search of a practical way of bringing God into their personal lives. This apostolate distributes information on the Way of the Cross and includes a blessed cross as a reminder of the Cross of Our Lord as well as a brief and simple meditation for making the Way of the Cross at home

HOLY WEEK

From the very beginning of Christianity, Holy Week has been devoted to special commemoration of Christ's Passion and death. After the time of the persecutions, Christian emperors of both the East and West issued various decrees forbidding amusements and games, and directed that the sacred days were to be spent free from worldly occupations and entirely devoted to religious exercises. Pardons were granted to those in prison, and many charges in court were dropped in honor of Christ's Passion. In medieval times, all secular business was prohibited; the time was spent in recollection and prayer. Kings and rulers often secluded themselves in a monastery. During the Middle Ages, the Sacred Triduum of Holy Week — Thursday, Friday, and Saturday — was a time of obligation. No servile work was done and the faithful were present at all of the impressive ceremonies of those days. In 1642, due to the changed conditions of social life, Pope Urban VIII rescinded this obligation.

PALM SUNDAY

By the fourth century, the faithful in Jerusalem began to reenact the solemn entry of Christ into their city on the Sunday before

Easter, holding a procession in which they carried branches and sang the "Hosanna." In the early Latin Church, the faithful held aloft twigs of olives during Mass. The rite of the blessing of the palms seems to have originated in the Frankish kingdom; an early mention of the ceremony is found in the Sacramentary of the Abbey of Bobbio in northern Italy, which dates from the eighth century. The rite was soon incorporated into the liturgy and celebrated in Rome. A Mass was held outside the walls of the city at some church where the palms were blessed. Then the faithful walked in solemn procession into the city to the basilica of St. John Lateran or to St. Peter's, where the Pope said a second Mass. The first Mass was later discontinued, and only the ceremony of blessing was performed.

During medieval times, a procession composed of the clergy

and laity carrying palms moved from a chapel or shrine outside the town, where the palms were blessed, to the cathedral or main church. Christ was represented by the Blessed Sacrament or by a crucifix adorned with flowers and carried by the celebrant. Later in the Middle Ages, a wooden statue of Christ

Palm crosses

sitting on a donkey, the whole image on wheels, was drawn in the center of the procession. These statues known as *Palmesel*, Palm Donkeys, may still be seen in a number of museums in European cities. Today's blessing of palms and the procession are usually held within the churches, and the blessing is short and simple compared to the former elaborate ritual.

In most countries, real palms are unattainable, so a variety of other branches are used. Centuries ago, not only branches but flowers were blessed, which is why in some countries the day is called "Flower Sunday." The term *Pascua Florida*, which in Spain originally meant just Palm Sunday, was later applied to the entire festive season of Easter Week. Thus the state of Florida received its name, when Ponce de León first sighted the land on Easter Sunday, 1513, and named it in honor of the great feast.

In central Europe, large clusters of plants interwoven with ribbons and flowers are fastened to a top of a wooden stick, and are called palm bouquets. The main plant used, however, is the pussy willow bearing their catkin blossoms. In the Latin countries and the United States, palm leaves are often braided or shaped into little crosses or other symbolic designs. The faithful reverently keep these in their homes during the year.

HOLY THURSDAY

In the early Christian centuries the bishop celebrated three Masses on Maundy (Holy) Thursday. The first, the Mass of Remission, was for the reconciliation of public sinners. The second was the Mass of the Chrism for the blessing of holy oils, and

Photo courtesy Basilian Fathers Missions

In many Latin countries, bread is blessed and distributed to the faithful on Holy Thursday.

Many Hispanic countries have the custom of building a special altar in the church, known as the *monumento,* for Holy Thursday. Typically, it is decorated with flowers and candles as a tribute to the Eucharist. In some regions, the people walk to as many churches as possible that night to visit the Blessed Sacrament and to offer prayers of adoration. The altar is taken apart on Good Friday and replaced with a representation of Calvary.

the third commemorated the Last Supper of Christ and the institution of the Eucharist. Today the Mass of the Chrism is still celebrated in every cathedral. During this Mass the bishop blesses the holy oils — oils of the sick, holy chrism, and oil of the catechumens. In the evening the Mass of the Lord's Supper is celebrated in all churches as one of the most solemn and impressive ceremonies of the year. The altar is decorated, and white, the liturgical color of joy, is used. After Mass, the Blessed Sacrament is carried in solemn procession to a decorated side altar, where it is kept in the tabernacle until the Good Friday service.

After the Mass the altars are stripped, and decorations except those at the repository shrine are removed in symbolic representation of the body of Christ, which was stripped of its garments.

Finally, there is the ancient rite of the washing of the feet, *Mandatum.* From ancient times, all religious superiors and the Popes performed the Maundy; the Synod of Toledo prescribed the rite as early as 694. In medieval times, and in some countries up to today, Christian emperors, kings, and lords washed the feet of old and poor men, to whom they afterward served a meal and distributed alms.

GOOD FRIDAY

Good Friday was celebrated from the earliest centuries as a day of sadness, mourning, fasting, and prayer. The first part of the

Good Friday service is the only example of the ancient Roman *Synaxis* — prayer meeting without Mass — that has survived to the present. After the synaxis, one of the most moving ceremonies of the year takes place, the Veneration of the Cross. The priest unveils the crucifix in three stages, and it is placed on a pillow in front of the altar. The priest and his assistants approach it, genuflecting three times, and devoutly kiss the feet of the image. The lay people follow performing a similar humble act of homage.

Veneration of the Cross was adopted by the Roman Church from Jerusalem, where from the fourth century, the True Cross of Christ was venerated every year on Good Friday. After Muslims conquered Jerusalem in 1187, the major relics were taken away and no trace of them was ever found. Small pieces of the cross, however, had previously been sent out and thus are extant today. Possibly the most famous of these is known as the Cross of Caravaca (p. 74).

(Photo courtesy Basilian Fathers Missions)

Preparing for a Good Friday procession

Following the Veneration of the Cross, the Blessed Sacrament is carried in procession from the repository shrine to the main altar and the Communion service is celebrated. Then, once the solemn ceremonies of Good Friday are concluded, the altar is stripped again, the tabernacle (if one remains) is left open, no lights burn in the sanctuary, and only the crucifix takes the place of honor on the naked altar or in front of the empty tabernacle.

The faithful practice various extraliturgical devotions in most countries of the world, which are today celebrated with solemn piety. The faithful of some countries have a ceremony and vigil of the Holy Sepulcher. In Spanish-speaking countries, a representation of Calvary is erected, and the priest detaches the body of Christ from the Cross and places it in the shrine of the Sepulcher. The faithful visit the shrine, praying all through the evening and on Holy Saturday.

In the Byzantine Church, the elders of the parish carry a cloth containing a picture of Our Lord's body resting in death and walk in procession to the shrine of the Sepulcher, where the cloth is placed on a table to be venerated by the people. The Ukrainians and other Slavs of the Oriental Church call this ceremony *Platsenitsia*.

From the second century, it was a widespread custom for people to fast day and night for forty hours, from Good Friday afternoon until Easter Sunday morning. To this fast was added a forty hours' prayer at the Holy Sepulcher shrine. This custom remained through the Middle Ages, and later; liturgically speaking, however, only the fasting is provided in the Roman Rite, and the Eastern Rites have a "burial" service in their Good Friday

(Photo courtesy Basilian Fathers Missions)
Carrying a statue of Mary during a Good Friday procession

ritual. The Forty Hours' Devotion, which grew out of the ancient forty hours' "wake," was separated from its original place and officially established as a liturgical devotion at various other times of the year. Devotions connected with the seven last words of Christ, processions, Passion plays, and other paraliturgical ceremonies have developed as well over time.

HOLY SATURDAY

Holy Saturday commemorates Christ's rest in the tomb; no service occurs in the Western church during daylight hours. In the early centuries, the catechumens would assemble in the church during the afternoon, and the rites that are still practiced in baptism were performed. But otherwise, as Christ rested in the grave, the faithful wait in prayer and fasting until the evening star announces the Easter Vigil.

Now, this day is traditionally spent around the home in preparing the home and food for the Easter celebration. In Central Europe, the Easter ham and other foods for the great feast are prepared. Eggs are boiled and painted, and the entire house is decorated with flowers. In the Slavic countries, baskets of food — especially the decorated eggs — are taken to the church to be blessed. In some regions, the priest goes from house to house to bless the Easter foods. All who come to visit are presented with a decorated egg.

In Russia, traditionally the people carried their *paska* (Easter bread) to the priest to be blessed after the midnight benediction. It was then was taken home and given the place of honor on the Easter breakfast table.

In Ukraine, the blessing of the traditional foods is called *Sviachenia*. Each of the foods in the specially decorated Easter basket has a symbolic meaning. The beautiful eggs are symbolic of the tomb from which Christ arose, and hold a special meaning of hope. The meat products of ham, roasted lamb, and sausage represent the animals used for sacrifice in the Old Testament, thus recalling for us of the sacrifice of Christ. The ham symbolizes freedom from the Old Law, and the lamb, symbolic of Jesus, reminds us of the New Law. Butter, cheese, Easter breads, and horseradish complete the contents, and each has a symbolic meaning as well. Ukrainians took their baskets to the church early on Easter morning, and afterwards the families met outside the church to admire them. Each also held a lighted candle, symbolic of the Light of Christ. Just as the meals at home were a sign of family unity, today's Ukrainian families living in the United States and Canada have begun a new unity tradition called the *Sviachene dinner*, which usually takes place on the Sunday following Easter. Sponsored by the parish churches, these dinners symbolize the unity of the parish family.

In Italy, bread was formed in fanciful shapes, including Easter baskets holding an egg, which was sometimes used as an *ex voto* offering.

EASTER VIGIL

From the beginning of Christianity, the feast of the Resurrection of Christ was celebrated as the most important and festive day of the whole year. For Christians, every Sunday is a "little Easter," consecrated to the memory of the risen Christ.

The word Easter originally meant the celebration of the spring sun, which had its birth in the East and brought new life to the earth. This symbolism was transferred to the supernatural meaning of our Easter —the new life of the risen Christ, Who is the eternal and uncreated Light. The Jewish Passover and the Christian Easter are significantly linked because Christ died on Passover Day. The lamb that had to be sacrificed for the deliverance of Israelis was considered by the Church as prophetic of Him Who is the "Lamb of God, who takes away the sin of the world" (Jn. 1:29).

In the early centuries, the faithful embraced with the words *Surrexit Dominus vere* (Christ is truly risen), to which the reply was *Deo gratias* (Thanks be to God). From the fourth century on, the mood of Christians turned into radiant joy at the sight of the first stars in the evening of Holy Saturday. The churches began to blaze with the light of lamps and candles, and the homes of the people shone with light. Multitudes crowded into the churches, joining in prayer. In later centuries, the vigil service began with the lighting of the Paschal candle, a sacred symbol of Christ's Person. After the blessing of the candle, a prayer service was held, Bible passages were read, and the priests and people recited psalms, antiphons, and orations. The faithful spent the entire night in church.

Near midnight, the bishop and clergy went in procession to the baptismal font, usually found in a structure outside the church. There, the baptismal water was consecrated with the same prayers used today. The catechumens were baptized, anointed, and given garments of white linen, which they wore at all services until the end of Easter week. The vigil was concluded about dawn of Easter Sunday with the celebration of the Holy Sacrifice. During later centuries some other rites, such as the blessing of the Easter fire, were added. This blessing was incorporated into the Roman liturgy during the latter part of the ninth century, and the blessing of the fire became the opening rite of the ceremonies on the Vigil of Easter.

EASTER

The solemn words of the official calendar of the Western Church announce the celebration of Easter Sunday: "This is the day the Lord has made, the Feast of Feasts, and our Pasch — the Resurrection of our Savior Jesus Christ according to the flesh." Although there are no special ceremonies other than the Mass itself, the Latin Church celebrates Mass in all churches with festive splendor and great solemnity on Easter Sunday.

EASTER LAMB

The lamb is the most significant symbol of Easter. The lamb, representing Christ, is usually shown with a flag of victory.

Prayers for the blessing of lambs date back to the seventh century. From the ninth century, the main feature of the Pope's Easter dinner was roast lamb. The ancient tradition of the Paschal lamb inspired the use of lamb as a popular Easter food among all the faithful. In Europe, small figures of a lamb made from butter, pastry, and sugar are popular.

EASTER EGGS

The custom of Easter eggs developed among the nations of northern Europe and Christian Asia soon after their conversion to Christianity. Their history stems from the fertility lore of the Indo-European races. It was a startling event to see a living creature emerge from a seemingly dead object, and so to our pre-Christian ancestors, the egg became a symbol of spring and fertility. Converts to Christianity gave the egg a religious interpretation, seeing it as a symbol of the rock tomb out of which

Making Easter eggs

Christ emerged to new life. Additionally, since eggs were forbidden during the fast of Lent, they became a special sign of Easter joy, and the faithful painted them in gay colors. They were blessed and eaten, or presented as gifts to friends.

A special blessing in the Roman Ritual read thus: "We beseech Thee, O Lord, to bestow Thy benign blessing upon these eggs to make them a wholesome food for thy faithful, who gratefully partake of them in honor of the Resurrection of our Lord Jesus Christ."

In medieval times, eggs were traditionally given at Easter to all servants, and to the children, along with other gifts. In most countries, the eggs are stained in plain vegetable-dye colors. Among the Chaldeans, Syrians, and Greeks, the eggs were dyed crimson in honor of the blood of Christ. In Poland and Ukraine, simple designs are found on eggs called *krasanki*, and a number of eggs are made each year in a very distinctive design. These latter are masterpieces of patient labor and exquisite workmanship. These, called *pysanki*, are unique and are saved from year to year as heirlooms.

In Central Europe, eggs used for cooking Easter food are pierced with a small needle and the contents blown out. The shell is reserved and given to the children for use in egg games. Armenians decorate these empty eggs with religious pictures as gifts, and in parts of Germany, the eggs are decorated and hung from shrubs and trees much like Christmas ornaments. The custom of hiding the eggs is universal.

EASTER BUNNY

The rabbit was the most fertile animal our pre-Christian ancestors knew, serving as a symbol of abundant new life in the spring season. The Easter Bunny has never had a religious symbolism, although the white meat is sometimes said to suggest purity and innocence. The Church has never had either a special blessing for rabbits, nor any link between them and the spiritual meaning of the sacred season. Throughout history, however, the Easter Bunny has acquired a cherished role as the provider of Easter eggs for children in many countries.

The first mention of the Easter Bunny and his eggs seems to be from a German book of 1572. In many sections of Germany, the children believed that the Easter Bunny laid red eggs on Maundy Thursday and multicolored eggs the night before Easter Sunday. The first Easter Bunnies of sugar and pastry were popular in southern Germany at the beginning of the last century.

VIA LUCIS – STATIONS OF LIGHT

The *Via Lucis*, from the Latin for "the Way of Light," is a recent devotion proper to the post-Easter liturgical period.

The new practice has characteristics similar to the Way of the Cross (*Via Crucis*) and can be prayed personally or in community.

A Paschal candle or icon of the Resurrection is carried, rather than a cross.

Stations of Light

The *Via Lucis* includes fourteen stations for reflection on Christ's Pasch, from his Resurrection to Pentecost. The service may include readings of the biblical narratives corresponding to each station, followed by silence, meditative prayer, and a hymn.

Promotion of the devotion began in 1994 by a group called TR2000 (TR standing for *Testimonio del Risorto*, Italian for "The Witness of the Risen [Christ]"). Its primary function is to remind the faithful to live the Easter spirituality according to 2 Tim. 2:8.

VIA LUCIS

One suggested set of stations for the *Via Lucis* is:

1. Jesus rises from the dead.
2. The disciples find the empty tomb.
3. Jesus appears to Mary Magdalen.
4. Jesus walks with the disciples to Emmaus.
5. Jesus reveals himself in the breaking of bread.
6. Jesus appears to the disciples.
7. Jesus confers on his disciples the power to forgive sins.
8. Jesus confirms Thomas in faith.
9. Jesus appears to his disciples on the shore of Lake Galilee.
10. Jesus confers primacy on Peter.
11. Jesus entrusts his disciples with a universal mission.
12. Jesus ascends into heaven.
13. Mary and the disciples await the Holy Spirit.
14. Jesus sends the Spirit promised by the Father to his disciples.

The *Via Lucis* was presented in 1989 to Don Egidio Vigano, the seventh successor to Don Bosco as head of the Salesian Order, who offered his support and help to TR2000. In 1990, the *Via Lucis* was first solemnly celebrated by Don Vigano in Rome at the catacomb of St. Calixtus, during the general chapter of the Salesians. The stations, sculpted by the artist Dragoni, were erected in the catacomb in 1996, and they were celebrated there during a World Youth Day in Rome.

PENTECOST TREE

The Pentecost Tree is a German custom in which, either on Pentecost eve or the day itself, a young man planted a tree in front of the house of a young woman he liked. It was considered an honor to have a *Pfingstbaum*, or Pentecost tree, planted in front of one's house. Today, Pentecost trees can be presented to the honoree in a decorated pot and trimmed with doves symbolic of the Holy Spirit, as shown below.

Decorated Pentecost tree

IMAGES

One of the major criticisms that Protestants have leveled at the Catholic Church deals with the Catholic veneration of images, which fundamentalists have at times misinterpreted as Catholic "idolatry." However, Catholic doctrine is quite clear on this point: the pictures and statues in the Church are *honored*, not *adored*. Just as people cherish photographs of their family and friends as reminders of them, so, too, we cherish our sacred images as reminders of Our Lord, the Blessed Virgin, and the saints. We honor our national flag not because of the cloth out of which it is made, but because of what it represents. It is this type of honor and respect that belongs to sacred images.

Holy images have a holy purpose. Sacred images help us avoid distractions while praying by fixing our attention. They serve as a silent admonition, encouraging us to imitation. Finally, they are a good means for instructing the faithful in religion. The greatest artists in the world have been Catholic artists, and their greatest masterpieces are treatments of religious subjects. Even an illiterate person can understand a picture.

We honor Christ and the saints when we pray before crucifixes, relics, and sacred images. We honor them because of the persons they represent; we adore Christ, and we venerate the saints. We venerate the saints for God's sake and our own — to increase in ourselves the wish to imitate their virtues. We venerate these images by praying before them, adorning them with flowers or precious objects, burning lights before them, and kissing them with reverence. We make visits to the tombs or shrines of the saints, just as on civil holidays we honor our heroes by placing wreaths on their graves. Veneration of sacred images can help us obtain effective and sometimes supernatural graces.

Catholics do not pray *to* the crucifix or to the sacred images, but to the *persons* they represent. In that sense only, disrespect to a sacred image is disrespect to the one represented. But Catholics do not believe that any divine power resides in any sacred image, and it is not the image that works any miracles. The numerous miracles worked through the use of relics and images are a result of God acting through them. Even today, relics and images continue to play a part in the working of miracles and the suspension of the natural law, but always and only as mere instruments of Almighty God.

There are literally hundreds of thousands of famous or well-known sacred images. Although paintings and statues are more common in the Western church, and icons (ikons) more prevalent in the Eastern churches, there is no form of artistic expression that has not been used in the creation of sacred images. The history of art itself cannot be separated from religion, for man has always given of his best artistic talents to his God. Just as with the case of relics, Christianity is not alone the custodian of sacred images.

Each painting, statue, or icon has its own unique history in the church. In this section, only a few representative images are included.

"Crowned" images are those accorded a special recognition in the form of a papal crown. The wealthy Italian nobleman Alexander Sfirzo left in his will a large sum of money for the purpose of crowning certain images as directed by the pope. Images crowned must meet three conditions: 1) the devotion to the image must be approved by the bishop of the area, 2) the devotion must have a long history, and 3) the picture or statue must have a reputation for being divinely chosen and an instrument of miracles.

TRAVELING IMAGES

Traveling, or pilgrim, images are those statues, icons, or other images transported from home to home, parish to parish, and country to country to promote devotion. Among the best known of these are the images of Our Lady of Fátima, San Juan de los Lagos, and *Santo Niño de Atocha*.

Traveling image of
Our Lady of Fátima

Another type of traveling image is the portable icon. These were popular from the thirteenth to the sixteenth centuries and are still common among the members of the Eastern Church. Made of many different materials, some of them were meant to be worn suspended around the neck. Others were made in the form of a triptych (*skladen*). Folding icons were widely used in Russia, made for being carried while traveling as a substitute for the domestic iconostases. Some miniature icons were made with a loop at the top, to be worn about the neck. This latter type was often donated to churches and monasteries, either as *ex voto* appendages to venerated icons, or under the wills of their owners after their deaths.

Two images deserve special mention here, although they are not paintings or another form of manmade artwork. Both the Shroud of Turin and the *tilma* of St. Juan Diego, containing the

Portable icon

image of Our Lady of Guadalupe, are considered miraculous and not made by man, but imprinted by the Divine.

SHROUD OF TURIN

Also known as the Holy Shroud, the Shroud of Turin is a worn, yellowed, and partially scorched linen cloth that has long been venerated as the burial sheet in which Jesus' body was wrapped immediately after he was taken down from the cross on Golgotha. It is best known for bearing a clear depiction of Christ's crucified body, although precisely how the image was imprinted upon the cloth remains today a mystery. Additionally the date of the shroud is the source of controversy among scientists and experts. Nevertheless, the shroud has been the source of private devotions since at least from the fourteenth century and evidence indicates it was known and revered for centuries before its appearance in Western Europe.

The shroud measures 14 feet 3 inches in length and 3 feet 7 inches in width. On the linen is the image of a Semitic man with long hair and a beard who bears the clear marks of crucifixion. All of the wounds described in the New Testament account of Jesus'

Passion are present in the hazy brown pigmenting. Including the marks from the crown of thorns on the head, bruises on the shoulders and severe cuts or lacerations on the back where the flogging would have occurred.

The Shroud is first mentioned in the Gospel of Mark. Chapter 15:43-46 details its purchase by Joseph of Arimathea and his use of it as a burial shroud for Christ. There is a long history in the lands of the Eastern Empire of a cloth bearing the image of Christ, but it disappeared after the fall of Constantinople in 1204 (i.e., there are no extant documents which prove its whereabouts). It was not until 1354 that the cloth was seen again, when a French knight, Geoffroi de Charny, presented a cloth bearing Christ's crucified image to the canons of Lirey near Troyes. From that time, the history of the relic is well documented. The shroud was venerated in a number of different cities and damaged in a fire before finally being permanently placed in Turin, Italy, in 1578.

A lawyer, Secondo Pia, made the first photographs of the Shroud in 1898. These sparked a renewal of interest in determining the true origin of the relic. The photos, startlingly, revealed a positive image on the negatives.

Radiocarbon dating in 1988 seemed to prove that the shroud dated only from medieval times, but reputable scientists have subsequently questioned these results. Recent scientific tests, although not well publicized, have shown traces of myrrh and aloes and other botanicals in the fibers of the cloth, which indicate that the origin of the shroud can be traced to the area around Jerusalem in Palestine as well as the time of Christ. During a major restoration in the summer of 2002, the patches sewn on the cloth at the time of the fire were removed and it was given a new backing cloth.

Although the Church has never officially pronounced the relic genuine, a number of Popes have written encouragingly about the message it presents to us: the message of the means of our redemption.

OUR LADY OF GUADALUPE

In the beginning of the sixteenth century in Mexico, an idolatrous worship of Quetzalcoatl and other gods flourished. Although Cortez had conquered Mexico for Spain, the Indians still held to their ancient religion, which emphasized human sacrifice. In the Aztec nation alone, 20,000 human lives were sacrificed annually to their gods.

Our Lady of Guadalupe

Our Lady appeared to Juan Diego, a Christian convert, on the hill of Tepayac on December 9, 1531. She requested that he go to the Bishop of Mexico, in Mexico City, and ask that a church be built on the spot. The hill held special significance in the pagan religion of the Indians. At first, the bishop refused the appeal, thinking that Juan was merely imagining things. The next day, Our Lady appeared again and repeated her request. This time, Juan was so sincere in his petition that the bishop was more inclined to listen and told Juan to ask the lady for some sort of a sign as proof of the apparition. At a third meeting, Juan mentioned the bishop's request, and the lady promised to give the sign the following morning. The morning of December 12, Juan awoke to discover that his aged uncle was very ill, and he left hurriedly to bring a priest from the city to administer the last rites. As he neared the hill, he remembered the request of the lady and, thinking that she would delay him, hurried around the bottom of the hill to avoid her. There she was, however, and when she asked him where he was going, he explained about his sick relative.

Our Lady assured Juan that his uncle would recover, and then sent him to the top of the hill to fetch some flowers for her. Juan knew that nothing grew there except some cactus, so he was greatly surprised to find many flowers in bloom. He picked a large bouquet, and so as not to drop them, he put them in his *tilma*, a cloak woven of vegetable fiber.

When Juan reached the lady again, she tied the ends of the *tilma* at his neck and charged him not to show the flowers to anyone until he was in the presence of the bishop.

On reaching the bishop's palace again, and after a lengthy wait, Juan was at last admitted to the bishop's presence. Only then did he unfold his *tilma*. Castillian roses cascaded to the floor. Immediately, all those in the room fell to their knees. A beautiful image of the Blessed Virgin was imprinted on the *tilma*.

Juan rushed home to tell his uncle, but his uncle was coming to meet him with the news that he too had seen the beautiful lady. She had spoken in his native language and told him that the image was to be known by the name of the "Entirely Perfect Virgin, Holy Mary," and that the image would be the means to crush or stamp out the religion of the stone serpent. That Our Lady's mission was successful is shown by the fact that within seven years, eight million Indians had come voluntarily to the Franciscans and other missionaries and requested instructions and baptism.

Juan and his uncle spoke to the Spanish bishop through the use of interpreters, and when they were telling about Mary's words to Juan's uncle — or so most modern scholars believe — the words they spoke were not translated correctly. To the Spanish ears of the translator, their words seemed to say that the image was to be known by the name "Virgin of Guadalupe," the name of a popular shrine in Spain dedicated to the Virgin.

Is the image really miraculous, or only a painting? Experts from various fields have studied it over time and have come to agree that no artistic process currently known on earth was used to make the picture. The gold on the picture is a precious gold powder not held on by any fixative or glue. The fine black lines that outline the picture were drawn on by human hands at a later date, as was a crown, not originally on the image. (It is interesting to note that the crown, although of real gold, has tarnished and almost disappeared, whereas the other gold on the image is still in good condition.)

The image is 66 by 41 inches, and the figure is four feet, eight inches tall. This makes the image life size, with colors that have stayed fresh in spite of the fact that, for centuries, it was not covered by glass or protected in any way.

In 1921, during the revolution and the persecution of Catholics in Mexico, a stick of dynamite hidden in a bouquet of flowers was placed on the altar to destroy the image. It exploded, causing a great deal of damage: it broke all of the windows in the church, tore out marble blocks from the altar, and knocked a heavy bronze crucifix standing under the image to the floor, leaving it bent and twisted. Nothing, however, happened to the image. The glass covering it was not even cracked. The preservation of the image in this case is miraculous in itself.

In 1976, work on a new basilica was completed and the shrine re-dedicated. Study and research on the image continues, and annually thousands flock to the site to pay homage to Mary under the title Our Lady of Guadalupe; twenty popes have issued decrees concerning the image.

Our Lady of Guadalupe is patroness of all the Americas.

Statues and *Santos*

THE INFANT JESUS OF PRAGUE

Devotion to the Child Jesus under the title "Infant Jesus of Prague" is over three and a half centuries old. The devotion originated in Spain, spread to what is now Czechoslovakia, and from there to all parts of the globe. Replicas of the original statue dressed in royal priestly vestments can be found in thousands of churches and private homes. In the United States, a national shrine in honor of the Christ Child under this title is located in Prague, Oklahoma.

In 1556, Maria Manriquez de Lara brought a precious family heirloom, a statue of the child Jesus, with her to Bohemia when she married the Czech nobleman Vratislav of Pernstyn. The statue of the child is eighteen inches tall, carved of wood, and thinly coated with wax. The left foot is barely visible under a long white tunic. The statue stands on a broad pedestal, in a waist-high silver case that holds it upright. The left hand holds a miniature globe surmounted by a cross, signifying the worldwide kingship of Christ. The right hand is extended in blessing in a form usually used by the Supreme Pontiff; the first two fingers are upraised to symbolize the two natures in Christ, while the folded thumb

Infant Jesus of Prague

and last two fingers touch each other to represent the mystery of the Holy Trinity. The statue wears a wig of blond human hair.

Since 1788, there have been two jeweled rings on the fingers of the statue, gifts in thanks for a miraculous cure, and in 1655, the statue was solemnly crowned by the supreme *Burgrave* of the Czech kingdom. The original garments are still preserved, but since 1713, the garments of the statue have been changed with the liturgical season. During the change of vestments, devotional objects are touched to the statue to be distributed to all parts of the world.

Princess Polyxena Lobkowitz inherited the statue of the infant from her mother, Maria, and honored it devotedly in her home until after the death of her husband. In 1628, she presented her beloved statue to the Discalced Carmelites of Prague — telling them, prophetically, that as long as they honored the Child

Jesus as king and venerated His image, they would not want. Her prediction was verified; as long as the Divine Infant's image was honored, the community prospered, spiritually and temporally. When the devotions relaxed, it seemed as if God's blessing departed from the house.

The statue was set up in the oratory of the monastery, and twice daily special devotions were performed before it. The novices were particularly devoted to the Holy Infant. One of them, Cyrillus of the Mother of God, was suffering interior trials. After prayers to the Child Jesus, he found a sudden relief from his worries and became the greatest apostle of the holy image.

During the Thirty Years' War, the novitiate was moved to Munich, Germany, but in 1631, King Gustavus Adolphus of Sweden — an inveterate foe of Catholicism — invaded. Many inhabitants of Prague fled, including all of the Carmelites except two, who remained to protect the monastery. The enemy took possession of the monastery in November of 1631, and the house was plundered. The image of the Infant was thrown in a heap of rubbish behind the high altar, where it lay forgotten for seven years.

In 1637, Father Cyrillus returned to Prague. The monastery had suffered many reverses in recent years, and the city was again overrun with hostile troops. The prior of the community called the monks together to offer prayers. Father Cyrillus remembered the favors formerly received through the intercession of the Infant, and he asked permission to search the monastery in hopes that the statue might have been left behind when the monastery was plundered. At last the statue was found, and Father Cyrillus placed the dusty little image on an altar in the oratory, where the long-forgotten devotions were renewed with vigor.

One day, after the other monks had left the oratory, Father Cyrillus remained kneeling in front of the statue for hours, meditating on the divine goodness. In a mystical ecstasy, he heard the statue speak these words: "Have pity on me, and I will have pity on you. Give me my hands, and I will give you peace. The more you honor me, the more I will bless you!" Startled, the priest noticed for the first time that the statue's hands had been broken off. He went immediately to the prior to beg him to have the statue restored. The prior denied his request, saying that the monastery was too poor.

Shortly thereafter, a wealthy and pious man came to Prague and fell ill. Father Cyrillus was called to the dying man, who offered financial help to repair the statue. The prior, however, used the donated money to buy an entirely new statue instead of having the old one repaired. On its very first day, a falling candlestick shattered the new statue. To Father Cyrillus, this was an indication that the wishes of the Infant must be fulfilled — literally.

The sorrowing priest took the damaged statue to his cell, where he prayed, through the intercession of the Blessed Virgin, for the money to repair the statue. No sooner had he finished his prayer than he was called to the church. There, he found a noble lady waiting for him; she handed him a considerable amount of money, and then disappeared.

Happily, Father Cyrillus took the money to the prior and, again, requested the repair of the statue. At last, the prior agreed, provided the repairs did not exceed a certain amount. Unfortunately, the estimates were too high, so again the statue was not repaired. Interiorly, the priest heard a voice telling him to place the statue at the entrance of the sacristy. He did so, and soon a stranger came and noticed the broken hands of the statue. The stranger offered to have the statue repaired at his own expense, an offer that was joyously accepted.

At last, the repaired statue was placed in the church. A pestilence was raging in Prague at the time, and the prior himself nearly died. He vowed to spread the devotion of the Infant if he were cured. Shortly thereafter, he ordered a general devotion to the Infant in which all the friars took part. At last, the Infant had completely won the hearts of the Carmel of Prague and become a cornerstone of their devotion.

In 1641, a generous benefactress donated money to the monastery for the erection of an altar to the Blessed Trinity with a magnificently gilded place for the miraculous statue, which was then exposed for public veneration. In 1642, a baroness financed the erection of a handsome chapel for the Infant, which was blessed in 1644 on the feast of the Most Holy Name of Jesus. This has remained the principal feast day of the image ever since. In 1648, the Archbishop of Prague gave the first ecclesiastical approval of the devotion when he consecrated the chapel and gave permission to priests to say Mass at the chapel altar. In 1651 the Carmelite general made a canonical visitation to the monastery to examine the devotion. The statue was solemnly crowned in 1655.

In 1741, the statue was moved to a magnificent shrine on the epistle side of the church of Our Lady of Victory. It became one of the most famous and popular shrines in the world and the Carmelites of the Austrian Province made the spread of the devotion a part of their apostolate. The popularity of the little King of Prague spread to other countries in the eighteenth century. Pope Leo XIII confirmed the Sodality of the Infant of Prague in 1896 and granted many indulgences to the devotion. Pope St. Pius X unified the membership into a confraternity, under the guidance of the Carmelites, which increased the spread of the devotion in our own century.

SANTO NIÑO DE ATOCHA

Portrayed as a small boy, the image of the child Jesus known as *Santo Niño de Atocha* (Holy Child of Atocha) is usually dressed in a long gown with a cape that has a wide lace collar and frilled cuffs. A cockleshell is on his cape, a Spanish symbol of a pilgrim. Seated on a small chair, the Infant holds a basket of food, and a water gourd is suspended from a staff in his hand. The image shows the child shod with sandals and wearing a large hat with a feather.

The story of *Santo Niño de Atocha* is a story rich both in history and pious devotion. Although the Holy Child is the miracle worker, the devotion began as a Marian one.

Tradition says devotion to Our Lady of Atocha originated in Antioch, and that St. Luke the Evangelist was the sculptor of the first mother-and-child image. ("Atocha" could be a corruption of "Antiochia.") By 1162, devotion had begun to Our Lady under this title and an image of her could be found in Toledo, Spain, in the Church of St. Leocadia. In 1523, Charles V of Spain paid for an enormous temple and placed the statue under the care of the Dominicans. The image of the Divine Child was detachable, and devout families would borrow the image of the infant when a woman was about to give birth to her child.

The pious legend tells that during the dark days of the Moorish invaders, many of the Catholic men of Atocha, a suburb of Madrid, had been imprisoned in Moorish dungeons. Their jailors did not feed the prisoners, relying on food brought by their families. At one point, the caliph ordered that no one except children twelve years old and younger would be permitted to bring food to the prisoners. How would families with no children feed their men?

Our Lady of Atocha and *Santo Niño*

The women begged Our Lady of Atocha to help them find a way to feed their husbands, sons, and brothers. Soon the children came home from the prison with a strange story. Those prisoners who had no young children to feed them were being visited and fed by a young boy. None of the children knew who he was, but the little water gourd he carried was never empty, and he always had plenty of bread in his basket to feed all the hapless prisoners with no children. He always came at night, slipping past the sleeping guards or smiling politely at those who were alert. Those who had asked the Virgin of Atocha for a miracle began to suspect the identity of the little boy. As if in confirmation of the miracle they had prayed for, the shoes on the statue of the child Jesus were worn down. When they replaced the shoes with new ones, those too were quickly worn out.

After Ferdinand and Isabella drove the Moors from Spain in 1492, the people continued to invoke the aid of Our Lady and her Holy Child. They especially asked help for those who were in jail and those who were "imprisoned" in the mines.

When the Spaniards came to the New World, they brought along the devotions of their native regions. In 1540, silver mines were found in Mexico, and mineworkers migrated, some to the area of Plateros, a tiny village near the mines of Fresnillo, Zacatecas. One of the mine owners donated a beautiful Spanish statue of Our Lady of Atocha to the parish church. It, like its counterpoint in Spain, had a removable infant, which at one time was lost. The replacement was carved with darker *mestizo* features and became much loved by the people.

Those whose prayers were answered left *retablos* in thanksgiving. The shrine has *retablos* dating from the 1500s to our own times. Through its turbulent history, Mexico has provided many prisoners for the Holy Child to aid. Annually, many other miraculous cures and favors are reported here.

The Holy Child of Atocha is a little pilgrim, often taken in procession and sometimes on "visits" to other churches in other cities.

In the 1800s, a man from New Mexico made a pilgrimage to Fresnillo and took back with him a small image of the Holy Child, which he enshrined in Chimayo, near Santa Fe. There, the devotion grew, just as it had when it came to the New World. Some of the first American troops to see action in World War II were from the New Mexico National Guard. They fought bravely on Corregidor, with its underground tunnels and defenses. The Catholics remembered that the *Santo Niño de Atocha* had long been considered a patron of all who were trapped or imprisoned. Some of them made a vow that if they survived the war they would make a pilgrimage from Santa Fe to Chimayo in thanksgiving. At the end of the war 2,000 pilgrims — veterans of Corregidor, the Bataan death march, and Japanese prison camps, together with their families — walked the long, rough road from Santa Fe to Chimayo, some barefoot, to the little adobe shrine.

The prayers and novenas to the miracle-working little Child Jesus all begin with prayers to Our Lady of Atocha. As Jesus is shown as a small child, first His clients have to ask His mother's permission for him to go to their aid. Then the miracle-working child Jesus hastens to assist those who need His help.

THE HOLY CHILD OF ARACOELI

A crowned, jeweled, life-size figure of the child Jesus is venerated in a special chapel at the Basilica of Santa Maria, in the Aracoeli section of Rome. The statue is world-famous, and pilgrims flock to venerate it because of many reported miracles and favors.

The statue of the Holy Bambino dates back to the end of the fifteenth century, when a pious Franciscan friar carved it from the wood of an olive tree from the Mount of Olives, near Gethsemane. According to a quaint legend, the friar lacked the necessary paints to complete his work, so an angel miraculously finished the statue. As the friar returned to Rome, a severe storm at sea caused him to throw the small case containing the statue overboard. The case floated to the port of Livorno by itself in the wake of the ship.

In the Eternal City, the statue soon became famous for reported miracles and was treated with special honor. One day during the Christmas season, a noble Roman matron stole the statue and hid it in her home. She became severely ill, and her confessor ordered her to return the statue. The legend has the statue leaving her house by itself during the night, and returning to its place in the church, as the bells of the basilica ring in joy at the miracle.

The Holy Child of Aracoeli

Rich gifts of gold and precious stones give witness to the gratitude of the faithful for the innumerable graces received. A number of attempts have been made to harm the statue. In 1798, Serafin Petrarca, a Roman citizen, paid a huge ransom to save the statue from being burned by Napoleon's troops.

Pregnant women often visit the Holy Bambino to receive a special blessing, and many return bringing their infants to be consecrated to the Divine Child. The statue has sometimes been carried out to the bedside of the sick faithful. It received a papal crown in 1897.

At Christmas, a special crèche is set up in the church. Sometimes the Infant is placed in the lap of a statue of the Virgin. Other times he is placed in a crib. Throughout the season, the children of Rome come to sing, recite poems, and perform plays for the Infant King. At dusk on the Feast of the Epiphany, a special blessing is given to the pilgrims gathered on the Capitoline Hill.

EL DIVINO NIÑO

This image of the Holy Child is a twentieth-century Colombian image of the Child Jesus first promoted by Salesian Father Juan del Rizzo. Miracles have been attributed to *El Divino Niño* (The Divine Child), and it remains probably the most popular devotion in Colombia today. After visiting the shrine in 1995,

El Divino Niño

Mother Angelica of Eternal Word Television seemed to hear the image of *El Divino Niño* speaking to her, asking her to build a temple for him. She set to work, and the new shrine at Our Lady of the Angels Monastery in Hanceville, Alabama, is dedicated to the Blessed Sacrament and *Divino Niño*.

SANTO NIÑO DE CEBU

Patron of the Philippines, *Santo Niño de Cebu* is an image of the Christ Child that bears a startling resemblance to the Infant of Prague. The Legazpi-Urdaneta expedition arrived in the Philippines at Cebu on April 27, 1565. On landing, Legazpi's soldiers made a house-to-house inspection and, in the home of Juan Camus, found a box holding a painted wooden image of the Holy Child Jesus. The image was taken to a provisional chapel, where the Augustinian Fray Andres de Urdaneta said a thanksgiving Mass for the success of the expedition, a mission to Christianize the islands. Fray Urdaneta observed that the image was like those made in Flanders during the sixteenth century. It is believed to be the image

Santo Niño de Cebu

that Magellan gave to Rajah Humabon's wife on her conversion to Christianity. During World War II, American bombing damaged the church where the image was kept, but the little Infant of Cebu was found hanging by its clothes, intact and unharmed.

So many miracles became associated with the little image that, in the seventeenth century, King Charles III awarded it the *Toison de Oro*, or the Golden Fleece. During the rites held to commemorate the fourth centennial of the Christianization of the Philippines, then Prince Juan Carlos — later Spain's king — gifted the image with a golden crown.

A special ritual dance, known as the *sinulog*, is performed to honor the Holy Child on His feast. This dance, of pre-Christian origin, is accompanied by the rhythmic sound of drums, which resembles the sound of the current of the river.

CHRIST OF THE ANDES

The most famous statue in South America, the Christ of the Andes, is found in Uspallata Pass, on the borderline between Argentina and Chile. After a number of disputes between Chile and Argentina over the boundary line between the two countries, war seemed certain. Then, the two countries decided to divide the disputed land between them. The people wanted to erect a monument to remind future generations that peace is better than war.

A figure of Christ was commissioned, then made out of the melted cannon of the two countries, but then came the problem of how to move the tremendously heavy statue up steep mountain trails. Mules were used for part of the distance, but finally even they were unable to complete the chore. Thousands of soldiers and sailors of the two countries hitched themselves to the ropes and dragged the statue to the place where it now stands, twelve thousand feet above the sea. Dedicated on March 13, 1904, the statue bears an inscription which reads: "Sooner shall these mountains crumble into dust than the Argentines and Chileans break the peace sworn at the feet of Christ the Redeemer."

Christ of the Andes

Jesus Entierro

JESUS ENTIERRO

In the Latin countries, a special image of Christ is taken down from the cross on Good Friday and "interred" or "buried" in the *monumento*. In some churches, this life-size figure is kept as a devotional image in a glass casket on a side altar during the year, and only removed for the Holy Week processions. The images are made with jointed arms and legs so the limbs may be stretched out to hang on the cross and folded to the sides when placed in the tomb. They are generally made of gesso-coated wood and ornamented with human hair and a crown of thorns. During the procession, they are dressed in purple robes. They are very realistic and lifelike, and the sight of the figure often moves the viewer to tears.

DIVINA INFANTITA – THE IMMACULATE CHILD MARY

The cult of the Immaculate Child Mary in Mexico began with a little-known apparition in Mexico City in 1840, to a Conceptionist sister of the convent of St. Joseph of Grace. Magdalena of St. Joseph, a distinguished, educated, and wealthy young woman, gave up her dowry so that another girl might enter as a choir sister, and she herself entered as a lay sister. On the feast of the Three Kings, she was praying in front of the manger scene, adoring the child Jesus, when she began to think, "Why isn't the Virgin honored in her infancy and celebrated with happy songs like the child Jesus?"

Just as she thought this, she saw a beautiful little girl, dressed like a queen, floating in the air in a reclining position. The vision seemed to say, "I will give those who honor me in my infancy the things they ask me for, because this is something the people have forgotten to do." Profoundly moved, Sister Magdalena wanted to begin the devotion at once.

She told the abbess, Sister Guadalupe of St. Lawrence, what had happened in the oratory, and of her great desire to do as the little virgin had asked. She requested permission to have a little image made in the form of the apparition, but the superior refused, seeming to receive the story with indifference. Her feeling was that if the apparition was from God, He would insist.

Sister Magdalena prayed daily for God's will, and one day while cleaning the sacristy, she found the head of a little angel that had broken off of a monstrance. She took it to the abbess, who gave her permission to have it made into an image of the little virgin. The sculptor did a beautiful job at a small cost. With fervor and great happiness, Sister Magdalena began to spread the cult; the devotion extended rapidly, and graces and extraordinary favors began to be reported.

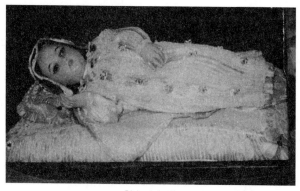

Divina Infantita

Opposition is always part of confirmation; this came on the part of Ecclesiastical authorities, who prohibited the new devotion. But this was changed when a pious and wealthy woman went to Rome to petition Pope Gregory XVI. He not only approved the devotion, but also enriched it with indulgences. Through the medium of this first image, the Immaculate Little Mary worked many miracles, including the conversion of sinners and the restoration of sight to a blind girl.

Sister Magdalena was as simple in her faith as a child and made many childish demonstrations of her love for the little image of the virgin. She labeled one of the cells in the convent with a sign that read "Cell of the Holy Little Mary." Novenas were made with grand solemnity, especially on September 8, the Virgin's birthday. Money to clothe the image regally, and decorations for her altar, came from the generous gifts of wealthy devotees. One September, the sisters had no money to buy the traditional new clothes for the image before the feast on September 8. Sister Magdalena put a crate in the window with the door open and asked the little Virgin for a bird that she could sell for the funds to buy the new clothing. A bird flew into the cage, singing beautifully. Sister Magdalena then took the bird to a wealthy friend, who gave her enough money to purchase a queenly new dress for the little image. The beautiful and mysterious bird that had charmed everyone with its lovely songs then disappeared from its closed cage.

Shortly before her death in 1859, Sister Magdalena charged the abbess to continue to spread the devotion. Although the abbess intended to comply, the devotion was stilled for more than twenty years. These were turbulent times in Mexico, so Sister Guadalupe had a sculptor make a small copy of the image, which she planned to have taken out to the people, hoping in this way to continue the devotion. When the sculptor brought the copy to her, however, she thought it was ugly so she put it away in her wardrobe, and the devotion began to languish.

Just as the cult had almost disappeared, a saintly mystic, Rosario Arrevillaga, was born. She would later resurrect the devotion. At nineteen, Rosario met the Conceptionist Sisters through an introduction by a friend. Because of the anti-religious laws of the reform, the sisters were living in small groups in regular houses, hiding from the government. Only those persons well known to the sisters were invited to visit them. Rosario gained their trust and was invited to see the image of the *Divina Infantita*. At the first sight of the little queen, Rosario fell to her knees, saying, "Here is what raises up my heart!" From that moment, Rosario became completely devoted to the nativity of Mary. Seeing her pious love, Sister Guadalupe decided to give her the little statue she had commissioned so many years ago and put away in her closet.

Rosario accepted the gift happily, and took her treasure home determined to spread the devotion and to do great things for the mother of God. She told the sisters, "Many miracles will be worked before this image, and the grandest of people will ask for her favors." Jokingly, she predicted further that one day there would be a great church in the little virgin's honor, religious orders to serve her, and many good works done through her intercession.

Although she was intelligent, sociable, and attractive, Rosario was simply a poor, middle class girl. But she was rich in the love of God and of the virgin, and before her death this simple girl was able to raise a temple, found a congregation, and begin a work to care for orphans, and the most unhappy and discriminated against of God's children. All of the things she had told the sisters, seemingly in jest, eventually came to pass.

Rosario and her mother lived in a modest house, which was the first home for the little wonder-working image of the child Mary. Rosario made an altar of boxes covered with paper and placed the statue in the largest room of the house. She made candlesticks out of bottles and crafted flowers from shiny paper. One day Rosario felt sad because she had no oil for the little vigil lamp before the altar. So she went to her neighbor, a baker, told him she had a miraculous image, and that he should bring oil for the lamp and ask the virgin to grant him favors. His request was granted rapidly, and the news began to spread around the neighborhood. Soon the most distinguished persons began to visit, attracted by the news of the miracle-working little queen. The image and its humble little altar began to be adorned with gifts from her devotees. Dresses of rich fabric, jewels, and a silver cradle were given in thanksgiving.

Rosario began to feel the voice of God urging her to build a church in the virgin's honor. Frightened of such a great undertaking, she prayed constantly for His will. Although there were many difficulties to overcome, she was eventually able to obtain the permission of the archbishop, get property donated, pay a large tax to the government, and find the money for construction of a beautiful temple. Wealthy and influential people came to her aid, including the daughter of the President of Mexico.

At the same time that the material temple was being constructed, a spiritual temple also began to rise. Father Federico Salvador y Ramon and Rosario began to talk of the formation of a group of nuns who would dedicate themselves to the child Mary. The first refuge for orphans was opened in September, and by February of 1901, a new religious congregation, the Slaves of the *Divina Infantita*, was formed with the approval of the archbishop. The Slaves were dedicated to the educational and moral formation of children; they opened refuges for the most underprivileged children and orphans. Today, their official name is the Slaves of the Immaculate Child, and their goal is to establish, through Mary, the reign of Jesus Christ in the world. Although Rosario was not one of the original members, she received the habit in December of 1901 and was professed in May of 1902. The church was finished and solemnly blessed on August 29, 1903, and the little image of the Virgin was translated there the following day, in a lavish ceremony that included the orphans dressed in their white First Communion clothes, as well as the rich and famous of the city.

In 1910, Pope Pius X silenced the devotion by a Decree of Reprobation, but this was rescinded in 1921 with a Decree of Approbation, just as the bitter persecution of the church in Mexico was beginning to boil up. Later, at the height of the persecution, the beautiful temple raised in honor of the *Divina Infantita* was confiscated by the government and destroyed.

Father Salvador had returned to Spain in 1907 and planted the seeds of the devotion in his homeland. He returned to Mexico in 1930, but died unexpectedly in 1931 and thus did not live to see the establishment of a religious community of men dedicated to the little virgin — although he had written a constitution for them. Madre Almita (Maria del Carmen Muriel), who succeeded Mother Rosario as superior of the Slaves, inspired in the hearts of the children under her care the love of the priesthood and of the *Divina Infantita*. The eventual founder of the men's group dedicated to the *Divina Infantita* was Father Vicente Echarri Gil, born in Spain in 1903. When he began to study for the priesthood, he developed tuberculosis that threatened to stop his ordination. He begged the Virgin of Guadalupe to save him, promising that if he were cured, he would go to Mexico as a missionary. He was cured, ordained in 1930, and left as soon as possible to fulfill his vow, arriving in Mexico in 1931.

In 1944, Father Echarri accepted a small group of aspirants who had been influenced by Madre Almita and formed a seminary in Tlalpan. The following year, he arranged for a group of them to be accepted at the Diocesan Seminary for Leon. The first priests of the new institute were ordained on April 2, 1949, in the Cathedral of Leon.

In its earliest days, the community was known as the Congregation of Missionaries of the Slaves of the *Divina Infantita* or "The *Infantitos*." The name of the order was changed to the Missionaries of the Nativity of Mary in 1970, and Pope John Paul II gave pontifical recognition to the community in 1988. With steady growth, they continue to spread the love and devotion to the Little Immaculate Mary to this day, through their work in Mexico, the United States, and Puerto Rico.

MARIA BAMBINA

Images of both the Infant Jesus and the baby Mary were popular objects of veneration throughout Europe during the eighteenth century. In Milan, Italy is an image of Mary made of wax, known as the *Maria Bambina*. Only the face is seen; she is wrapped in "swaddling" after the style of the Middle Ages, when infants were wrapped and bound tightly to ensure that their limbs grew straight.

Today a replica of this image can be seen at St. Thomas Catholic Church in Huntington, Massachusetts, where pilgrims are welcome to come and venerate the little Virgin in her infancy. The Sisters of Allegany also have a copy of the image at their convent in Allegany, New York, where the image is venerated in the Sacred Heart Oratory.

A life-size, realistic image of *Maria Bambina* was made about 1735 by a Poor Clare nun in Todi and brought to Milan in 1738

Maria Bambina

by Bishop Alberico Simonetta. After his death, the image was in the custody of several groups before it was given to the Sisters of Charity of Lovere, who took it with them when they assumed the direction of the Ciceri Hospital in 1842. In 1876, it was moved to its current location at the sisters' motherhouse. Originally kept in the novitiate, during the octave of the Nativity of Mary, the image was moved to the chapel in celebration of the feast. With the passage of time, the image became dirty and discolored, so eventually it was put away in storage, brought out for veneration only during the octave.

On the feast of the Nativity in September of 1884, one of the sick sisters begged the superior to bring the little image of *Maria Bambina* to the infirmary and let it remain with her during the night. On the following morning, the superior was inspired to take the image around to the other sick sisters. A devout novice took the little *Bambina* in her arms and begged for the return of her health. Immediately, she was miraculously cured of a crippling paralysis. Two of the other sisters in the infirmary were also cured. The following month, the statue was given new clothing and placed in a beautiful cradle in a temporary chapel.

The sisters began to venerate the image and request favors, and the *Bambina* began to answer their pleas. By January of the following year, an amazing and inexplicable transformation began to occur. The faded gray complexion of the image slowly changed to warm flesh tones that made the statue seem almost alive, and gave it the appearance of a living baby. Soon, people from the city heard of the miracle and they began to come to venerate the miraculous image. A new chapel, open to the public, was dedicated in 1888. Cardinal Ferrari solemnly crowned *Maria Bambina* in 1904, and in 1909, St. Pope Pius X enriched the devotion with indulgences.

As the devotion began to spread throughout Italy a small wax copy of the image became a popular wedding gift. The small images are still made today, although few of the younger sisters know the ancient art of working in wax.

Bombing during World War II destroyed the shrine and the motherhouse, but the image had been taken to safety. It remained in the temporary motherhouse of the sisters until the new motherhouse and shrine were built in 1953. Annually on September 8, the sisters touch small pieces of cotton to the image, which are then distributed as sacramentals. Today, numerous supplicants come to bring their petitions to her. Young couples who want the gift of a child are among the most fervent of her devotees. Many return, holding their newborns, to thank her for prayers answered.

Devotion to *Maria Bambina* has spread throughout the world. For many years, an image of *Maria Bambina* was on display in a niche in the altar of the crypt of St. Anne's Church in Jerusalem, which, by tradition, marks the spot of the Virgin's birth. Although the devotion is still little known in the United States, that may be changing. Among her other advocations, *Maria Bambina* is seen by many as a wonderful advocate for the respect for life.

Sister Mary Lawrence Scanlan, a member of the Franciscan Sisters of Allegany, has always had a strong devotion to the childhood of Mary. In the late 1950s, she was appointed vocation director of her Order and was inspired to write a little chaplet in the virgin's honor called the Garland of the Holy Child Mary (see separate entry.) In the late 1950s, her Community began to disseminate leaflets of the Garland for the intention of obtaining vocations to the priesthood and the religious life. Fr. Benedict Ballou, O.F.M., brought the sisters a replica of the *Maria Bambina* of Milan from Italy that was in their novitiate for many years.

Another who has a deep devotion to the nativity of Mary is Father Donald Noiseux.

He obtained the replica of *Maria Bambina* now venerated in St. Thomas Church in Huntington, Massachusetts. A priest friend and one of his parishioners designed and built the beautiful reliquary that houses it. Another parishioner helps the parish to maintain a Web site, *www.mariabambina.org,* where people can learn more about the mystery of the nativity of Mary.

OUR LADY OF PROMPT SUCCOR

Although the Ursuline monastery of New Orleans was founded by a band of French Ursulines in 1727, by 1803 only seven Ursulines remained there. The superior appealed to a cousin of hers in France, Mother St. Michel, for aid and personnel.

Mother St. Michel had been driven from her convent by the Reign of Terror, and as soon as the first indication of religious tolerance appeared, she had, with another young woman, opened a boarding school for young girls. Her bishop did not want to lose her, so on receiving the appeal from her cousin, Mother St. Michel asked her spiritual director for advice. He demurred. On direct appeal to the bishop, the answer came, "Only the Pope can give you authorization." This reply amounted almost to a definite "no," as the Pope was in Rome, a virtual prisoner of Napoleon. His jail-

ers were under strict injunction not to allow either messages to him or correspondence from him. Nonetheless, Mother St. Michel wrote her request, concluding, "Most Holy Father, I appeal to your apostolic tribunal. I am ready to submit to your decision. Speak. Faith teaches me that you are the voice of the Lord. I await your orders. 'Go' or 'Stay', from Your Holiness will be the same to me."

The letter had been written for three months, but no opportunity had presented itself to send it. One day, as she was praying before a statue of Mary, Mother felt inspired to call on the Queen of Heaven with these words, "O Most Holy Virgin Mary, if you obtain a prompt and favorable

Our Lady of Prompt Succor

answer to my letter, I promise to have you honored in New Orleans under the title of Our Lady of Prompt Succor."

That Mother St. Michel's trustful prayer was pleasing to Our Lady, and that she wished to be honored in the New World under this title, were revealed in the prompt and favorable reply she received. Her letter was dispatched on March 19, 1809; the reply is dated in Rome on April 28.

The reply directed Mother to place herself at the head of religious aspirants and go to Louisiana — miraculous in itself. The Pope was well aware of the need for workers such as Mother in France. Many would be needed to regenerate what the Revolution had torn down. Nonetheless, he gave his approval of her voyage, and her bishop acknowledged that his hopes to keep her in France were defeated. He requested the privilege of blessing the statue of Our Lady that Mother St. Michel had commissioned, according to her promise.

On the arrival of the pious missionaries in New Orleans in December of 1810, this precious statue was solemnly installed in the convent chapel.

Prayers before this image are credited with saving the Ursuline convent from fire in 1812. The victory of Andrew Jackson's American forces over the British in the battle of New Orleans in 1815 is another favor attributed to the intercession of Our Lady of Prompt Succor. The chronicles of the Ursuline monastery record numerous favors, both spiritual and temporal, wrought through the intercession of Our Lady of Prompt Succor. In 1851, Pius IX authorized the celebration of the feast of Our Lady of Prompt Succor. The papal delegate solemnly crowned the statue in 1895. This was the first ceremony of this type in the United States. In 1928, a new shrine in Our Lady's honor was consecrated, and Our Lady of Prompt Succor was named the principal patroness of the City of New Orleans and the State of Louisiana.

OUR LADY, QUEEN OF PEACE

The miraculous statue of Our Lady, Queen of Peace, is venerated in the chapel of the Religious of the Sacred Hearts of Jesus and Mary in Paris, France. The statue is eleven inches high and is carved of chestnut-brown wood. The Virgin is represented holding her Divine Son on her left arm, while in her right hand she holds the symbol of peace, an olive branch. The Christ Child holds a cross, representing the price paid for the gift of peace to mankind.

Documents trace the statue to the possession of a noble French family of the sixteenth century. While praying before this statue, one of the family members, the Duc de Joyeuse, was inspired with a call to the religious life. He had a chapel built in her honor in the Capuchin house in Paris, later opened to the faithful, and it became a place of prayer and veneration of the Queen of Peace.

For about sixty years, the image was placed in a niche outside the door of the monastery. There for several years a clear light seemed to miraculously illuminate it during the night. Later, in 1651, the people heard the Salve Regina being chanted by unseen singers. A number of miraculous occurrences brought much attention to the image. The sacred image was moved to the place where the former duke, Father Ange, was buried; miracles kept multiplying, and a new chapel had to be built to contain the crowds who came to venerate her. At the beginning of the French Revolution, the Capuchins were forced to abandon the monastery, and gave the image into the keeping of a pious lady named Madame Pepin. The statue then passed through a number of hands until it was given to a certain Madame Riolet, who gave it to Father Coudrin, the founder of the Congregation of the Sacred Hearts of Jesus and Mary. The statue was placed in the chapel of the Religious in the Rue de Piepus, Paris, in 1806. Since that day, favors have been constantly granted through her intercession, and numerous gifts are left at the shrine in testimony. The statue was crowned in 1906 in the name of Pope St. Pius X.

OUR LADY OF LEBANON

For Lebanese Catholics, devotion to the Virgin Mary is like an inherited instinct from apostolic times. This devotion is the dominant note of the invincible Christianity of Lebanon, long under persecution, and it is a key point in the spirituality of Lebanese Catholics, most of whom are members of rites that came from the Antiochene tradition.

The shrine to Our Lady of Harissa, or Our Lady of Lebanon, was begun in 1904 to commemorate the fiftieth anniversary of the Proclamation of the Dogma of the Immaculate Conception. The idea for building the shrine was a joint dream of the Maronite Patriarch and the Papal Nuncio. Built in the region known as "the rock" on the hill of Harissa, which overlooks the city of Jounieh, the Mediterranean sea, and Beirut, the monument is set in a beautiful landscape high above sea level. The statue of the virgin was made in Lyon, France, of bronze and is painted white. It is 8 meters tall and stands on a pedestal 20 meters high. The pedestal is built of stone, and to reach the feet of the statue, pilgrims climb a spiral staircase of 104 steps. The monument was erected on May 3, 1908, and Mary was proclaimed Queen of Lebanon. A feast in honor of Our Lady Queen of Lebanon is celebrated in Lebanon on the first Sunday of May.

Photo courtesy of Our Lady of Lebanon Shrine, North Jackson, OH

Our Lady of Lebanon, seen from below

A replica of the Harissa monument was erected in North Jackson, Ohio, in 1963. This sanctuary in honor of the Blessed Mother is cared for and supported by all Maronites, and pilgrims of all religious backgrounds, from every part of America. The Eparchy of Our Lady of Lebanon of Los Angeles operates the national shrine. The image of Our Lady is carved from rose granite and weighs over 7 tons. It is twelve feet tall and mounted on a four-foot pedestal set on a stone tower 42 feet high. Sixty-four steps climb to the top, each step counting the prayer of the Rosary.

Our Lady of Lebanon, closeup

Photo courtesy of Our Lady of Lebanon Shrine, North Jackson, OH

The images of Our Lady of Lebanon show her standing, holding out her hands in invitation and love to all her children.

BLACK MADONNAS

Black Madonnas are those images of the Virgin Mary portraying her as dark-skinned. Among the better-known pilgrimage sites with Black Madonnas are those at Altotting, Germany; Czestochowa, Poland; Einsiedeln, Switzerland; Loreto, Italy; and Montserrat, Spain. In some cases, the pigmentation is unintentional, a result of discoloration through age and grime. In others, the dark hue is simply the color of wood from which the statue or image is made. There are also Madonnas whose facial characteristics and skin color match a particular, dark-skinned indigenous population, such at the image of Guadalupe.

SANTOS

The term *santos* refers to religious folk art which dates back to colonial times in New Mexico. In its earliest years, the region was so isolated that few religious articles were imported, and the Spanish in New Mexico began to produce sacred art for themselves. Working almost exclusively with home-crafted local materials, the artists, known as *santeros,* developed a dynamic iconic tradition. It was important that the painter be a holy man, and a *santo* made by a holy *santero* came to have a sacredness of its own. In other words, the art had a different relationship to the painter and viewer; it operated from the religious rather than the aesthetic plane. Once the coming of the railroad opened the area and the colony was less isolated, priests brought in many inexpensive copies of European art, and the *santos* were removed from the

A *santo* of St. Michael

churches. In recent years, however, an appreciation of the art has developed, and *santos* have become highly collectible pieces of art as well as religious items. Catholic artists in New Mexico have begun to revive the religious traditions of the *santeros* and their religiously inspired art.

Santos are also made today by artisans in Central America and some parts of Mexico.

On first sight, these *santo*s, whether in the form of *retablos santos* (paintings) or *bultos* (sculpture), seem only as rough representations, lacking all the grace and beauty of the European sculpture. Because of the way they are made, with true religious inspiration, *santo*s are translated to the eye of the devotee into true representations of the Divine.

Paintings, Icons, and *Retablos*

PAINTINGS

The *Pantokrator*

The *Pantokrator* is the name given in Eastern Rites to an image of Our Lord as the Ruler of Heaven and Earth. It is derived from the Greek word meaning "almighty" and corresponds to the title "Christ the King" in the Roman rite. This picture of Christ is the major one used in the Eastern Rites. The picture is generally located on one of the central domes of the church.

Divine Mercy

The image of Jesus as Divine Mercy so popular today was given in private revelations to a humble Polish nun, Sister Faustina Kowalska, now numbered among the Saints of the Church. The first image of the Divine Mercy was commissioned by Sister Faustina's spiritual director, Rev. Michael Sopocko, and painted by Eugene Kazimierowski in Vilnius under Sister's direction.

Not pleased with the way the painting was turning out, Sister Faustina complained to the Lord with tears, "Who will paint You as beautiful as You are?" In answer, she heard these words: "Not in the beauty of the color nor of the brush lies the sublimity of this image, but in My grace." Thus, Our Lord seems to be saying that in spite of the human work of the artist, the picture is to recall His grace. He directed Sister Faustina to write down this short prayer: "O Blood and Water, which gushed forth from the Heart of Jesus as a fount of mercy for us, I trust in you."

In 1931, Sister Faustina received the first apparition of Jesus as The Merciful One. She described it thus:

"In the evening, when I was in my cell, I saw the Lord Jesus clothed in a white garment. One hand [was] raised in the gesture of blessing, the other was touching the garment at the breast.

Image of Jesus as Divine Mercy

From beneath the garment slightly drawn aside at the breast there were emanating two large rays, one red, the other pale.

"In silence, I kept my gaze fixed on the Lord; my soul was struck with awe but also with great joy. After a while Jesus said to me:

'Paint an image according to the pattern you see with the inscription: Jesus, I trust in You. I desire that this image be venerated first in your chapel and [then] throughout the world.'"

Later, at the request of her confessor, Sister Faustina asked Our Lord about the symbolism of the rays and received, while at prayer, this clarification:

"The two rays denote blood and water — the pale ray stands for the water which makes souls righteous; the red ray stands for the blood which is the life of souls. These two rays issued forth from the depths of My most tender mercy when My agonized heart was opened by a lance on the cross. These rays shield the soul from the wrath of My Father. Happy is the one who will dwell in their shelter, for the just hand of God shall not lay hold of him."

Our Lady of Czestochowa

In the town of Czestochowa, Poland, is a church containing a painting of Our Lady regarded by many as an actual portrait of the Madonna, painted during her lifetime by St. Luke the Evangelist on the top of a cypress-wood table.

An ancient legend tells how the painting was brought to Poland. Nothing is known of the first years of the picture's history. In 326, when St. Helen went to Jerusalem to search for the true cross, she also found the picture of Our Lady. She gave the picture to her son, Constantine, who had a shrine built for it in Constantinople. There it was credited with saving the city from attacking Saracens when it was displayed from the city's walls during battle.

Our Lady of Czestochowa, Black Madonna of Poland

Years later, the Emperor Charlemagne visited Constantinople, and when he was offered his choice of any of the treasures in the city, he chose only the portrait of Our Lady. Charlemagne presented the painting to Prince Leo of Ruthenia.

For hundreds of years, the picture remained at the royal palace. Then enemy troops invaded the country. Urgently the king prayed to Our Lady to aid his tiny army. Through the intercession of Our Lady, a heavy darkness fell on the enemy, and in the confusion they began destroying their own troops. Later, the Ruthenian king had a dream in which the Blessed Mother requested him to take her picture to the Mount of Light (*Jasna Gora*) in Poland. He took the picture at once and left it with a group of Paulite fathers.

The monks built a shrine for the painting at Czestochowa, and a number of miraculous events occurred there. Soon it became the most famous shrine in Poland.

An attempted theft resulted in a slash on the face of the virgin. Later, vandals set fire to the shrine and only the picture remained unburned. The smoke (or centuries of vigil lights) darkened the picture, which resulted in its popular name, "The Black Madonna."

In 1655, in gratitude for a military victory, the King of Poland placed the country under the protection of Blessed Mother and named Our Lady of Czestochowa the queen of the crown of

Poland. Today, Poland is no longer a monarchy; however, The Black Madonna remains queen in the hearts of Polish Catholics everywhere.

Our Lady of the Rosary of Pompeii

Blessed Bartolo Longo, while visiting the valley of Pompeii on business in 1872, was shocked and filled with great pity at the ignorance, poverty, and lack of religion of the inhabitants of the area. His generous heart was moved, and he promised Our Lady to do all in his power to promote devotion to the Rosary among the people of the area. In order to encourage the people, he determined to purchase a picture of Our Lady with her Rosary to be exposed for veneration. A Dominican sister offered him a large painting which had been bought at a junk shop for three francs. Seeing his hesitation, as the picture was in poor condition and rather ugly, she told him not to hesitate about taking the picture and predicted that it would work miracles. Bartolo accepted the picture and made arrangements for a wagoner to transport it to Pompeii.

Blessed Bartolo himself described the picture, which was dilapidated, wrinkled, soiled, and torn — "Not only was it worm-eaten, but the face of the Madonna was that of a coarse, rough countrywoman . . . a piece of canvas was missing just above her head . . . her mantle was cracked. Nothing can be said of the hideousness of the other figures. St. Dominic looked like a Street idiot. To Our Lady's left was St. Rose. This latter I had changed later into a St. Catherine of Siena . . . I hesitated whether to refuse the gift or to accept."

The wagoner arrived at the chapel door with the large painting wrapped in a sheet on top of a load of manure, which he was delivering to a nearby field! Thus did Our Lady of Pompeii arrive in the desolate valley which, one day, would become one of the major places of world pilgrimage in her honor.

At first, everyone who saw the picture was disappointed. An artist refurbished the unsightly canvas and ornamented it with diamonds donated by the faithful. A crown was placed on the head of the Madonna, and the painting was solemnly mounted on a throne of marble imported from Lourdes. Bartolo later commented, "There is something about that picture which impresses the soul not by its artistic perfection but by a mysterious charm which impels one to kneel and pray with tears."

Our Lady of the Rosary of Pompeii

Immediately on its exposition, the picture became a veritable fountain of miracles. First, a young epileptic girl in Naples was restored to health on the very day that the picture was re-exposed for veneration. Her aunt had heard of the plans to form a Rosary confraternity in Pompeii and vowed to assist in the building of the church if the child got well. Next, a young woman dying in agony recovered completely, immediately after her relatives had made similar promises to Our Lady of Pompeii. A Jesuit priest who had been persuaded by the Countess di Fusco to put his faith in the Virgin of Pompeii was cured of terminal disease immediately, and the following Feast of the Holy Rosary he sang the Mass and acknowledged his cure from the pulpit at Pompeii. In less than ten years, over 940 cures were reported at the shrine.

Today, the picture is framed in gold and encrusted with diamonds and precious gems which hide all but the faces of the saints and the Holy Child. Daily, pilgrims plead with Our Lady for her graces and favors. In this valley where once a pagan religion thrived, Our Lady reigns over her subjects whom she calls to adoration of her son.

Our Lady of Grace

Our Lady of Grace is the title of a picture of the Madonna found by Venerable Dominic of Jesus and Mary, a Spanish Discalced Carmelite. In 1610, Ven. Dominic bought an old dilapidated building to convert into a convent. On a rubbish heap he found a bust painting of Our Lady in bad condition. He cleaned it, repaired it, and began to venerate it. Legend has it that one night, while he prayed before the picture, the face became animated, and Our Lady spoke to Dominic. She promised to answer favors and especially hearken to prayers for those in Purgatory.

The portrait shows the Madonna wearing a full veil, a blue mantle decorated on the right shoulder with a rosette-backed star, and a red gown. A jeweled crown and a necklace were added later. The head is slightly inclined to the left, and the image is sometimes called "Our Lady of the Bowed Head."

A number of miracles were associated with the picture. It was moved several times, and finally enshrined in the Carmelite Church in the District of Dobling in Vienna. In 1931, on the occasion of the third centenary of its appearance in Vienna, the revered picture was given a papal crown, presented by a legate of Pope Pius XI.

There are some other famous images popularly called Our Lady of Grace.

- Our Lady of Ipswich, a famous medieval statue in England, was taken to London and ordered burned at Chelsea; however, some sources indicate it may have escaped the flames of the Reformation and been spirited away to Nettuno, Italy.
- Another famous statue sometimes called Our Lady of Grace is also known as Our Lady of the Globe. St. Catherine Labouré was praying in front of a copy of this statue when she received the apparitions in which Mary gave the world the Miraculous Medal. It is this depiction of Our

Two images popularly known as Our Lady of Grace: *left,* Our Lady of the Bowed Head
(after portrait found in 1610); *right,* Our Lady of the Globe

Lady, with her hands outstretched and her feet on a serpent, which has been the most celebrated in art; copies of the image are found throughout the world.

Our Lady of Providence

Scipione Pulzoni, a native of Gaeto, Italy, painted the original picture of Our Lady of Providence about the year 1580. In 1664, this painting was placed in the Church of San Carlo ai Catinari in Rome. Trusted to the keeping of the Barnabite Fathers, the picture was enshrined in a monastery corridor and given the title *Mater Divinae Providentiae.* Many people who visited the shrine reported remarkable favors received through the intercession of Our Lady of Providence. Under this title, Our Lady is the Patroness of Puerto Rico.

Our Lady of Providence

Desatanudos — The Virgin Who Unties Knots

An ancient German devotion to Mary with an unusual title has recently taken Argentina — and the United States — by storm.

The devotion to *La Virgen Maria Desatadora de Nudos,* or the Virgin as Untier of Knots, became enormously popular a few years ago in Argentina after Argentinean movie stars, boxers, singers, and soccer players began referring to the *Desatanudos* as though it were some kind of talisman or New Age divinity. The Catholic Church in Buenos Aires reacted promptly to this trend of public invocation to clarify the true Marian character of the devotion.

La Virgen Maria Desatadora de Nudos was brought to Argentina in the early 1980s by Jesuit Father Jorge Bergoglio, who was then rector at the Jesuit University of El Salvador and went on to become the cardinal archbishop of Buenos Aires. He had found the image at the church of St. Peter am Perlach during a visit to Augsburg, Germany. He was intrigued by the odd name and image of Mary called *Knotenloserin,* The One Who Unties Knots.

The seventeenth-century Baroque painting, attributed to the German artist Johann Melchior Georg Schmittdner, represents the Virgin with an angel on her left side handing her a white ribbon filled with knots. As the ribbon winds through Mary's hands, it falls to her right side, with the knots untied, into the hands of a second celestial denizen. The dove of the Holy Spirit seems to shower graces on the humbly inclined head of Mary, while a choir of cherubim looks on.

Father Bergoglio brought several postcards with the image back to Argentina and commissioned the painting of a replica of the image, which remains today in the chapel of the University. For nearly twenty years, the devotion remained mostly unknown, except among the university's students, professors, and visiting Catholic scholars. Then, in 1996, three parishioners of San José de Talar (a suburban parish of Buenos Aires) asked Father Rodolfo Arroyo for permission to promote devotion to *La Virgen*

Maria Desatadora de Nudos. Knowing nothing of the devotion, Father Arroyo approached Cardinal Antonio Quarracino who, in turn, referred him to his then-Vicar General and auxiliary, Bishop Bergoglio, who was both surprised and delighted with the idea. Devotees at the parish decided to build a small chapel for her, which they dedicated on December 8 of that year. Devotion grew rapidly; in May, 2003, a copy of the image was enthroned at St. Joseph's Church in Del Rio, Texas, the first to be enshrined in the United States.

The Virgin Who Unties Knots

Mario H. Ibertis Rivera, a married Catholic businessman and father of four from Buenos Aires, did extensive research to find the origin and background of the image. In particular, he wanted to counter the esoteric practices he saw creeping into the true Marian character of the devotion because of its enormous upsurge of popularity at the end of the 1990s. Eventually, he was able to discover the name of the painter and unearth records showing that Father Hieronymus Ambrosius Langenmantel, a priest and doctor of canon law from 1666-1709 at St. Peter am Perlach, commissioned the painting. In 1612, a noble named Wolfgang Langenmantel was on the verge of divorce from his wife, Sophie. He visited with the learned Jesuit Jakob Rem in the city of Ingolstadt for council and prayer, and venerated an image of the Blessed Virgin in company with the priest. Changes in their family life occurred and the troubles of the marriage were resolved in 1615. Father Hieronymus, the grandson of Wolfgang, donated the painting as an *ex voto* altar in gratitude to the Virgin for her favors to his family and in commemoration of the turn of the century.

The image of *La Virgen Maria Desatadora de Nudos* presents a beautiful symbol of Mary as the one who unties the knots of our lives, in particular those of married life. An old wedding custom in Germany is probably the basis for the ribbon the artist has painted in Mary's hands. At the wedding ceremony, the arms of the bride and groom were tied together with a white ribbon as a symbol of unity. The couple kept the ribbon as a keepsake. In some families, the couple would tie a knot in the ribbon when they had a problem, and untie it when the problem was solved. A remnant of this custom can be seen today among the Pennsylvania German and Dutch in the United States.

In Latin American countries it is a prevalent custom during the wedding ceremony for the bride and groom to be physically united, or joined, with a bridal ribbon or lasso to symbolize that the couple is united forever. They see the ribbon in the hands of the Virgin in the painting as a lasso, and the Virgin as the one who will untangle the knots of troubled marriages.

Priests, too, can find a special appeal in this image if they look on the ribbon in the virgin's hands as symbolic of the *manutergium*. Formerly, after the bishop anointed a new priest's hands with chrism, an acolyte wound the *manutergium*, or ribbon of white linen, around his folded hands. Standing as *regina cleri*, *La Virgen Maria Desatadora de Nudos* will then aid the clergy in untying the knots of their lives.

Himself a staunch devotee of Mary as Untier of Knots, Mario Ibertis-Rivera wrote a novena and 28-day devotion in honor of the Virgin and began a prayer group with the hope of spreading the devotion's fraternity worldwide. Rosie and Henry Aguilar, active parishioners of St. Joseph's Catholic Church in Del Rio, Texas, brought the devotion to the United States. With the blessing of Archbishop Patrick Flores of San Antonio, and their parish priest, Father Ramiro Cortez, they spearheaded the campaign to enthrone the image in their parish church. They received two copies of the *Desatanudos* image from Ibertis–Rivera; a large painting to be enshrined in the church and a smaller one to be used as a pilgrim virgin.

ICONS

An icon (ikon, in the Oriental rite) is a form of religious art whose name comes from the Greek *eikon* for "image." The word is also a theological term central to the Eastern understanding of the world: visible things are revealed images (*eikones*) of the invisible.

Icon (Ikon)

The subject matter of an icon is not the natural flesh and blood of the subject. It lies rather on the border between the visible and the invisible and is focused on the point where the boundary between these two worlds is transcended through the Incarnation.

In art, the symbol of light is gold, and the golden background of an icon signifies the unapproachable light that existed before creation and in which St. Paul says God dwells (see 1 Tim. 6:16). The faces of the saints depicted in icons are not left to the artist's imagination, as in Western art, but are fixed by tradition. The proportions of the face represent qualities of sanctity rather than realistic portraiture of the person: the eyes are large, the forehead broad, the nose finely elongated, and the lips devoid of sensuality. The spiritual nature of the entire icon is expressed through stylization.

Iconoclasm, from the Greek for "image-breaking," was a prominent heresy in the Eastern Church in the eighth and ninth centuries. Its proponents claimed that veneration of pictures and images was against the commandment to worship God alone. At an ecumenical council in Nicaea in 787, the Church defined the distinction between adoration given to God (*latria*) and veneration (*dulia*) given to the saints. The Council Fathers said veneration is an act of homage to the person depicted in an image, not to the image itself.

Our Mother of Perpetual Help

One of the best-loved and most widely known images of Our Lady is that of Our Mother of Perpetual Help. From 1865, when Pope Pius IX gave custody of the image to the Redemptorist Order, the members of this congregation have followed his command to "make Our Mother of Perpetual Help known throughout the world." Today, copies of the original Byzantine Madonna are found worldwide, and devotion is strong for this mother who always stands ready to help her children.

The picture of Perpetual Help is similar in many ways to the Byzantine Madonna known as the *Hodegetria*, which tradition holds St. Luke painted from life. However, the theme of the Perpetual Help image is a portrayal of sorrow and thus falls into the "Passion type" of Byzantine Madonnas.

Our Mother of Perpetual Help

In this image, Mary's head is titled maternally toward her Child. Her hand loosely clasps the tiny hand of her Son. The Christ Child has a look of fright and sorrow as He gazes into the future and sees the vision of His Passion and death awaiting him. Hastily He has run to find refuge in the arms of His Mother. So swiftly has He run to her that His little sandal has come loose. The background of the picture is a simple, unadorned field of gold, symbolizing divinity. The Greek letters identify the persons portrayed in the picture: the Mother of God, Jesus Christ, and the Archangels Michael and Gabriel, who hold the symbols of the Passion.

The Mother of God is the central figure of this picture. Her eyes are gazing toward those looking at the picture. In sorrow and love, she invites all to place their confidence in her. With her left arm, she supports her Child so closely that the lines of His body blend into hers. On Mary's forehead is a simple eight-pointed star of gold, and a four-pointed ornamental cross (which may have been added to the original picture by a later artist). Around her head is a plain golden halo, while the halo of the Child is decorated with a cross to show His dignity and office. Her tunic, visible at the neck and sleeves, is red and fringed with golden stripes. A green inner veil holds back her hair. A cloak of rich blue covers her head and drapes over her shoulders. In typical Byzantine artistic style, shadows are omitted, so thin gold lines indicate the folds of her clothing.

The image of Christ seems to gaze with wide-open eyes into space. His face shows serious contemplation. Christ foresaw His crucifixion, and when the realization of the anguish and suffering He was to undergo seemed to overwhelm Him, He knew He could find refuge in the loving embrace of His Mother. The Child's fingers hold His Mother's right hand, although they rest loosely. Though Mary is the Mother, He is her God, and to Him she owes all her graces. The features of the Child closely resemble those of the Mother. His head is covered with curly auburn hair and is surrounded with an embellished halo, a sign of His divinity. He is clothed in a full-sleeved green tunic, held in at the waist with a reddish sash. A yellowish-brown mantle is draped over His right shoulder and covers most of His body.

To the left of the picture is the Archangel Michael. The Archangel Gabriel is on the right. Both are clothed in purple tunics and their wings are green, streaked with gold. In order to show great reverence to the instruments of the Passion, the angels are carrying them in veiled hands. Michael holds the urn containing the gall, mixed with myrrh, offered to Our Lord by the soldiers. In the urn are the lance and a reed topped by a sponge. Gabriel carries the cross and holds the nails.

Inscriptions in Latin are found on some of the copies of this ancient picture. On a few copies are found these words: "Behold Thy Son! Behold Thy Mother!" Other copies carry a longer inscription which gives the full significance of the picture: "He who first brought to the Most Pure Lady the news of joy now shows beforehand the signs of the Passion; but Christ, clothed in mortal flesh and featuring death, is frightened at this vision."

The first known part of the story of the image of Our Mother of Perpetual Help was written on a large piece of parchment affixed to a wooden tablet which hung, along with the picture, for many years in St. Matthew's Church in Rome. Later the parchment was fastened to the picture itself. Written in both Latin and Italian, the document gives a history of the picture's arrival in Rome in 1499 and its enthronement in the Augustinian church of St. Matthew. Copies of this parchment are in the Vatican Library.

A condensed translation of the document tells that a merchant, native to Crete, stole the picture of the Virgin that had been the instrument of many miracles on the island. He boarded a ship, and at sea a storm arose. Although the sailors knew nothing of their precious cargo, their fervent prayers to the Mother of God were heard, and they were saved from the storm. The merchant came to Rome and was stricken with a fatal disease. He asked a Roman friend to care for him, and he was taken into his friend's home and nursed tenderly. Before his death, the merchant begged his friend to fulfill a last request. He told him about the theft of the famous picture and asked his friend to put the picture in a church where it could be properly venerated.

After the merchant's death, the picture was found among his belongings, but the Roman's wife fancied it and hung it in her bedroom. The Blessed Virgin, in a number of visions, told the Roman to put the picture in a more honorable place, but he ignored her requests. Finally, the Virgin appeared to the Roman's six-year-old daughter, telling her to warn her mother and her grandfather to take the picture out of the house. After further delays, she appeared to the child again and commanded her to have her mother place her picture between St. Mary Major and St. John Lateran in the church dedicated to St. Matthew. At last, the mother obeyed the heavenly injunction and called the Augustinian fathers who were in charge of that church. Thus the picture was enshrined in the church of St. Matthew in March 1499. Here the image of the Mother of Perpetual Help reigned from her own chosen place for three centuries until the destruction of the church by the French invaders in 1798. During these centuries, the Church of St. Matthew was one of the most important pilgrimage sites in Rome, and pilgrims came from all corners of the world to worship at the shrine of Our Mother of Perpetual Help.

In 1798, the French military governor of Rome ordered that thirty churches be destroyed and the land put to better use. The Church of St. Matthew was one of those to be destroyed. The Augustinians hastily removed some of the artworks and the church furnishings, taking some items to St. John Lateran and some, including the miraculous image, to St. Eusebio's. Our Mother of Perpetual Help was sent into exile and oblivion.

The picture remained at St. Eusebio's until 1819, when the Augustinians were transferred to the small church and monastery of Santa Maria in Posterula on the other side of the city. This church already held a picture of Our Lady, so the image of Perpetual Help was put in the monastery chapel, where it remained until 1865. One of the Italian lay brothers was transferred to this monastery in 1840. He recognized the picture and remembered his devotion to the picture when it was in St. Matthew's. Brother Augustine told the story of the picture to his favorite altar boy, Michael Marchi.

St. Alphonsus Mary Liguori founded the Congregation of the Most Holy Redeemer, also known as the Redemptorists, in

1732, to minister to the most abandoned. The congregation grew rapidly, and in 1853 the Pope commanded the vicar general of the order to establish a house in Rome to serve as their worldwide headquarters. The property they bought was on the Esquiline Hill and was shaped like a triangle. The estate lay along the base of the hill, and at the tip of the triangle were the ruins of the old St. Matthew's church. As the Redemptorists built, they also began to research the history of their property. In 1859, their historian discovered some documents telling of a famous image of Our Lady which used to be enshrined in the church of St. Matthew. Father Michael Marchi, the former altar boy, told his Redemptorists brothers that he knew about the famous image and where its current location was.

During 1862-63, a Jesuit preacher named Father Francis Blosi delivered a series of sermons on some of the famous pictures of Our Lady that hung in the churches of Rome. One picture that he spoke about was the image of Perpetual Help. In his sermon he spoke of the previous fame of the picture and asked if any of his hearers knew where the picture was. He expressed the wish that the picture, if it could be located, be returned to Mary's chosen place on the Esquiline Hill so that all the faithful might come and pray before it.

When the Redemptorists heard of Father Blosi's sermon and realized that Our Lady had designated a spot for her shrine, they became excited. Again Father Michael Marchi was called on to tell his story of the picture and of its hidden repose in the chapel of the Augustinian monastery. The community brought the news to the highest superior of the Redemptorists, Father Nicholas Mauron. Father Blosi was contacted and sent a copy of his sermon for the consideration of the superior. Instead of hastening to claim the picture, Most Reverend Father Mauron directed the men at St. Alphonsus to pray for the guidance of the Holy Spirit in this matter. They complied with his directive and prayed for almost three years until December, 1865, at which time Father

Mauron obtained an audience with the Holy Father Pope Pius IX. To him Father Mauron unfolded the detailed story of the picture of Our Mother of Perpetual Help. After reading the sworn statement of Father Marchi, the Holy Father, a great devotee of our Blessed Mother, took the paper and on the reverse wrote directions that the image of Perpetual Help be given into the care of the Redemptorists at the church of St. Alphonsus, with the provision that the Redemptorist superior substitute a suitable picture to the Augustinians. The Augustinians chose a careful copy of the image, and rejoiced that the picture would receive the honor she deserved at the site which she herself had chosen almost four centuries before.

The image was brought to St. Alphonsus on January 19, 1866. Although the picture was more than four centuries old, and possibly four times that age, the colors were still bright and fresh. Only a small section of one of the sleeves had faded. The picture, painted on wood, had suffered some small damage on the reverse from worms. There were a number of nail holes left in the picture, but no irreparable damages. A skillful Polish artist was chosen and entrusted with restoring the picture. His work was done, and a solemn procession was held April 26, 1866. During the course of the procession, a number of striking miraculous events were reported.

When the picture reached the Church of St. Alphonsus, it was placed on the high altar. The image of Mary had at last come home and remains there to this day.

The Image of Perpetual Help was solemnly crowned in 1867.

Iveron Mother of God of Montreal

Tradition holds that the apostle Luke painted the original icon of the Iveron Mother of God, which has been in the Iveron Monastery on Mount Athos from the year 999.

In 1648, an exact copy of the icon was made and taken to Russia, where it soon acquired the reputation of being a miracle-working image. The Russian people especially revered this icon until the Revolution of 1917, when the Bolsheviks destroyed the chapel and the icon disappeared.

In 1982, José Muñoz Cortes, a young Chilean convert to Orthodoxy who was living in Canada, went to Mt. Athos on pilgrimage. A talented artist himself, he taught art at the University of Montreal and had begun studying iconography. He intended to visit some of the monasteries

Iveron Mother of God

and their *sketes*, which specialize in the writing (painting) of icons.

He and a friend who had accompanied him had been climbing up hill on rough terrain for about eight hours, intending to visit the famous Danilov *skete* when, worn out by the climb, they stopped to rest at a small *skete* which they happened to notice. Dedicated to the Nativity of Christ, the *skete* is a poor one whose 14 monks keep a strict monastic rule. The abbot, Father Klimentos, greeted them and offered them hospitality. After their refreshment, the abbot showed the guests to the *skete's* icon painting studio. As soon as he entered the room, José felt an immediate attraction to a copy of the Iveron Icon hanging on the wall. He asked to purchase the icon, but was told that it was not for sale. That night at divine service, José prayed fervently, asking the Mother of God to be allowed to take her icon back with him "where we have need of you." The following morning, as José and his companion were leaving, the abbot appeared and offered the icon to José, saying that it pleased the Mother of God to go with him to North America. Before his return, José took the icon to the

Iveron monastery and with permission touched the icon to the original Portaitissa.

On returning to Montreal, José placed the icon in the icon corner of his home and began to read a daily *Akathist,* or hymn of praise, before it. Early on the morning of November 24, 1982, José woke up to the smell of a very strong fragrance as if someone had spilled a bottle of perfume. Puzzled as to the source of the odor, he was standing before the icon corner to say his morning prayers when he noticed that the hands of the Virgin were streaked with oil. Assuming that his housemate had spilled oil on the icon from the vigil lamp hanging over it, he wiped the icon and discovered that it was the source of the beautiful fragrance. After consulting with a local Orthodox clergyman, José took the icon to church and placed it on the altar. During the entire liturgy, myrrh flowed from the hands of the Christ Child. From that time, with the exception of a few days during Holy Week, the myrrh continued to flow almost continuously.

The phenomenon amazed and delighted all who saw it. His Eminence Metropolitan Vitaly, First Hierarch of the Russian Orthodox Church Outside of Russia, asked that the icon be examined for evidence of fraud. No one could find a natural explanation for the myrrh; the icon was painted on plain pine board, which remained dry on the back, while the myrrh streamed only from the front. His Eminence and the Holy Synod then declared the phenomenon a miracle. After some years, the Roman Catholic Bishop of Montreal also recognized the supernatural character of the myrrh. Orthodox and Catholic faithful, and even some Protestants, began to ask to see the wondrous icon and to venerate the Holy Mother of God.

José began to take the icon to many cities and parishes, where it was venerated with great joy by the faithful. The icon was placed in a wooden frame about 12" by 18" with a lip at the bottom, where cotton wool was placed to catch the flow of myrrh. The cotton was then distributed to the faithful as a precious sacramental.

The flow of the myrrh varied, at times in greater abundance than others. It flowed from the hands of the Mother of God, from the star on her left shoulder and, occasionally, from the hands of the infant Jesus. In 1985, even the frame and glass of the icon began to exude myrrh in such quantity that the cloth of the *analogion* on which it lay was completely saturated.

From childhood, José had been taught to love and venerate the holy Virgin, but he never asked for any miraculous sign. He considered himself the guardian, not the owner, of the icon, which he insisted belonged to all the faithful. In the presence of the icon, people of all faiths became as brothers and sisters, sons and daughters of her who, at the foot of the Cross, became the mother of all believers. Although a number of physical cures have been claimed, the healing property of the icon seems most directed at the healing of souls. Many have testified to experiencing repentance and consolation in front of the icon.

For fifteen years, Brother José accompanied the miraculous image of the *Theotokos* throughout the world. In a magazine article, José wrote about death. He said, "Believers must be ready to die for the truth, and not to forget that in acquiring enemies here we acquire the Heavenly Kingdom." It seemed as if he had a presentiment of his coming death. The day before his death, Brother José visited the monastery of St. Nicholas the Wonderworker on the Island of Andros, Greece. As he entered the monastery, an ancient fresco of the Mother of God painted on the wall began to weep. José was tortured and murdered in a hotel room in Athens, Greece, on the night of either October 30 or 31, 1997, possibly by a group of Satanists. He had planned to return to Canada the following day to celebrate the fifteenth anniversary of the appearance of the miraculous myrrh on the icon. José's body was shipped back to Montreal for identification and then taken to Holy Trinity monastery in Jordanville, New York, where he is buried.

A man was tried for the murder in 1998, but was acquitted for lack of evidence. Conspiracy was suspected, as the blood and D.N.A. of another man was found in the room where José was killed. Although this second man was investigated, he was never brought to trial, and the murder remains unsolved.

Brother José had taken the icon with him to Greece, but kept the fact silent so as not to attract the usual crowds and to be able to rest for a few days. After the murder, the icon was not found among his effects. Its whereabouts remain unknown.

In March of 2002, Archpriest Victor Potapov of St. John the Baptist Russian Orthodox Cathedral in Washington, D.C., visited with the monks at the Optina Hermitage near Moscow. Here, they met a Father Michael who told them that an exact copy of the Montreal icon had been written on one of two boards which had belonged to Brother José, and which had been given to the monks of Optina after his death. He told them that in his cell, the copy had been streaming myrrh for three months, and brought it out so the American visitors could venerate it. After an hour, while they visited other parts of the monastery, Father Michael came toward them holding the icon. Father Michael signed Father Potapov with the icon, and then handed it to the startled priest, saying "While reading the Psalter, I got the sensation that the icon must return with you to Washington." After making a prostration, he quickly returned to the *skete*.

Potapov brought the icon back to the cathedral, where it is installed next to the reliquaries along the wall of the left *kliros*. Although the icon is no longer streaming myrrh, signs of the previous phenomenon are visible on its surface, and it exudes a sweet aroma. Devout members of all faiths are welcome at the cathedral to venerate the holy Mother of God, who wishes to remain with her American people.

Two *Retablos ex voto*

RETABLOS

Retablos are traditional paintings of religious images popular in the Latin cultures. In Mexico, these were originally painted on thin sheets of tin-plated iron. Anonymous artists produced thousands of these paintings from the early nineteenth to the early twentieth century.

The word *retablo* is derived from the Latin *retro tabula* — "behind the altar table." The artistic tradition of decorating the space behind the altar was imported to the Americas, along with the Catholic religion, during Spain's conquests in the New World.

Retablos are of two types: *laminas* and *ex votos*. A *retablo ex voto* is a gift offered in completion of a vow or in thanksgiving or petition for divine intervention, favors, or aid, and is placed in a public shrine or church. Now, most *retablos* are *ex votos*, found hanging in shrines throughout the world. Although the tradition of *retablo santo* died out around the beginning of the last century (except in the American Southwest, where it has seen a revival), the *retablo ex voto* tradition continues. Today, *retablos* are considered highly collectible works of popular art.

Retablos santos, or *laminas*, were intended for private devotion and were hung near home altars. The majority of extant *laminas* are found today in museums or private collections as works of art. Hispanic artists in New Mexico and the American Southwest are producing many, some of which are available to be purchased for their original intention, as private home sacramentals.

ENTHRONEMENT OF THE SACRED HEART

Many beautiful images of the Sacred Heart of Jesus have been popular throughout the world for centuries. The ceremony of establishing the Sacred Heart as the head of the household is known as the Enthronement of the Sacred Heart.

The great modern apostle of devotion to the Sacred Heart, especially of priestly and family consecration, was Father Mateo Crawley-Boevy (1875-1960). A priest of the Sacred Heart

Fathers, he founded the Catholic University of Valparaiso, Chile, and then requested Pope St. Pius X to allow him to devote himself to bringing the "entire world, home by home, family by family," to the Sacred Heart. Instead of granting permission, the Pope commanded Father Mateo to dedicate his life's work to this aim. Father Mateo, who spoke five languages fluently, traveled worldwide to do just that.

The Enthronement ritual is a paraliturgical family celebration in which Jesus Christ is proclaimed the Lord of the home. Father Mateo wrote, "The Enthronement can be defined as the official and social acknowledgment of the sovereignty of the Heart of Jesus over a Christian family, an acknowledgment made tangible and permanent by a solemn installation of the picture of the Divine Heart in the place of honor, and by an act of consecration."

Father Mateo saw the sanctification of the family as the ultimate goal of the apostolate. He believed the Enthronement fulfilled all of the requests of the Sacred Heart made to St. Margaret Mary at Paray-le-Monial. To him, the family as a social cell must be the living throne of the King of Love.

In the Enthronement ceremony, a representation of the Sacred Heart is installed in a prominent place in the home. Preferably, the father or the head of the household does this. Then, the family is consecrated to the Heart of Jesus, Lord. In their voluntary dedication, they are set aside as something holy and pleasing to the Lord. The consecration is a covenant or pact that the family freely makes with the Heart of Jesus. It is like a collective renewal of the baptismal commitment made by each member of the family.

Holy Cards

Hand-size printed religious images, typically of Christ, Mary, an angel, or a saint are commonly known as "holy cards." The cards are used as devotionals, slipped in prayer books and, often, distributed to children during catechism classes or given on the occasion of certain religious ceremonies.

The history of holy cards is linked with the history of paper and printing itself. The very first holy cards were made by hand, in imitation of miniatures, illuminated manuscripts, book illustrations, stained-glass windows, and paintings. The prints or cards served as religious texts for the almost illiterate public. The first holy cards were xylographs, or woodcuts, created initially in monasteries, on paper or parchment. The

Holy cards

earliest dated European wood-block print is a picture of St. Christopher, printed in 1423. By 1550, production from the monasteries decreased, and holy picture making passed progressively to engravers and print-sellers. Antwerp became the world center for picture-engravers. The Jesuits encouraged their distribution as a means to counteract Protestantism. Jesuit missionaries also used the holy cards to catechize the people in mission lands.

As print technology developed, the pious activity of creating handmade devotional cards — in France known as *dévotes dentelles* and, in German lands, *Andachtsbilden* — was exceptionally popular from the fourteenth to eighteenth century. Only a few well-preserved specimens of cutouts are found today. These cards were the likely forerunners of greeting cards and present-day holy cards, and they became popular as gifts and remembrances of special events.

By the seventeenth century, Augsburg, Munich, Lyons, Nuremberg, Vienna, and Prague had joined Antwerp to become centers of religious engravers, publishers, and sellers of religious holy cards, and continued to be so up to the nineteenth century. Holy cards from the seventeenth and eighteenth centuries are works of art comparable to the engravings of the great artists of that period; many are currently found in European museums.

The history of modern religious cards dates back to the work of a German map inspector named Aloys Senefelder (1771-1834), the inventor of the printing process known as lithography. His process, a versatile and inexpensive means of multiplying drawings, rapidly gained popularity in Europe. Within twenty-five years, European printers were producing floods of lithographed devotional prints, and industrialization brought a radical increase in the quality of prints available to worldwide markets. By 1825, the new technology was being used successfully in the United States. By the 1840s, the reproductive color process known as "chromolithography," also a Senefelder invention, was in wide use.

With the invention of lithography, the art of the cutout holy card disappeared in 1820, replaced with cards made by industrial processes. Whole pictures were made of die-cut lace; they were found in Prague and in Paris in the first third of the nineteenth century. Later, just the edging would be perforated and, in the nineteenth century, some of the finest lace cards had swirling cuts reaching deep into the card and surrounding the image.

As early as the 1840s, French companies in Paris in the area of Rue St. Jaques and the Church of St. Sulpice generated a good deal of Catholic religious material. In 1862, there were at least

120 firms that made and marketed mass-produced religious goods, including holy cards, much of which was sold in America. The design style of this time, characterized by soft, feminine-looking images, came to be known as *l'art St. Sulpice.*

Catholics commonly exchanged holy cards as gestures of affection. Some bought fancy lace cards and tied medals on them; other cards were hand-decorated with flowers and designs. Small pictures of Christ and the saints were assembled on velvet. These intimate gifts were exchanged between Catholic women, nuns, and children as signs of mutual friendship.

To increase sales in America, some European printers set up branches in the United States. Carl Benziger and Sons, in operation since 1792 in Switzerland, opened in Cincinnati as early as 1838. Later known as Benziger Brothers, the company became the most important Catholic publishing house in the United States, with branches in a number of cities. Local competitors exploited the lucrative print market by setting up their own shops where European compositions were often pirated or adapted.

Records exist of how and when holy cards were used in the lives of some famous saints of the nineteenth century. St. John Neumann (1811-1860) distributed holy cards to children who, in their old age, cherished their cards as relics. St. Anthony Maria Claret distributed more than 83,500 holy cards as he evangelized the Caribbean. Mementos of St. Thérèse of Lisieux's life from 1873 to 1897 include numerous holy cards that she received from family members.

Early Catholic holy cards were most commonly used to commemorate funerals. These cards, with somber black borders and black-and-white lithographs of crucifixion, crosses, and other images, were common at the turn of the century. Funerals are still a prime occasion for the distribution of holy cards.

Religious subjects were represented as well in the "scrap" and die-cut lace style in the Victorian era. Pasting commercially printed die-cut scrap into scrapbooks was a popular pastime of the late 1800s. Another Victorian innovation was the mechanical folding and stand-up holy card.

HOLY CARDS IN *L'ART SACRE*

In the steps toward sainthood, holy men and women are first declared venerable, then blessed, before they are canonized. Holy cards with an image and biography of the saint-to-be are usually published by those advancing a canonization cause, in efforts to solicit reports of favors and miracles achieved through the intercession of the potential saint. These are often produced with small cloth relics mounted onto the cards.

In 1935, Dominican Marie-Alain Couturier founded the influential religious art journal *L'Art Sacre*. Modern liturgical art, or *l'art sacre*, was represented by simpler, often abstract, and masculine-looking images in contrast to the much more ornamented, stereotyped images of the *l'art St. Sulpice*. This trend in Catholic art was reflected in the images of holy cards as well. One example of the *l'art sacre* style is the work of Ade Bethune, whose woodcut-looking art was popularized in the *Catholic Worker* Magazine. Bethune's series of saints' illustrations are still popular today.

From the 1930s through the 1950s, devotions to Mary and the saints swelled in popularity, resulting in an increased production and distribution of holy cards, which became a staple presentation token in parochial schools.

A German nun, Sister Mary Innocentia Hummel, produced more than 600 drawings of cherub-like figures of children while living at the Seissen Convent before and during World War II. Some of these were published as holy cards in the Netherlands in the 1940s and 1950s.

Publishers began to trim cards with gold borders during the 1950s and '60s. In the years after the Second Vatican Council (1962-65), calligraphic quotations from Scripture and symbols such as the fish and *Chi Rho* were offered in place of the more old-fashioned images.

EPHEMERA

Though holy cards have been collected in Europe for centuries, paper collectibles known as *ephemera* only became popular in America in the 1970s and 80s. Possibly the largest collection of holy cards worldwide is contained in the Liturgy and Life Collection at the Burns Library of Rare Books and Special Collections at Boston College. The collection includes some 100,000 Mass cards, posters, programs, leaflets, and holy pictures.

Catholic archivists and genealogists view religious paper, such as holy cards, as a very under-explored genre of heritage material. Today, holy cards are experiencing a revival. The new cards are often encased in or printed on plastic, although paper versions are still available. In order to appeal to today's children, publishers have begun to print holy cards in a collectible trading-card format. "Superhero art" might be used to characterize the styles used for much of the recent religious trading-card art of the 1990s.

Card collectors are making use of modern technology and using the Internet to locate and purchase items for their collections. Various Catholic Internet web sites allow computer users to send electronic holy cards. An image is selected along with a verse, and then sent via e-mail to a friend anywhere in the world.

CINCTURES AND CORDS

The liturgical girdle, or cincture, is a long rope of linen or hemp, tasseled at the end, with which the alb is confined at the waist. It may be the color of the other vestments, but is usually white. Its practical use is to control the loose alb, but symbolically it also refers to sacerdotal purity. The cincture has been recognized as a part of liturgical attire since the ninth century (although it may date back as far as the seventh century), and from early times prayers were recited in putting it on. The cincture was not always the simple cord it is now; surviving examples are made of silk and other precious cloths, sometimes richly embroidered, or interwoven with gold and silver thread.

Some form of cincture is included in many religious or ecclesiastical costumes. In certain religious orders it receives a special blessing, and is sometimes sanctioned or indulged by the Church as a sign of allegiance or affiliation to a particular institute.

In the early Church, virgins wore a cincture as a sign of purity. Wearing a cord or cincture in honor of a saint is of ancient origin, and an early mention of this practice is found in the life of St. Monica. During the Middle Ages, cinctures were often worn by the faithful in honor of saints; a cincture in honor of St. Michael was general throughout France. Later on, ecclesiastical authority set special blessings for cinctures in honor of Our Lady, the Most Precious Blood, St. Francis of Paola, St. Francis of Assisi, St. Thomas Aquinas, and St. Joseph, among others. The blessing of a cincture in honor of the Blessed Virgin Mary was originally reserved to the Hermits of St. Augustine; that of the cord in honor of St. Francis of Assisi was originally reserved to the Order of Friars Minor Conventual. The Order of Minims blessed and invested wearers with a wool cincture in honor of St. Francis of Paula; the Dominicans blessed and distributed cinctures, in honor of St. Thomas Aquinas, for the preservation of chastity. The Roman Ritual contains blessings for cinctures to be worn in honor of Our Lord, Our Lady, or a canonized saint.

THE CORD OF ST. THOMAS AQUINAS

St. Thomas Aquinas, the great medieval doctor of the church, was born near Aquino, one of many children of a nobleman of Lombardic descent. After receiving a good education, he decided to join the Dominicans. His wish to be a mendicant friar shocked his noble relatives, so his brothers kidnapped him and attempted to change his mind.

The devotion known as the Angelic Warfare, or the Cord of St. Thomas, stems from an event that occurred during this period of family imprisonment. While Thomas was held in the castle Montesangiovanni, his brothers attempted to destroy his holy purity and thereby discredit his vocation. But Thomas repulsed the advances of the woman sent by his brothers, forcing her out of his room by threatening her with a firebrand. He then burned a cross on the door of his room, and prayed in thanksgiving for the preservation of his virtue. That night in a dream, two angels came to him from heaven and girded his loins.

Although early historians romanticized this episode, his mystical experience is recorded in the acts of his canonization process and by his earliest biographers. Serious historians see in the account of the girdle of chastity not a material cord, but a spiritual "cord of fire." One account in the canonization process states that Thomas nevermore experienced the "movements of sensuality," and indicates that he was never again to suffer any temptation against chastity. The account of the angel's speech seems more realistic: "On God's behalf we gird you with the girdle of chastity, a girdle which no attack will ever destroy."

Although it is difficult to determine how soon after his death the practice of wearing the cord or girdle in memory of St. Thomas's chastity began, it was probably a fairly common devotion before the first local confraternities of the fifteenth and sixteenth centuries were founded in Spain and Italy.

The Dominican Francis Duerwerdes is considered the founder of the Angelic Warfare Confraternity, instituted at the University of Louvain in 1649 and constituted as an apostolic confraternity in 1727 under Pope Benedict XIII. Pope Pius XI (and seven other popes) recommended the confraternity to youth and granted permission to wear a medal in place of the cord.

One part of the enrollment ceremony in the confraternity is the beautiful prayer of St. Thomas for purity:

Dear Jesus, I know that every perfect gift and especially that of chastity depends on the power of your Providence. Without you, a mere creature can do nothing. Therefore, I beg you to defend by your grace the chastity and purity of my body and soul. And if I have ever sensed anything that can stain my chastity and purity, blot it out, Supreme Lord of my powers, that I may advance with a pure heart in your love and service, offering myself on the most pure altar of your divinity all the days of my life. Amen.

The object of this devotion includes the young St. Thomas, the excellence of his chastity, and the benefits of a religious vocation. The confraternity venerates the Angelic Doctor and directs its members to imitate not only his chastity, but all his virtues.

The cord is white and sometimes made of linen. It is worn around the waist to remind the wearer that he is a temple of the Holy Spirit. There are fifteen knots on the cord as reminders of the mysteries of the Rosary. Each knot has three twists, a reminder of the Holy Trinity and the three theological virtues. A loop is made at one end of the cord, and its two strands represent the natural and supernatural life in each man. The circular loop serves as a reminder that the supernatural life leads us to God.

The confraternity medal has on one side an image of St. Thomas being girded by angels, and on the other side Our Lady, Queen of the Holy Rosary. In the mid-'60s, an American Dominican nun, Sister Mary of the Compassion, a well-known religious artist from Union City, New Jersey, designed a new confraternity medal. One side has an image of St. Thomas with the two angels as bearers of God's help. The border is made up of the design of the cord itself. On the other side, the moon symbolizes Our Lady, and the sun of justice symbolizes Our Lord. The sun is held in the moon as a symbol of the Incarnation of God through Mary. This side has a border whose design is a reminder of the fifteen mysteries of the Rosary.

ST. JOSEPH'S CORD

In 1657, in Antwerp, Belgium, an Augustinian nun named Sister Elizabeth was dying. Her physicians had given up hope and expected her death within a few days, but Sister Elizabeth, a devotee of St. Joseph, prayed to him. Then, she asked for a cord to be made and blessed in his honor. The dying sister's wish was granted.

Sister Elizabeth put on the cord and implored the intercession of St. Joseph for the recovery of her health. While praying, she felt her strength return and rose from her sickbed, instantly cured.

In 1858, the Cord of St. Joseph was approved by the Sacred Congregation of Rites, and indulgenced by Pope Pius IX. The cord is made from simple cotton twine. Seven knots at one end of the cord remind the wearer of the seven joys and the seven sorrows of St. Joseph.

Father John Drumgoole, a New York priest who founded the Mission of the Immaculate Virgin for the care of needy children, placed his life and his work under the protection of St. Joseph. He established St. Joseph's Union to further the work of the mission. This union today is in charge of the Cord of St. Joseph in the United States.

St. Joseph's Cord

CORD OF ST. PHILOMENA

The cord blessed and worn in honor of St. Philomena is red and white and has two knots, representing her purity and martyrdom, at the end. The cord is worn under clothing like a belt.

BRIDAL CINCTURE

This is a cincture, similar to the ropelike belt sometimes worn by a priest at Mass, and also called *El Lazo* (from the Spanish for "the Lasso" and similar appellations). The sponsors (*padrino* and *madrino*) of the cincture at a Hispanic wedding are responsible for placing it over the bridal couple after the Gospel, and removing it after Communion. It symbolizes the binding tie of marriage.

An old German wedding custom dictates that at the wedding ceremony, the arms of the bride and groom are tied together with a white ribbon as a symbol of unity. The couple then keeps the ribbon as a keepsake. In some families, the couple would tie a knot in the ribbon when they had a problem, and untie it when the problem was solved. (See Our Lady Who Unties Knots, p. 162.)

In former days, at ordination a new priest's hands were tied with the *manutergium*, a white ribbon wound around his folded hands after the anointing with chrism. The ribbon was then presented to his mother, who kept it as a blessed reminder and who was usually buried with it. This custom has almost died out today.

MEDALS

The custom of wearing medals is an ancient one. In general, medals are flat metal disks, usually in the form of a coin, which are struck or cast for a commemorative purpose. Religious medals are enormously varied and are used to commemorate persons (Christ, the Blessed Mother, the saints), places such as famous shrines, past historical events (dogmatic definitions, miracles, dedications), or personal graces such as First Communion, ordination, etc. Medals can also be concerned with ideas, such as the mysteries of our faith, and some serve as badges of pious associations.

Medals are worn around the neck or on the person and serve as a reminder, as does a photograph or other relic of a loved one. Medals should be regarded in the same way as any other image; they are merely signs of the prototype inscribed thereon and, in themselves, have no efficacy. To consider them otherwise would be superstition. The medal is to be used as a reminder to honor the subject displayed on the medal, and of the need to advance in Christian perfection. The benefit of the medal, used as a sacramental, is the blessing called down from God on the wearer. Indulgences have sometimes been attached to various types of the innumerable medals struck.

The roots of medal wearing go back to pagan antiquity, where the use of amulets was widespread. These were talismans worn about the neck. It is possible that the early Church tolerated an analogous practice; some early medals have been found in the catacombs. Christians sometimes wore *phylacteries* containing relics or other devotional objects; in Africa, ancient molds for crosses have been found. Unfortunately, the wearing of these phylacteries and *encolpia,* or *pectoral crosses,* soon lent itself to abuses when magical formulas began to join the Christian symbols. Thus, we find record of protests from many of the Church fathers from the fourth century on. Sometimes, alternatively, regular coins were overprinted with a Christian symbol and holes were drilled in them, so the medals might be hung around the neck. We have no way of telling, however, how popular the custom was prior to the Middle Ages.

By the twelfth century, well-known places of pilgrimage began casting tokens of lead or other metals which served as souvenirs, objects of piety, and proofs that a pilgrim had reached his destination. These *signacula,* or pilgrims' signs, came in a variety of forms and were worn prominently on the hat or breast.

By the sixteenth century, these had begun to be replaced by medals cast in bronze or silver with more artistic work on them. Beginning in the thirteenth century, jetons, or counters, began to be used for religious purposes. These were flat pieces of metal, generally a form of brass but later more precious metals, used as vouchers for attendance at ecclesiastical functions, or given as souvenirs. Commemorative medals began in the last years of the fourteenth century. The first ones were elaborate works of art, and therefore restricted to the wealthy. Papal Jubilee medals began as early as 1417.

During the sixteenth century, the custom began of giving papal blessings to medals. One of the first of these was a medal worn by the Spaniards during the revolt of the Gueux in Flanders in 1566. This medal bore an image of Our Lord on one side and an image of Our Lady of Hal on the other. Pope Pius V granted an indulgence to those who wore this medal on their hats. This vogue soon spread throughout Catholic Europe, and soon each city had craftsmen of its own.

Medals became so popular, and were struck for so many reasons and in so many designs, that it seems almost impossible to even classify them. Only a few are outlined here.

Plague medals were struck and blessed as a protection against pestilence. Popular subjects for these are St. Sebastian, St. Roch, and shrines of the Virgin, sometimes with a view of a particular city on them. These medals often carried letters as abbreviations for prayers or mottoes.

Eucharistic miracles were often commemorated with medals, especially on jubilees or centenaries. These were issued in the different places where the miracles were believed to have happened, and some carry picture stories of the miraculous events.

A large number of private medals were struck to commemorate incidents in the life of individuals and be distributed to friends. Among these were *baptism medals,* which often contained precise details of the date of birth.

The cross of St. Ulrich of Augsburg is an example of a medal commemorative of a particular legend. Supposedly, an angel brought a cross to St. Ulrich so that he might carry it into battle against the Huns in 955. More than 180 examples of this one commemoration have been found.

Papal medals, especially in conjunction with the opening and closing of the Holy Door during jubilee years, have been struck since 1417. Almost all major events of the reigns of the popes since that time have been commemorated in medals. Other semi-devotional medals have been struck by religious associations such as the Knights of Malta, and by abbeys in commemoration of their abbots.

ST. CHRISTOPHER MEDAL

Practically nothing is known about St. Christopher other than his name and the fact of his martyrdom, probably about the third century. Although his veneration was widespread in both the Eastern and Western Church from the earliest centuries, early legends supplied with abundant fantasy what history could not provide; all manner of startling details were told of him.

A pious — and the most popular — legendary biography of him is found in the thirteenth-century Golden Legend. This legend tells of a heathen king who, through the prayers of his wife to the Blessed Virgin, had a son whom he named Offerus. This young man grew to great size and strength. The boy decided to serve only the strongest lord in the world and began in the service of an emperor. Discovering the emperor was frightened of the Devil, Offerus then served the Devil for a while until he saw how the Devil trembled at the sight of a crucifix. Thus, the young giant determined to serve Christ and, asking advice from a hermit, was instructed to make a home by a deep and treacherous river and carry Christian pilgrims across.

One night a little boy asked to be carried, so Offerus placed the child on his shoulders and entered the churning water. As he forded the river, the child became heavier and heavier, until Offerus thought he would fail. When he reached the other side, he asked with surprise why the child was so heavy. The child replied that Offerus had carried not only the whole world, but also He who made it. The child identified Himself as Christ, then took Offerus into the water and baptized him, giving him the name Christopher ("Christ-bearer"). He instructed the saint to jam his staff into the ground; it immediately burst forth into leaves and blossoms, and the Christ child disappeared. Christopher later went joyfully to persecution and death for his beloved Lord. One account of his martyrdom has him being shot with arrows for twelve hours and finally beheaded.

St. Christopher Medal

Christopher's legends have inspired many devotions. He was venerated as a patron against sudden and unexpected death, especially during the times of epidemics and plagues. The faithful believed that if they prayed before his picture in the morning, no harm would come to them that day. The custom began of hanging his picture over the door of the house, or painting it on the walls outside so that others could also venerate the saint. He is the patron of ferryboats, pilgrims, travelers, gardeners, and freight ships. He is also known as a patron of skiing.

Churches and monasteries were dedicated to St. Christopher as early as 532. A breviary from the early seventh century has a special office in his honor. In 1386, a brotherhood was founded under his patronage in Tyrol and Vorarlberg to guide travelers over the Arlberg. Temperance societies were established in his name as early as 1517.

Although coins with his image are from a much earlier period, use of the medals and plaques — which people now carry on keychains or in their cars — began in the sixteenth century. Their original purpose was to serve as a picture of the saint for travelers to gaze on in the morning and to protect them from sudden death that day. Although the original custom has long died out, the medals remain as a token of St. Christopher's help and protection in modern traffic. Today many Christians, not just Catholics, keep these medals, which honor the saint as patron of travelers — even though Christopher's feast was dropped from the liturgical calendar, and the Church no longer promotes his *cultus.*

MEDAL OF THE HOLY FACE

Twelve-year-old Giuseppina de Micheli was praying in her parish church, St. Peter in Sala (Milan), on Good Friday. Quite distinctly, she heard a voice tell her, "Nobody gives me a kiss of love in my face to make amends for the kiss of Judas." As she believed all in the church had heard the voice, she was pained to observe that the pious members of the congregation passed by the statue of Jesus, kissing devoutly the wounds, yet not the face.

To herself she thought, "Have patience, dear Jesus, I will give You a kiss of love." In turn this young soul, already filled with a spirit of reparation, kissed the countenance of the replica of Him who would become her Divine Spouse.

Medal of the Holy Face

In 1916, Giuseppina joined the Daughters of the Immaculate Conception, taking the name of Sister Maria Pierina. From the earliest days of her postulancy, Sister Pienna began to experience mystical meetings with Our Lord, who taught her the devotion of reparation to the Holy Face. In 1936, Our Lord told her, "I wish that my face, which reflects the deep pains of my soul, the sorrow and love of my heart, be better honored; who contemplates me consoles me." Later, he also told her, "Every time my face is contemplated, I will pour out my love into the heart of those persons, and by means of my holy face the salvation of many souls will be obtained."

In 1940, under Sister Pierina's direction, a medal of the Holy Face was cast and approved by the Curia of Milan. The design for this medal had been given to her during one of the manifestations she had experienced from Our Lady.

The front of the medal has the Latin words for "May, O Lord, the light of Thy countenance shine upon us" (cf. Ps 66:10). The words encircle a picture of the face of Christ. On the reverse of the medal is a radiant host with the words "Stay with us, O Lord." This medal is to be worn in a spirit of reparation for the outrages committed against the Holy Face of Our Lord during His Passion, and for those committed against Him every day in the Sacrament of His divine love. If possible, the wearer should make a visit to the Blessed Sacrament each Tuesday.

QUEEN OF ALL HEARTS MEDAL

"Mary is Queen of heaven and earth by grace, as Jesus is King of them by nature and by conquest. It is principally in the hearts that she is more glorified with her Son. And so we may call her, as the saints do, the Queen of All Hearts" (St. Louis de Montfort).

The Queen of All Hearts Medal is worn by the members of the Confraternity of Mary, Queen of All Hearts, a pious union of the faithful established in 1899. Pope Pius X erected the confraternity as an archconfraternity in 1913.

The purpose of this confraternity is to help the members live and publicize the Marian Way of Life (as explained in the writings of St. Louis de Montfort) as a way to sanctify themselves and restore the reign of Christ through Mary. The confraternity promotes consecration to Mary, Queen of All Hearts, and its members share in all the good works and prayers of the members of the Company of Mary and the Daughters of Wisdom.

The medal is heart-shaped. On the front is a design of the Queen of All Hearts statuary group found in the Regina dei Cuori Chapel in Rome. Mary is seated, holding the child Jesus. Kneeling at her feet are St. Louis de Montfort and an angel. The book *True Devotion to Mary* is pictured under the group. On the obverse of the medal is a shield with a monogram of Mary surmounted by a crown. The shield is circled with a Rosary entwined with a lily, symbolizing Mary's purity.

MEDAL OF ST. BENEDICT

The medal of St. Benedict is one of the oldest and most highly honored medals used by the Church. Because of the extraordinary number of miraculous occurrences, both physical and spiritual, attributed to this medal, it became popularly known as the "devil-chasing medal."

On the face of the medal is an image of St. Benedict standing before an altar. He holds the cross in one hand and the Benedictine rule in the other. On either side of the altar are an eagle and the traditional chalice. Inscribed in small letters beside two columns are the words *Crux E. Patris Benedicti* ("Cross of our Father Benedict"). Written in larger letters in a circular margin of the medal are the words *Ejus in obitu nostro praesentia muniamur* ("May we be protected in our death by his presence"). St. Benedict is considered one of the patrons of the dying because of the circumstances of his own happy death. He breathed his last while stand-

Medal of St. Benedict

ing in prayer before the Most Blessed Sacrament. Below the figure of the saint is the year the medal was struck — 1880. This is known as the Jubilee medal, as it commemorates the fourteenth centenary of the birth of the saint. Near this is the inscription of Monte Casino, the abbey where the medal was struck.

The back of the medal has a cross of St. Benedict surmounted by the word *Pax* (Peace), the Benedictine motto, and a circular margin, which bears the inscription *VRSNSMVSMQLIVB.* This inscription stands for *Vade Retro Satana* ("Get thee behind me, Satan"), *Nunquam Suade Mihi Vana* ("Persuade me not to vanity"), *Sunt Mala Quae Libas* ("The cup you offer is evil"), and *Ipse Venena Bibas* ("Drink the poison yourself"). On the upright bar of the cross are found the letters *C.S.S.M.L.,* which stand for *Crux Sacra Sit Mihi Lux* ("May the sacred cross be my light") and on the horizontal bar of the cross is inscribed *N.D.S.M.D., Non Draco Sit Mihi Dux* ("Let not the devil be my guide"). The four large letters around the arms of the cross stand for *Crux Sancti Patris Benedicti* ("Cross of the Holy Father Benedict"). The older version of the medal-cross carried the letters *U.I.O.G.D.,* which stand for *Ut In Omnes Gloriam Deum* ("That in all things God be glorified").

Much of the origin and early history of this medal is hidden in the twilight of antiquity. St. Benedict, the founder of the Benedictine Order, was born at Nursia, Italy, in 480 and died at Monte Cassino in 548. This saint had a profound veneration for the Holy Cross and performed many miracles by its means. He taught his followers to have great reverence for the cross, the sign of our redemption, and to rely on its use in combating the world, the flesh, and the devil.

To a large extent, European culture spread from the medieval monasteries of the Benedictines. St. Benedict has even been called the Father of Europe. His name came to be associated with the cross of Christ, and in the course of time a medal was struck in his honor.

Shortly after the year 1000, the Cross of St. Benedict miraculously cured a saintly youth named Bruno of a deadly snakebite. In 1048, this young Benedictine became Pope Leo IX. His reign marked the end of a deplorable period in the history of the papacy. As Pope, St. Leo IX carried out vigorous reforms of the clergy and prepared the way for the future popes to be elected by the cardinals of the Roman church alone. He did much to spread the devotion to the Holy Cross and to St. Benedict. He enriched the medal of St. Benedict, which replaced the Cross of St. Benedict, with many blessings and indulgences. A later Pope, Benedict XIV, gave the solemn approval of the Church to the use of this medal and urgently recommended it to all the faithful.

The life of St. Benedict was characterized by a powerful and all-embracing love for God, a serene dedication to a life based on prayer, and absolute trust in the providence of God. The medal of this saint acts as a reminder to the wearer of those virtues that the saint practiced during his life, and serves as an outward and concrete sign of the person's interior commitment to a life marked by a constant prayerful disposition, trust in God, and practice of charity. The wearing of the medal is in itself an unspoken prayer, a plea for heavenly protection, and a loving token of our attachment to God.

The medal of St. Benedict may be worn or carried. No special prayers are prescribed, but the wearer should cherish a special devotion to Christ Crucified, and have great confidence in St. Benedict.

THE MIRACULOUS MEDAL

"Catherine, Catherine, wake up. Come to the chapel; the Blessed Virgin is waiting for you."

Sleepily, Sister Catherine Labouré, a novice of the Sisters of Charity at the motherhouse on the rue du Bac in Paris, France, opened her eyes. "About half past eleven [July 18, 1830], I heard myself called by my name. I looked in the direction of the voice and I drew the curtain. I saw a child of four or five years old dressed in white [who told me to come to the chapel]. Immediately the thought came to me: 'But I shall be heard.' The child replied: 'Be calm . . . everyone is asleep; come, I am waiting for you.'

"I hurriedly dressed and went to the side of the child. I followed him wherever he went. The lights were lit everywhere. When we reached the chapel, the door opened as soon as the child touched it with the tip of his finger. The candles were burning as at midnight Mass. However I did not see the Blessed Virgin. The child led me to the sanctuary and I knelt down there. Toward midnight, the child said: 'Here is the Blessed Virgin!' I heard a noise like the rustle of a silk dress . . . a very beautiful lady sat down in Father Director's chair. The child repeated in a strong voice: 'Here is the Blessed Virgin.' Then I flung myself at her feet on the steps of the altar and put my hands on her knees.

"I do not know how long I remained there; it seemed but a moment, the sweetest of my life.

"The Holy Virgin told me how I should act toward my director and confided several things to me . . . "

On hearing these words, the young novice's spiritual director, Father Aladel, a young Lazarist, cannot be blamed for thinking Sister Catherine possibly the victim of an overactive imagination.

Later, Catherine wrote of the things the Virgin confided to her that night:

> "The good God, my child, wishes to entrust you with a mission. It will be the cause of much suffering to you, but you will overcome this, knowing that what you do is for the glory of God. You will be contradicted, but you will have the grace to bear it; do not fear. You will see certain things; give an account of them. You will be inspired in your prayers."

Catherine's mission was revealed to her on November 27, 1830. While at community prayer, Catherine again saw the Blessed Virgin, standing dressed in a robe of white silk, with her feet resting on a globe. In her hands she held a smaller globe, and her eyes were raised toward heaven.

"Then suddenly, I saw rings on her fingers, covered with jewels . . . from which came beautiful rays . . . At this moment, she lowered her eyes and looked at me, and an interior voice spoke to me: 'This globe which you see represents the entire world, particularly France, and each person in particular. This is a symbol of the graces which I shed on those who ask me.'

"At this moment, where I was or was not I do not know, an oval shape formed around the Blessed Virgin, and on it were written these words in letters of gold: 'O Mary conceived without sin, pray for us who have recourse to thee.'

"Then a voice was heard to say: 'Have a medal struck after this model. Those who wear it will receive great graces; abundant graces will be given to those who have confidence.' Some of the precious stones gave forth no ray of light. 'Those jewels which are in shadow represent the graces which people forget to ask me for.'

"Suddenly, the oval seemed to turn. I saw the reverse of the medal: the letter M surmounted by a cross, and below it, two hearts, one crowned with a crown of thorns and the other pierced by a

Miraculous Medals

sword. I seemed to hear a voice which said to me: 'The M and the two hearts say enough.'"

After this last account, Father Aladel still had his doubts, but he requested an interview with the Archbishop of Paris. The Archbishop could find nothing against the faith in the idea and authorized the medal to be struck. In May of 1832, the first medals were distributed. Soon afterward came a flood of reported cures and conversions associated with it — so many, in fact, that the people soon began calling it the "Miraculous Medal."

On July 27, 1947, Pope Pius XII canonized St. Catherine Labouré, calling her the "Saint of Silence."

The Miraculous Medal became a sign for a renewal of devotion to Our Lady and an evangelical revival. Millions of Catholics worldwide wear the Miraculous Medal as a reminder of the blessings Our Lady is waiting for them to request.

The Vincentians maintain the National Shrine of the Miraculous Medal in Perryville, Missouri.

THE ST. JOSEPH MEDAL

In 1871, Pope Pius IX, declared St. Joseph the patron of the Universal Church. Just as Joseph was the guardian and protector for the Holy Family, he also is guardian and protector for all the family of God . . . the Church. In 1971, the St. Joseph medal was struck to commemorate the centennial of this declaration. This medal summarizes some of the salient points of the devotion to St. Joseph.

"A medal can be anything from an object of superstition or mere ornament to a valuable means of grace. It can be a silent encouragement in times of stress and trial, a call to virtue in temptation, a bond of union with a great personality, a symbol of loyalty and dedication" (Father Christopher Rengers, O.F.M. Cap.,

St. Joseph Medal

originator of the St. Joseph Medal). Father Rengers expressed the hope that people would wear the St. Joseph medal intelligently and fruitfully, to encourage devotion to the saint, to encourage unity in the family and in the Church, and to encourage loyalty to the Pope. As with all approved medals, this medal is meant to be a means of grace, an aid against temptation, and a bond of union with God and St. Joseph.

An artist named Norbert Schrader carved the design for the medal from dense pine, using fine chisels. Then the plaque was sent to Germany, where the medal was struck. The medal is enameled with the colors purple and white to symbolize Joseph's purity, justice, and humility. A touch of red symbolizes the Holy Spirit and the redeeming love of Christ. The medal is rectangular in shape to preserve the memory of the St. Joseph Scapular, approved by Pope Leo XIII in 1893 and given to the Capuchin Order to promote.

On the face of the medal, St. Joseph is shown in a protective stance, with his arms about the child Jesus and Our Lady. The Child rests his head against the heart of the saint. The circular position of the family conveys unity. Joseph's short-sleeved garment, and the chair on which Our Lady is seated, remind us

Joseph was a carpenter, a worker. The petition inscribed on the face of the medal reads, "That all may be one: St. Joseph Our Protector Pray for Us." The letters *GIJM* stand for Joseph's fidelity to grace in his interior life and his love for Jesus and Mary.

The obverse of the medal has the words, "Feed my lambs, feed my sheep. The spirit of the Lord his guide." It depicts sheep underneath the shepherd's staff and crossed keys, a symbol of the papacy; the whole is surmounted by a dove symbolizing the Holy Spirit. This side of the medal reminds us to invoke St. Joseph as protector of the Church, on behalf of the Holy Father.

Thus, the St. Joseph medal honors St. Joseph as patron of the Church, fosters family and Church unity, and encourages loyalty to the Holy Father. It is distributed by the Workers of St. Joseph.

THE SCAPULAR MEDAL

Scapular medal, front and back

In 1910, Pope St. Pius X introduced a scapular medal, which may be substituted in most cases for any of the various scapulars. Valid enrollment in the scapulars must, however, be made before the substitution.

The decree, in translation, reads thus:

"For the future all the faithful already inscribed or who shall be inscribed in one or other of the real Scapulars approved by the Holy See (excepting those which are proper to the Third Orders) by what is known as regular enrollment may, instead of the cloth scapulars, one or several, wear on their persons, either round the neck or otherwise, provided it be in a becoming manner, a single medal of metal, through which, by the observance of laws laid down for each scapular, they shall be enabled to share in and gain all the spiritual favors (not excepting what is known as the Sabbatine Privilege of the Scapular of Our Lady of Mount Carmel), and all the privileges attached to each.

"The right side of this medal must show the image of Our Most Holy Redeemer, Jesus Christ, showing His Sacred Heart, and the obverse that of the Most Blessed Virgin Mary. It must be blessed with a separate blessing for each of the scapulars in which the person has been enrolled and for which the wearer wishes it to suffice. Finally, these separate blessings may be given by a single Sign of the Cross (*unico crucis signo*), whether in the act of enrollment or later at the convenience of those enrolled, it matters not how long after the enrollment or in what order they may have taken place; the blessing may be given by a priest other than the one who made the enrollment, as long as he possesses the faculty, ordinary, or delegated, of blessing the different scapulars — the limitations, clauses, and conditions attached to the faculty he uses still holding their force. All things to the contrary, even those calling for special mention, notwithstanding" (Holy Office, Rome, December 16, 1910).

MEDAL OF ST. MARIA GORETTI AND OUR MOTHER OF CONFIDENCE

In 1950, a little Italian peasant girl, Maria Goretti, was canonized as a martyr — not for the Christian faith, but for the Christian life. At the age of twelve, Maria was attacked and stabbed by a young man who wanted to seduce her. She heroically resisted, in defense of her purity, and died 24 hours later, after having forgiven her murderer. After eight years in prison, unrepentant, her murderer had a change of heart after experiencing a vision of Maria and, when released from prison in 1937, received Communion at the side of Maria's widowed mother.

Maria's canonization stands as one of the fastest modern canonizations on record; she was raised to the honors of the altar only 48 years after her death (only St. Maximilian Kolbe's was

Medal of St. Maria Goretti *(left)* and its reverse, displaying Our Lady of Confidence *(right)*

faster — 41 years). A medal in her honor was struck about the time of the canonization.

The reverse of this medal displays a picture of Our Lady of Confidence, surrounded by the aspiration "My Mother, My Confidence." The picture of Mary under this title has been venerated in Italy for centuries. Sister Clare Isabella Fornari, a Poor Clare of Tadi, Italy, whose beatification process has begun, stated that Our Lady promised to grant a particular tenderness and devotion toward herself to everyone who venerates her image under the title of Our Lady of Confidence.

MEDAL OF OUR LADY OF FÁTIMA

A young Portuguese priest, Father Joseph Cacella, was driven out of his native country when the radical party came to official power. After spending five years as a missionary in the Amazon, he came to America in 1914 to die; he had contracted jungle fever while on the mission, and his doctors had given him a mere six months to live. In America, he found residence with the Friars at Graymoor in Garrison, New York. But instead of dying, he lived to become the great apostle of Fátima.

While at Graymoor, Father Cacella received letters from his mother in Portugal, telling of the apparitions to the three shepherd children of Fátima. Her letters were intimate and full of details, as she knew and had spoken with the parents of the children and with the children themselves. She was convinced the children were speaking nothing but the truth.

A classmate of Father Cacella at the seminary in Portugal, a Msgr. Formigao, visited the children and questioned them. He was the first representative of the Church to question the children and he missed no detail. He began to write inspiring accounts of the apparitions, although he prudently published them under a pen name.

However, the radical communist government — which was suppressing all information about Fátima — tracked down the identity of this priest, and he was suspended, silenced, and imprisoned for months. Not to be deterred, Msgr. Formigao appealed to Father Cacella's mother to send information to her son. America, with its freedom of the press, would be the herald of the news of Fátima. Father Cacella joyfully agreed, and took up the task of making Fátima known worldwide.

As the message of Fátima spread, so did the demand for pictures, statues, and medals of Our Lady. Father Cacella went to the religious-goods houses that made medals and statues, but they were not interested in his proposition. Since the Fátima movement at that time was still in an unknown stage, they did not want to produce a medal that might be a risk on their hands. As a last resort, Father Cacella went to an old friend, Vincent Hirten, the head of a company, who agreed to turn out the medals if Father would furnish the die. Unfortunately, with no medals, there were no dies.

Actually, Father Cacella had one medal of Fátima, one his mother had sent him from Portugal in 1920. This was probably the only medal of Fátima in the United States. He finally decided to allow it to serve as the design for a medal. Since that day, millions upon millions of medals have been struck — from the design of the one medal that Father Cacella had received from his own earthly mother.

MEDAL OF ST. DYMPHNA

Nervous and mental diseases present one of the most serious problems facing our nation today. On the grounds of the Massillon State Hospital in Massillon, Ohio, is the National Shrine of St. Dymphna, the patroness of those afflicted with nervous and emotional

St. Dymphna Medal

illness. St. Dymphna has been honored and loved for centuries, and thousands have been helped through her intercession.

St. Dymphna was born in the seventh century in Ireland, the daughter of the king or chieftain of Oriel. Although her father was a pagan, Dymphna's mother was Christian, remarkable both for her piety and her beauty. She had Dymphna instructed in the Catholic faith.

When Dymphna was about fifteen, her mother died and, through grief and bereavement, her father slowly lost his sanity. His advisors advised him to marry again, so he sent messengers throughout the countryside looking for a replacement for his wife who shared her same qualities. No new bride could be found to suit him, however, and eventually, he decided that his daughter was the only one in the kingdom who would make a suitable wife.

Dymphna and her confessor fled to Gheel in Belgium to escape the incestuous advances of the chieftain, but after a lengthy search, Dymphna's father tracked down the escapees, beheading both the priest and his own daughter. The people of Gheel first buried the martyrs in a cave. Later, according to the legend, when workers excavated the cave in the thirteenth century to rebury the remains more fittingly, they found the relics in two white marble coffins. A red tile identified the relics of the teenage girl saint.

When the bodies were removed to a small church, a woman suffering from nervous disorder touched the tomb and was instantly cured. People began to flock to Gheel, and when St. Dymphna's relic was touched to those suffering mental and emotional disorders, the number of cures defied belief.

Through the centuries, the fame of Gheel grew, until caring for the emotionally disturbed became the major occupation of the inhabitants. The people loved their little princess, and she in turn showered graces on those who — like her once-beloved father — suffered from an illness no scientist could lay under a microscope and examine. To this day, the town of Gheel continues to befriend those who come to honor her.

A shrine in Ohio is the first church in America to be built in honor of St. Dymphna. It was dedicated in 1938, and since then has served as a storehouse of grace for those suffering from depression, anxiety, and all other mental disorders. Medals, as well as statues and information about the Irish martyr, are distributed from this national shrine. The shrine is the home of the League of St. Dymphna, a group of members throughout the country whose intentions are remembered at the shrine. She who died at the hands of her insane father intercedes graciously and willingly for those who suffer and for their families.

Medal of Our Lady of Olives

MEDAL OF OUR LADY OF OLIVES

A medal of French origin based on a fourteenth-century image of Our Lady. Traditionally, people wear the medal as a protection against lightning in a storm; women also wear it at the time of childbirth, asking the Virgin to assist them in the hour of delivery. The prayer to Our Lady of Olives refers to her as the Olive of Peace and pleads for harmony between all nations.

CLOTHING AND JEWELRY

RINGS

A ring is a piece of jewelry traditionally used to symbolize power or commitment. Today there are also many styles of rings with Christian symbolism.

WEDDING RINGS

As a sacramental, a symbol of the love and union of husband and wife. The Christian use of wedding rings apparently developed from the Roman custom of betrothal rings. In the archdiocese of Westminster, England, an indulgence may be gained by a married couple who kiss the blessed ring and recite with contrite heart the following prayer: "Grant us, O Lord, that loving You, we may love each other and live according to Your holy law."

The earliest betrothal rituals involved an exchange of gifts or property, usually from the groom to the bride's family. Gold rings date back to the early days of marriage by purchase when gold rings were often used as currency. During medieval times, the groom-to-be placed a ring on three of the bride's fingers to represent the Holy Trinity. This custom was adapted in some religious orders of women who wear a ring indicative of their vows as a "bride of Christ." Their rings are conferred at the time of their solemn profession.

EPISCOPAL RINGS

Episcopal rings are first mentioned as an official part of the bishop's insignia in the early seventh century. The pope's ring is known as the Fisherman's Ring. It is a gold seal ring engraved with St. Peter in a boat and the pope's name around it. At the pope's death, it is ceremonially broken.

Rosary Ring

ROSARY RINGS

Rosary rings with ten beads to indicate a decade became popular in the fifteenth century; their popularity has revived in recent times, and several styles are available.

CHASTITY RINGS

A fairly new and popular sacramental in the form of a ring worn by youth pledged to abstain from sex until marriage.

JESUIT RINGS

Rings made of brass or bronze showing religious representations. In the second half of the seventeenth century, Jesuit missionaries used to award rings to converts, particularly in the area of present-day New York State.

BLESSED DRESSES

In the 1950s and 60s, it was a pious custom for young ladies to wear blessed dresses as a promise or to obtain some special favor. The most commonly used blessed dresses were those in honor of our Lady of Lourdes, our Lady of Sorrows, the Immaculate Conception, of Carmel, of Mary Help of Christians, of St. Anthony, and of St. Joseph. The color of the dress indicated in whose honor it was worn. The dress of Our Lady of Lourdes was white with a blue sash tied in front. That of Our Lady Help of Christians was coral pink with a powder blue sash tied in a bow at the left side. All blessed dresses were to be modest with long sleeves and closed necklines. Although the custom died out by the end of the decade of the 60s, in some Hispanic areas today, young children are occasionally dressed in clothing specially blessed in honor of the Virgin. In some Hispanic paraliturgical ceremonies, special clothing is worn sacramentally.

HABITS

Among religious orders that still wear habits, these are also sacramentally blessed.

CROSSES AND OTHER CHRISTIAN SYMBOLS

Crosses, crucifixes, and other Christian symbols are popular as jewelry and other clothing adornments.

SCAPULARS AND BADGES

The scapular began in the early Middle Ages as a long, narrow piece of cloth about the width of the shoulders, with an opening in the center so that it could be slipped over the head and hang in equal lengths. It was worn over the tunic and, sometimes, under a belt. Some, such as those worn by the early Benedictines, had a hood attached. Originally, the scapular was a work garment meant to protect the tunic; through the years it became considered part of the habit. A number of the scapulars worn by the religious orders had great religious significance, stemming from the way the scapular was received by the order.

Later, an abbreviated form of the scapular came into proper use and was given to the laity in order to give the wearer a share in the merits and good works of the particular group of which it served as a badge. These scapulars are connected to third orders and confraternities. The wearer is invested in the scapular by religious authority, and the scapular is worn according to specific directions. These abbreviated scapulars are generally formed from two pieces of cloth about three inches long and two inches wide, and are connected with strings so that it may be worn front and back. The scapulars generally have embroidered or stamped representations on them. There are nearly a score of scapulars which have received approval for use in the Universal Church, although several of these are little known in America. Just as with many other sacramentals, care must be taken that the wearers understand fully the devotion connected with the scapular and that they must guard against superstition.

In 1910, Pope St. Pius X authorized the wearing of a blessed medal as a substitute, under certain conditions, for wearing one of the small scapulars. This medal, commonly called the "scapular medal," (see separate entry) has a representation of the Sacred Heart on one side and a representation of the Blessed Virgin on the other. Investing in any scapular, however, cannot be done with just the medal; the actual scapular must be used. The priest who blesses the medal must also have the faculties to invest in the scapular it represents.

In addition to the scapulars, cloth badges will be treated in this section.

THE BROWN SCAPULAR OF OUR LADY OF MOUNT CARMEL

Along with the Rosary, the brown scapular is one of the most ancient and best loved of the sacramentals. Its Carmelite tradition of Marian devotion extends back to 1251, when Our Lady herself presented the first one to St. Simon Stock (or, as he is sometimes called, St. Simon of England).

The Brown Scapular of Our Lady of Mount Carmel is the habit of the Carmelite Order. For the religious Carmelites, it takes the form of two long undecorated panels of brown cloth joined at the shoulders and falling, one panel to the front and the other to the back. For the laity it is in the form of two smaller pieces of brown or dark cloth, preferably plain, joined over the shoulders by ribbons and falling in the same manner as the larger scapular.

As the order's habit, the scapular signifies some degree of affiliation to the Carmelites such as the religious men and women of the order and aggregated institutes, including the Third Order (a secular, or lay, order), as well as members of public associations and confraternities of Our Lady of Mount Carmel such as active communities of the Scapular Confraternity. Those who have been invested in the scapular practice the order's spirituality and have been granted some association with the order; those who wear

Brown Scapular of Our Lady of Mount Carmel, with medals

the scapular out of devotion, practice the order's spirituality, but have no formal association with the order; and, those who are committed to practice the Marian characteristics of Carmelite spirituality but use outward forms other than the Brown Scapular to express this devotion.

It should be noted, too, that the scapular is the common habit of all the branches of the Carmelite family and a sign of unity of that family. Therefore, the Scapular Confraternity, and similar associations of the faithful that center around the Scapular of Our Lady of Mount Carmel, belong not to any one branch of Carmel, but to the entire Carmelite family.

According to the Rite for the Blessing and Enrollment in the Scapular of the Blessed Virgin Mary of Mount Carmel, approved by the Holy See in 1996, any priest or deacon has the faculties for blessing the scapular. And a person given authority to act in the name of the order may receive people into the confraternity of the scapular. Part of the ceremony of investiture reminds the wearer, "Full of faith in the love of such a great Mother, dedicate yourself to imitating her and to a special relationship with her. Wear this sign as a reminder of the presence of Mary in your daily commitment to be clothed in Jesus Christ and to manifest him in your life for the good of the Church and the whole of humanity, and to the glory of the Most Blessed Trinity."

THE GREEN SCAPULAR OF THE IMMACULATE HEART OF MARY

THE SCAPULAR OF THE IMMACULATE CONCEPTION

BADGE OF THE IMMACULATE HEART OF MARY

Although commonly called the green scapular, this sacramental is not the habit of any confraternity and is improperly styled a scapular, as it does not have a front and back part but only two pious images attached to a single piece of green cloth which hangs on a single string of the same color.

On one side of the cloth is a picture of the Blessed Virgin Mary. She is dressed in a long gown over which hangs a mantle. No veil covers her head, and her hair fails loosely over her shoulders; her feet are bare. Her hands are folded inward, and she holds her heart from the top of which brilliant flames issue. On the other side of the cloth is a picture of a heart ablaze with flames, pierced with a sword and dripping blood. The heart is surmounted by a cross and encircled by the words: "Immaculate Heart of Mary, pray for us now and at the hour of our death."

No special formula is required for blessing the green scapular, and there is no investiture ceremony. All that is necessary is for the scapular be blessed by a priest and honored by the person wishing to benefit by its happy influences. It may be worn or carried. Additionally, if a person in need of grace is obstinate, the Green Scapular may be placed secretly upon his person on in his possession, and the giver should say the prayer for him. The prayer is that which encircles the heart, and should be said at least once daily.

The green scapular devotion was brought to the world through a series of private revelations to Sister Justine Bisquey-

Green Scapular (Immaculate Heart of Mary Scapular)

buru, a humble French sister of the Daughters of Charity of St. Vincent de Paul.

On January 28, 1840, Sister Justine was at prayer when suddenly the Blessed Virgin made herself visible to her eyes. Mary was dressed in a long white gown which reached to her bare feet, over which was a mantle of very light blue. Her hair hung loose, and she wore no veil. In her hands, she held her heart, from the top of which abundant flames gushed out. Several times more, Sister Justine was privileged to see this same vision of Our Lady. At first, these visions seemed intended only to increase the tender devotion of the young sister to Mary and her Immaculate Heart. Later, she had another vision. The Mother of God appeared to her during meditation, holding in her right hand her heart surmounted by flames and in the left a kind of scapular. One side of the scapular, or cloth badge, contained a representation of the Virgin such as she had appeared to Sister Justine in previous apparitions. The other side contained, in Sister Justine's words, "a heart all ablaze with rays more dazzling than the sun, and as transparent as crystal." That heart, pierced with a sword, was encircled by an inscription of oval shape and surmounted by a gold cross. It read, "Immaculate Heart of Mary, pray for us, now and at the hour of our death." At the time of this vision, an interior voice revealed to Sister Justine the meaning of the vision. She understood this picture was, by the medium of her order, to contribute to the conversion of souls, and to obtain for them a good death. She also understood that copies should be made as soon as possible and distributed with confidence.

Sister Justine wrote to her novice mistress, begging her to keep her communication secret, and telling her she feared it might have been an effect of her imagination. She asked if her novice mistress believed it necessary for her to speak of it to her spiritual director. The vision was repeated twice more in the next year, when Sister Justine at last confided it to her director, Father Aladel. At first, there was a delay in the making and distributing of these scapulars. (The Virgin herself complained about the delay in later visions to Sister Justine!) But at last, the scapulars began to be made and distributed. Pope Pius IX gave formal permission and encouragement for the sisters to make and distribute the scapulars in 1870.

Devotees of the green scapular say great graces are attached to the wearing or carrying of this sacramental. These graces, however, are more or less in proportion to the degree of faith and confidence possessed by the user. The scapular is known for drawing forth devotion to the Immaculate Heart of Mary, and for numerous conversions.

THE SCAPULAR OF OUR LADY OF MERCY

St. Peter Nolasco (d. 1256) devoted his life to the rescue of captives from the Moors, who were then occupying much of Spain. With this aim in mind, he founded the Order of Our Lady of Mercy (Mercedarians) between 1218 and 1234. The scapular contains a picture of Our Lady of Mercy or an embroidered M with a crown over it on one side and is backed by the arms of the order. It is commonly worn by members of the Third Order, but can be worn by anyone.

BLUE SCAPULAR OF THE IMMACULATE CONCEPTION

Venerable Ursula Benicasa, foundress of the Order of Theatine Nuns, tells in her autobiography how the habit worn by her sisters was revealed to her in a vision. This habit was to be worn in honor of the Immaculate Conception, and in return Our Lord promised great favors to the order. Venerable Ursula then begged the same graces for all the faithful who would devoutly wear a small sky-blue scapular in honor of the Immaculate Conception and for the purpose of securing the conversion of sinners.

Ursula herself made and distributed the first of these scapulars, after having them blessed by a priest. The scapular usually bears a symbolization of the Immaculate Conception on one side and on the other the name of Mary. The scapular received papal approval in 1671 from Pope Clement X. In 1992, Fr. Donald Petraitis, MIC, Superior General of the Marians of the Immaculate Conception, obtained for himself and his successors a perpetual permission from the Superior General of the Theatine Fathers to bless and confer the scapular. The Marians promote and distribute the scapular today.

THE BLACK SCAPULAR OF THE SEVEN DOLORS OF THE BLESSED VIRGIN MARY

Today's scapular of the Seven Sorrows is made of black cloth and usually bears a picture of Our Lady of Sorrows on the front panel. The back panel may also have a picture of Our Lady. Information about this scapular, as well as other devotions in honor of the Sorrowful Mother, may be obtained from the Servite Order, the trustee of this cult.

THE SACRED HEART BADGE

The most common token of the Sacred Heart is the Badge of the Sacred Heart, one of the most common of the Catholic sacramentals. This familiar badge owes its origin to St. Margaret Mary Alacoque.

The Black Scapular of the Seven Dolors of the Blessed Virgin Mary

St. Margaret Mary was a humble nun of the Visitation convent at Paray-le-Monial, France. She was favored in prayer by special revelations, beginning in 1693, in which Our Lord called her to reveal to the world the love of his Sacred Heart. On one occasion when Christ appeared to her, He expressed the wish that those who loved Him should wear or carry a picture of His Sacred Heart. St. Margaret Mary made some little pictures that she and her friends carried. These were the first Sacred Heart badges.

Sacred Heart Badge

In 1720, the city of Marseilles, France, was ravaged by the plague. Nearly a thousand persons a day were dying from the dread disease, and the people were panicked with fear. The bishop asked the nuns of the city to make up thousands of badges of the Sacred Heart. He then consecrated the city to the Sacred Heart and distributed the little badges. No new cases of the plague were reported, and the people were wild with joy.

Over the centuries, the style of the badge has changed. Today, the Badge is an oval shape with a serrated-edge print showing Christ with His Heart exposed on one side and the Heart itself on the other. The badge was brought to the United States by the Apostleship of Prayer and is used as an external sign of the union of the members with Christ. On the front of the badge are found the words "Apostleship of Prayer — League of the Sacred Heart." On the reverse are found two prayers: "Cease, the Heart of Jesus is with me," and "Sacred Heart of Jesus, Thy Kingdom Come."

THE SACRED HEARTS BADGE

In his great encyclical on the Sacred Heart, *Haurietis Aquas*, Pope Pius XII enjoined the faithful to join devotion to the Immaculate Heart of Mary to that of the Sacred Heart of Jesus. His words echoed those of Our Lady at Fátima, "The Heart of Jesus wishes to be venerated together with the Heart of His Mother."

Devotion to the Sacred Heart has been practiced for centuries. Since the apparitions of Our Lady to St. Catherine

Sacred Hearts Badge, front and back

Labouré in which she gave the pattern for a medal showing the two hearts, and since the messages of Our Lady at Fátima, the twofold devotion has increased in popularity. In 1793, Father Mary-Joseph Courdin founded the Congregation of the Sacred Hearts for its promotion.

The badge of the Sacred Hearts depicts, pictorially and symbolically, both the Sacred Heart of Jesus and the Immaculate Heart of Mary. It serves as a reminder of the great love Jesus and Mary have for us, and that we must love them in return. The badge reminds us graces come from the Heart of Jesus through the Heart of His Mother.

SCAPULAR OF THE HOLY FACE

A white scapular, worn by the members of the Archconfraternity of the Holy Face, bears the well-known Roman picture connected with the towel of St. Veronica. The members may wear the picture of the Holy Face on a medal or cross instead of the scapular — merely one of the pious practices of the archconfraternity — without any special indulgences or investiture.

Sister Marie de St. Pierre, a Discalced Carmelite nun of Tours, received special favors from Our Lord, who through her offered a number of promises to anyone who showed honor and reverence for His Holy Countenance. The wearing of this scapular is connected with this devotion.

THE PASSIONIST EMBLEM

Paul Francis Daneo (St. Paul of the Cross, 1694-1775) received many graces from God indicating he was to found a community to keep alive the memory of the Passion of Our Lord. Members of the order today are known as Passionists, and they have spread worldwide. The Passionist sign is the figure of a white heart surmounted by a cross with the inscription *JESU XPI PASSIO* (The Passion of Jesus Christ) and with three nails underneath the heart. The emblem is white on a black background.

Passionist Emblems

The badges or emblems worn by the saint himself often seemed to have a special, miraculous power. He frequently gave away those he no longer wore. He sometimes allowed those persons for whom he was spiritual director to wear these signs secretly.

St. Paul himself explained the symbolism of the sign. The white color of the heart means that the heart with the Passion imprinted on it ought to be already purified. He called the sign a "terror of hell" and a "sign of salvation." From this practice of the founder, the wearing of a small Passionist emblem gradually developed. The original emblems were of cloth; later metal ones were struck. At one time a black scapular of the Passion was used, but that is no longer promoted.

The faithful who wear a small sign of the Passion are encouraged to recite the pious aspiration "Passion of Christ, strengthen me." Today, the Passionists give small pins to their volunteers and others associated with the order as reminders of God's love for us and forgiveness of our sins, as seen in Jesus' Passion.

THE SCAPULAR OF THE MOST HOLY TRINITY

The scapular of the Most Blessed Trinity has its origin in a series of private revelations to St. John of Matha. The first of these revelations came as St. John was celebrating his first Mass. An angel clothed in a white garment appeared at the altar. Across his breast and shoulder was a cross of red and blue. His arms were crossed and held over what appeared to be two captives — a Christian and a Moor. St. John understood he was to found an order for the redemption of captives, Christian and non-Christian alike.

St. John retreated to the desert, where he met St. Felix of Valois. Together the two men lived, for a time, the eremitical life, fasting and praying fervently for guidance in their mission. At last, after a number of other apparitions, the two traveled to Rome in 1198 to seek the counsel of the Holy Father. Pope Innocent III, while

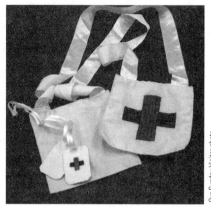

Holy Trinity Scapulars

deliberating on their proposals, also had a vision of an angel wearing a red and blue cross. He approved the new institute and ordered it to be called the Order of the Most Holy Trinity for the Ransom of Captives. He gave the members a white habit with a red and blue cross.

This habit became the basis on which the scapular of the Blessed Trinity was later made. This scapular is the badge of the members of the Confraternity of the Most Holy Trinity. There are several groups of the laity associated with the Trinitarians whose U.S. Headquarters are in Baltimore, Maryland.

THE PRECIOUS BLOOD HEART

American headquarters for the Confraternity of the Precious Blood is at the cloistered monastery of the Precious Blood Sisters in Brooklyn, New York. Its official emblem is a small heart made of red cloth. On one side is a reproduction of the mural behind the altar in the chapel of the Most Precious Blood in the monastery. A sunburst haloes the crucified figure of Our Lord.

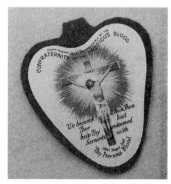

Precious Blood Heart

Above the crucifix is the name of the confraternity; about the foot are the words "We beseech Thee, help Thy servants whom Thou hast redeemed with Thy Precious Blood." On the back of the heart is a red drop of the Precious Blood on a white background with the saying of Pope Pius IX, "Place on thy heart one drop of the Precious Blood of Jesus and fear nothing."

THE RED SCAPULAR OF THE PASSION

THE SCAPULAR OF THE SACRED HEART OF JESUS AND OF THE MOST LOVING AND COMPASSIONATE HEART OF THE BLESSED AND IMMACULATE VIRGIN MARY

The red scapular of the Passion was revealed in a series of apparitions of Our Lord to Sister Apolline Andriveau from July 26, through September 14, 1846.

A beautiful, intelligent, talented young Frenchwoman, Louise Apolline Aline Andriveau joined the Sisters of Charity of St. Vincent de Paul at the age of twenty-three. Here she blended with the other sisters, humbly dedicating her life to the service of the sick and the poor. On receiving the habit, Sister Apolline was sent to St. John's at Troyes, where one of her duties was the care of the chapel. In the presence of the Holy Eucharist, she began to receive special graces from Our Lord.

"I went up to the Chapel before Benediction. I thought I beheld Our Lord; in his right hand he held a red scapular, the opposite ends of which were connected by two woolen strings of the same color. On one end of the scapular was represented our Savior crucified; the most painful instruments of the Passion lay at the foot of the cross . . . Around the crucifix were inscribed these words: 'Holy Passion of our Lord Jesus Christ, save us!' On the opposite end of the scapular were represented the Sacred Hearts of Jesus and of His holy Mother. A cross seemed to rise between these two hearts — and the scapular at this end bore the inscription 'Sacred Hearts of Jesus and Mary, protect us!' "

Red Scapular of the Passion

The apparition of Jesus holding in His hand the scapular of His Passion was repeated frequently. On one occasion, Our Lord told Sister Apolline that those who wore the scapular would, on Fridays, experience a great increase of faith, hope, and charity.

When someone remarked that it would be a difficult matter to secure authorization for this devotion, Sister Apolline told them with confidence that, as the devotion was wished for by Christ Himself, He would remove all the obstacles that usually oppose the introduction of new devotions. In fact, Pope Pius IX approved the scapular of the Passion in 1847, scarcely a year after the apparitions.

The front panel of the scapular pinpoints the central act of Redemption. In the center is a large oval of the crucifix, embellished with the other instruments of the Passion. A hammer and pincers in the upper left hand corner symbolize not only the tools used to drive and remove the nails, but also the hammer serves as a symbol of penance and the pincers remind us to pull out sin from ourselves and make room in our souls for the healing grace from the sacred wounds. In the upper right-hand corner three nails and the crown of thorns symbolize the mental and physical discipline that must go together for us to achieve integrity of spirit. Beneath the cross is a ladder whose steps symbolize the virtues by which we must ascend our own cross in union with the redeeming cross of Christ. The crowing rooster symbolizes that the time for repentance is at hand. The spear reminds us we must pierce our own hearts and break them free from every attachment save God. Other symbols displayed are the scourges, the sponge and water pot, and Veronica's veil.

The last apparition to Sister Apolline took place just five days before the apparition of Our Lady of La Salette. The crucifix and passion instruments shown to Sister Apolline were similar to the crucifix which Our Lady wore on a chain around her neck at La Salette. The instruments of Christ's Passion teach us how to meditate on His many sufferings. By this daily remembrance we come to understand that, if we hope to share the joys of His glory, we must first share His bitterness and humiliations in suffering.

Interestingly, the picture on the front of the red scapular is the same picture honored throughout the Latin world as the *Justo Juez*, or Just Judge. Devotion to the Just Judge has its roots in the gospels: Mt. 25:31, 26:64, and Jn. 5:22, as well as Acts 10:42. Devotion to Christ under this title is connected both with the picture and with an image. Sadly, like many other true Catholic devotions, the devotion to the Just Judge has been corrupted and transferred into an almost magical symbol in some places. Botanicas which sell items for Santaria, Voodoo, and some other spiritualists also often sell "magic" candles and "lucky mojo charms" of *Justo Juez* which claim to keep the user safe from judicial persecution without any mention of whether or not the petitioner is guilty. The initial devotion, however, is a valid one.

The red scapular of the Passion is promoted by the Archconfraternity of the Holy Agony, whose headquarters is at the Marian Center in Emmitsburg, Maryland. Investiture is no longer required for this scapular. The graces depend upon the faith and confidence of the wearer.

THE SCAPULAR OF ST. DOMINIC

The reception of the Dominican scapular by Blessed Reginald from the hands of Mary parallels the story of the brown scapular and St. Simon Stock. In 1903, St. Pius X granted the small Dominican scapular indulgences, as often as the wearer devoutly kissed it.

It is made of white wool and was approved by the order as the usual form of affiliation with the community. No images are necessary; however, the scapular, as given in the house of the Dominican general at Rome, has the picture of St. Dominic kneeling before the crucifix on one side and, on the other, the image of Blessed Reginald receiving the habit from the hands of the Mother of God.

SCAPULAR OF ST. NORBERT

St. Norbert, the great Eucharistic saint of his time, received the direction to found his order, an indication of the place where the order should begin, and the holy habit from the hands of the Blessed Virgin in a vision. St. Norbert and the Praemonstratensian Order, which he founded, became the wellspring of Eucharistic devotion and restored its place of primacy in Christian life.

Upon St. Norbert's true devotion to the Blessed Virgin and to the Blessed Sacrament, he built the first "third order" for laymen in the church. In 1128, St. Norbert gave a little scapular of white wool to Count Theobald of Champagne and Blois, as a proof and emblem of his union with the Norbertine family. Thus, the Norbertine scapular ranks as one of the oldest scapulars.

THE RED CROSS OF ST. CAMILLUS

About 300 years before the founding of the International Red Cross, the "red cross" had already become a symbol of organized charity and dedication to the sick. St. Camillus de Lellis, the founder of the Camillians (Order of the Servants of the Sick), obtained the privilege of wearing a cross made of red cloth on the

THE RED CROSS
OF ST. CAMILLUS

Patron of the Sick and Dying
Hospitals and Nurses

The Red Cross of St. Camillus de Lellis

black habits of the order. It served as an inspiration for the sick by reminding them of the Passion, death, and resurrection of Our Lord. Additionally, it reminded the priests and brothers who wore the habit of their dedication and solemn commitment of service to the sick.

During the battle of Canizza in 1601, the Camillians were busily occupied with the wounded. The tent in which they had stored their equipment and supplies caught fire, and everything in the tent was destroyed except the red cross of one of the habits. Other miracles gradually increased devotion to the red cross.

Today, the Servants of the Sick carry on the work of St. Camillus in 350 houses, hospitals, clinics and other health facilities in almost thirty countries. They distribute small, simple red cloth crosses worldwide. A special blessing was inserted in the Roman Ritual for the crosses. From the sick who have received these crosses come many reports of a deepening faith in Christ the Healer, miracles, and conversions.

MEMENTO MORI

Memento mori includes all those types of sacramentals that serve as reminders that all people die, from the Latin words "reminder of death."

During the Middle Ages, human mortality was a frequent topic of preaching, and the laity became fascinated with the physical properties of death almost to the point of overshadowing the Christian message of the Resurrection. This morbid fascination became enormously popular and resulted in works of art including painting, statues, plays, dances, and other daily reminders of death.

There are myriad customs concerning the dead throughout the world. Special foods, clothing, and beads are discussed in other sections of this book. Sacramentals that have served as *memento mori* are often found in antique shops and are highly prized by collectors. With the influx of Latin immigrants, new customs and *memento mori* are becoming popular in the United States, although our material society tends to attempt to avoid the subject of death, the final equalizer.

VANITIES

Vanities are images and objects that remind one of the swift passage of time, the illusions of this world, and even the tedium of life.

Vanities became popular in the sixteenth century; their use became rarer, but continued, through the early nineteenth. Today, the practice finds remnants in the folk art and celebrations of a number of countries.

Vanities

Symbols of the end of life were not relegated to paintings and sculpture, but spilled over to furniture and clothing. Girolamo Savonarola, an Italian reformer, recommended that everyone carry with him a small death's head made of bone and look at it often. Death-head rings were popular and were later distributed, along with mourning gloves, to those who attended burial services in New England. Watches and brooches were made in the shape of death's heads or coffins. Furniture was marked with skulls and skeletons.

As late as the mid-nineteenth century, the skeleton was still a favorite subject for earthenware dishes. Engravings recalling the uncertainty and brevity of life were commonly found over fireplaces.

MEMORIAM CARDS

It has long been a custom to distribute small cards (often also known as holy cards) to commemorate funerals. The cards, with somber black borders and black-and-white lithographs of crucifixion, crosses, and other images, were common at the turn of the century. Funerals are still a prime occasion for the distribution of holy cards, although the styles have changed through the years. Some of these cards contain a photograph of the deceased along with prayers; some simply contain the person's name and dates of birth and death and are backed with religious pictures of Our Lord or Our Lady. A crucifixion scene and Our Lady of Sorrows are popular images used on these cards.

Memoriam Cards

WYPOMINKI

Wypominki is a black-bordered paper used in a Polish custom of bringing paper to the parish priest on All Souls' Day.

The names of their beloved dead are written on the sheets. During November at evening devotions and Sunday Masses, the names are read from the pulpit and prayers are offered for the repose of their souls

DIA DE MUERTOS

Spanish for "day of the dead"; the *Dia de Muertos* is the Mexican celebration of All Souls. It is one of the most sacred and revered days in the Mexican cycle of feasts. The celebration includes the cleaning up of family burial plots as well as prayers, processions, special foods, and meals in the cemetery.

Dia de Muertos is an enrichment of the doctrine of the communion of saints. In Mexico, the celebration begins on November

Day of the Dead Altar

1 when the souls of the *angelitos* — children — are remembered. On November 2, deceased adults are honored. Folklore holds that the spirits return to earth to visit, so elaborate preparations are

Day of the Dead Altar

made to welcome them. In some parts of Mexico, offerings of bread and water are hung outside the houses or placed in a corner of the church on October 27 for the spirits which have no one to greet them and no home to visit. Cemeteries are cleaned and decorated and, in southern Mexico, the streets are paved with flowers.

The *ofrenda,* or home altar, commemorates the dead of individual families. The altars are covered with black cloth and decorated with *papel picado,* flowers, candles, food, religious images, and reminders of the family dead. Images of skeletons abound. *Calaveras* — skulls — made of sugar are exchanged as gifts.

The word *calaveras* has the double meaning of "skulls" and "scatterbrain." It is also the word for satirical poems, exchanged much as we exchange Valentine cards.

José Guadalupe Posada (1852-1913) was a Mexican artist particularly known for his illustrations of the *calaveras* filled with grinning, dancing cadavers miming every conceivable activity in human existence. Today, copies of his work are often seen at the *Dia de Muertos* celebrations.

In recent years, a number of American parishes have adapted this custom to celebrate the lives of the deceased members of the parish. But overall, in many places in the United States, celebrations of this deeply religious time have sadly fallen into the province of folk art and become secularized extravaganzas and political tools.

Dia de los Muertos, Calavera Cartoon by Guadalupe Posada

CHAPLETS, ROSARIES, CROWNS, AND BEADS

The practice of using a string of beads as an aid in meditation and prayer is an ancient one. Early monks, wishing to say a certain number of prayers, counted the prayers by moving small pebbles or stones from one container to another. Later, strings of beads were used for the counting. The Old English word *bede*, surviving today as the word *bead*, originally was a word for "prayer."

During the Middle Ages, the Rosary which we know today as the Dominican Rosary evolved and became one of the most popular sacramentals of the Church. The word *rosary* is from the Latin *rosarium*, or "rose garden." It signified a wreath or garland and was seen as a special favor of presentation to Our Lord and Our Lady. The word *chaplet*, from the Old French *chaplet* and the Latin word *corona*, also means a wreath or crown.

Today, the words *rosary, chaplet, corona*, and *beads* are used interchangeably to refer to prayer devotions that use special strings of beads to aid the Catholic in meditation. Chaplets are intended to honor and invoke the members of the Holy Trinity, Our Lady, the angels, or the saints. New chaplets are composed to honor and spread devotion to a particular saint or to reinforce devotion to a particular mystery or aspect of our religion. Some saints have even received these new chaplets from heavenly "authors" through private revelations. However, the origins of many of the older chaplet devotions — and even the origins of some of the more modern ones — are unknown.

What all of the chaplet devotions using designated beads have in common, however, is providing a tangible reminder of the spiritual.

THE ROSARY

According to tradition, Our Lady gave the Rosary to St. Dominic Guzman in 1206 as a form of Gospel-preaching and popular prayer, although history seems to belie that tradition. Nonetheless, for more than seven centuries, the Rosary devotion has been one of the most popular devotional practices in the Church. Its combination of vocal and mental prayer has made it a prime tool for contemplation. Jesus is the author and source of grace; Our Lady's Rosary is the key to open the treasury of grace to us.

Prayer beads have been found in many cultures and several religions. The earliest beads in Christian history were pebbles which monks moved from one pile to another as they repeated the Jesus Prayer. Later, they wove cords of knots, and this is the form that still prevails among Byzantine Christians. Strings of beads were first used as the layperson's psalter. Just as the literate monks and nuns chanted their 150 psalms, the illiterate recited 150 *Paternosters* (Our Fathers). In time, Scripture texts began to provide themes for meditation during the recitation of the *Paters*. Gradually, the use of the angelic salutation began to replace or be mixed with the *Paters*. It was thus in the time of Dominic (thirteenth century); the last half of the Hail Mary was not commonly used until the Reformation.

So, although prayer beads had been popular before Dominic's time, he and his friars quickly adopted the Rosary as an excellent way to teach the mysteries of Christianity to a largely illiterate European population. In 1470, Blessed Alan of Rupe founded the first Rosary confraternity, thereby launching the Dominican Order as the foremost missionaries of the Rosary. Through the efforts of Blessed Alan and the early Dominicans, this prayer form spread rapidly throughout Western Christendom.

The meditations on the fifteen mysteries serve as reminders of incidents in the lives of Jesus Christ and Mary, basic mysteries of our Christian faith. These are divided into the Joyful, Sorrowful, and Glorious mysteries. Thirteen of the mysteries come from incidents in the New Testament. One, the Assumption of Mary into Heaven, comes from Sacred Tradition. The fifteenth, the Crowning of Mary as Queen of Heaven, is thought to derive from images in the Book of Revelation.

In 2002, Pope John Paul II marked the 24th anniversary of his election by signing the apostolic letter *Rosarium Virginis Mariae*, "The Rosary of the Virgin Mary." In it he suggested five new "Mysteries of Light," or Luminous Mysteries.

The mysteries of the Rosary are as follows.

The Joyful Mysteries

1. The Annunciation
2. The Visitation
3. The Nativity
4. The Presentation
5. The Finding in the Temple

The Luminous Mysteries

1. Christ's baptism in the Jordan
2. Christ's self-manifestation at the wedding at Cana
3. Christ's proclamation of the kingdom of God with his call to conversion
4. The Transfiguration
5. Christ's institution of the Eucharist

The Sorrowful Mysteries

1. The Agony in the Garden
2. The Scourging at the Pillar
3. The Crowning of Thorns
4. The Carrying of the Cross

5. The Crucifixion

The Glorious Mysteries

1. The Resurrection
2. The Ascension
3. The Descent of the Holy Spirit
4. The Assumption
5. The Crowning of the Blessed Virgin

Through the years, Our Lady has reaffirmed her approval of this devotion and her pleasure in the title "Queen of the Rosary." Through Blessed Alan, she made fifteen promises to those who devoutly recite her beads. She told him, " . . . immense volumes would have to be written if all the miracles of my holy Rosary were to be recorded."

Our Lady also told Blessed Bartolo Longo to propagate the Rosary, promising those who would do so would be saved. In 1884, Our Lady of Pompeii appeared at Naples to Fortuna Agrelli, who was desperately ill. She told Fortuna the title "Queen of the Holy Rosary" was one that particularly pleased her, and she cured Fortuna of her illness.

At Lourdes, Our Lady told St. Bernadette to pray many Rosaries. When Bernadette saw the beautiful lady, she instinctively took her beads in her hands and knelt down. The lady made a sign of approval with her head and took into her hands a Rosary, which hung on her right arm. As Bernadette prayed, Our Lady passed the beads of her Rosary through her fingers but said nothing except the *Gloria* at the end of each decade. At Fátima, Mary told the children to pray the Rosary often.

POPES AND THE ROSARY

Popes throughout history have loved the Rosary. Not a single Pope in the last 400 years has failed to urge devotion to the Rosary. From Sixtus IV, in 1479, to the present day, the popes have urged the use of this devotion and enriched its recitation with indulgences. Pius XI dedicated the entire month of October to the Rosary. Pope St. Pius X said, "Of all the prayers, the Rosary is the most beautiful and the richest in graces; of all it is the one most pleasing to Mary, the Virgin Most Holy." Pope Leo XIII repeatedly recommended the Rosary as a most powerful means whereby to move God to aid us in meeting the needs of the present age. In 1883, he inserted the invocation, "Queen of the Most Holy Rosary, pray for us!" into the Litany for the Universal Church. Pope John XXIII, who was particularly faithful to the daily recital of the whole Rosary, has said, "We can never sufficiently recommend the saying of the Rosary, not simply with the lips but with attention of the soul to the divine truths, with a heart filled with love and gratitude." Pope John Paul II told us to "love the simple, fruitful prayer of the Rosary."

Many saints and religious orders have praised the Rosary as well:

- St. Charles said he depended on the Rosary almost entirely for the conversion and sanctification of his diocese.
- Founders of most religious orders have either commanded or recommended the daily recitation of the Rosary.
- The Benedictines speedily adapted this devotion in their ancient cloisters.
- The Carmelites were happy to receive the Rosary, as well as their rule, from the Dominicans.
- The Franciscans made their Rosaries out of wood, and preached this devotion as well as poverty.
- Inspired by the example of their founder, the Jesuits invariably propagated the devotion.
- St. Francis Xavier used the touch of his chaplet as a means of healing the sick.
- St. Vincent de Paul instructed the members of his order to depend more on the Rosary than upon their preaching.

Our ancestors had recourse to the Rosary as an ever-ready refuge in misfortune and as a pledge and proof of their Christian faith and devotion. St. Dominic used the Rosary as a weapon in his battle against the Albigensian heresy in France. In the last century, the Christian successes over the Turks at Temesvar and at Corfu coincided with the conclusion of public devotions of the Rosary. During the penal days in Ireland, the Rosary bound Irish Catholics together as a Church Militant. When it was a felony to teach the Catholic Catechism, and death for a priest to say Mass, Irish mothers used their Rosaries to tell their little ones the story of Jesus and Mary, and thus kept the Faith green in the hearts of their children. St. John Vianney, the Curé d'Ars, declared emphatically that in the nineteenth century, it was the Rosary that restored religion in France. Likewise, in the more recent dark days of persecution in Mexico, sturdy Mexican Catholics clung faithfully to their Rosaries. The martyr Miguel Pro's last request before being shot by a firing squad was to kneel and pray with his Rosary in his hand.

The Venerable Marie Pauline Jaricot in the city of Lyons, France, founded a special society, the Society of the Living Rosary, in 1826. She formed bands of fifteen members who each said one decade of the Rosary daily. Thus, collectively, the members of each circle said the entire Rosary daily.

Father Timothy Ricci, O.P., instituted the Perpetual Rosary, or Mary's Guard of Honor, in 1935. The aim of this devotion is to unite the members in such a way that some devoted watchers will ever be found in prayer and praise at Our Lady's shrine, telling their beads for the conversion of sinners, the relief of the dying, and the succor of the dead. In Belgium, the Dominican nuns of the Third Order established a monastery for the express purpose of maintaining the Perpetual Rosary; there, it became not merely the devotion of a society, but the distinctive work of a community. A number of shrines of the order are to be found in the United States. Here, members of the community say the Rosary day and night. Rosary processions are held, and pilgrims come to sing again and again the praises of their Heavenly Queen.

HOW TO PRAY THE ROSARY

When reciting the Rosary, one begins by making the Sign of the Cross and reciting the Apostles' Creed on the crucifix. After an initial Our Father, three Hail Marys are said, followed by the Glory Be to the Father. Then the first mystery is announced, after which one recites one Our Father and ten Hail Marys while meditating on that mystery. The Rosary is continued in this manner until all the mysteries have been contemplated, although often only five of the fifteen mysteries are recited at one time.

Many people add the Fatima angel's prayer at the end of each decade of the rosary. In the apparitions of Our Lady at Fátima in 1917, this prayer was taught to the children: "O, my Jesus, forgive us our sins, save us from the fires of hell, lead all souls to heaven, especially those in greatest need."

The conditions of the First Saturday devotion, which basically came from the Fatima apparition of June 13, 1917, include five decades of the Rosary, a communion of reparation, reparatory prayer and some sacrifice made for the same intention. During this apparition, Our Lady said: : "I promise at the hour of death to help with the graces needed for their salvation, whoever on the first Saturday of five consecutive months shall confess and receive Holy Communion, recite five decades of the Rosary, and keep me company for fifteen minutes while meditating on the fifteen mysteries of the Rosary with the intention of making reparation to me."

The devotion of the Five First Saturdays includes these conditions and adds confession and a fifteen-minute meditation on the mysteries of the Rosary. Confession may be in the eight days preceding or following the Saturday, and the intention, if forgotten, may be made at confession on the first opportunity. The meditation may include one or all of the mysteries.

Indian Corn and Job's Tears Rosaries

Rosaries have been manufactured from all materials, from precious gemstones to glass, wood, and plastic. One Rosary in the author's collection was crafted by Native Americans from corn seed. Another, made for her by a ship's engineer, is fashioned of metal chain links. Yet another is made from seed known as "Job's tears." A descriptive folder accompanying this Rosary reminds the user that Job's sufferings purified his love of God, and points out that frequent use of these Rosaries will make them shine more brightly.

Rosaries are made in all sizes, from tiny beads that fit entirely into one's palm to large family Rosaries with beads over an inch in diameter.

Sometimes, modifications have been made to Rosaries for aesthetic or other reasons. Some wear a Rosary ring, a single decade crafted as a ring which the wearer turns round and round to say successive decades. The Mexicans have a *decena,* a small single-decade Rosary easily carried in a pocket. Another beautiful Rosary from Mexico is called a ladder Rosary. With the beads hung crosswise like rungs, it seems a symbolic ladder to Heaven.

A single-decade Irish Penal Rosary was used during the dark years in Irish history when religious objects were forbidden to the Catholics. This Rosary became not only a reminder of the fifteen mysteries, but a symbol of the Passion as well. The crucifix is lavishly embellished with symbols, front and back, to recall all the events of the Passion.

One of the loveliest and most practical Rosaries available today is called the Special Favor, or Symbolic, Rosary. In place of the Our Father beads are sculptured metal symbols for each of the mysteries. This Rosary is an excellent teaching tool because of its visible reminders of the mysteries.

Standard Rosaries are often found with medals of particular saints or shrines attached to the centerpiece. Sometimes relics of saints or blessed (Beati) are attached, or a single drop of holy water is caught in the centerpiece. These medals simply serve as a reminder of that particular person or place. It is a popular custom in many parts of the world to touch Rosaries to the body or relics of saints. The Rosaries thus become what are known as "touch relics."

SCRIPTURAL ROSARY

The Scriptural Rosary, as composed in the 1960s, is a modern version of the way the Rosary was once prayed throughout Western Christendom in the late Middle Ages. A different thought taken from Scripture is assigned to each Hail Mary bead. These Scriptures have been arranged so the story of each mystery is told in consecutive steps. Popular versions of the Scriptural Rosary are available in Catholic bookstores; Our Sunday Visitor has a number of Scriptural Rosary books.

Rosary devotional booklets

OUR LADY'S ROSARY MAKERS

While a teacher at St. Xavier High School in Louisville, Kentucky, Brother Sylvan Mattingly, C.F.X., was haunted by the urgent requests by Our Lady at Fátima for people to pray the Rosary. This humble Holy Cross brother had a burning desire to do something for the Mother of God. In the 1940s, Brother Sylvan decided to share his talent for making Rosaries and taught a group of children how to make Rosaries for the missions. Brother's idea developed into a club, and the club developed into an international movement. Individuals and units of Rosary makers are in all 50 states and in at least 15 foreign countries. Today, the headquarters for Our Lady's Rosary Makers is at the Rosary Center in Louisville. It is a nonprofit organization. They furnish supplies at below-cost to members who make Rosaries for the missions.

MILITARY ROSARIES

A number of Rosary making groups around the country are making special dark-colored Rosaries for the military. These have become known as "Ranger Rosaries" or "G.I. Rosaries," although their originator, Staff Sergeant Frank "Bo" Ristaino, originally called them "Tactical Field Rosaries." An Army National Guard recruiter, Ristaino came up with the idea of making a simple, lightweight Rosary for servicemen and women which — following military regulations — would be made with no metal parts to reflect light or make rattling noises, so military members could safely carry them wherever they went. The Rosaries are made with plastic beads in dark colors — gray, dark blue, brown, black, and green — and use cords, rather than metal links.

SFC Ristaino, then serving in the Marine Corps, was going through the O.C.S. program at Quantico, Virginia, when the land navigation instructor explained how to keep track of distance with a "pace counter" using beads on parachute cord. The instructor made a humorous remark that the Catholics ought to do well at the exercise because the counter was like their Rosary. That gave Ristaino an idea, and years later, when his children learned to make Rosaries at a Junior Legion of Mary meeting, he turned his

Military or "Ranger" Rosary

Our Sunday Visitor photo

> There are hundreds of chaplets approved by competent authority for use by the faithful. Only a few are discussed in this book.

idea into a reality. Ristaino, his wife Barbara, and their oldest children worked with other home school families to make nearly a thousand Rosaries which were distributed by chaplains in Bosnia. Ristaino's unit chaplain, Chaplain Ray Williams, called him from Bosnia to request as many of the Rosaries as possible to be given to Chaplain Christian Connelly, who was serving with the 1-181 infantry, a unit with many Irish Catholics from Massachusetts. As requests from other Chaplains increased, Ristaino turned to Steve Beard, the youth coordinator of St. Mary's parish in Annapolis, Maryland, who enlisted the confirmation classes in the project. Steve then went to St. Mary's High School and Elementary School. The students were allowed to make the Rosaries during their special activity classes. St. Mary's Rosary guild, the Scouts, young adult groups, and many committee members in the parish continue the work. As the people make the Rosaries, they also pray for the military who will use them, and for peace.

THE ROSARY PRIEST

The Servant of God Father Patrick Peyton, C.S.C., inspired people all over the world by his holiness of life and his strong and tender devotion to Our Blessed Mother. He became known as "The Rosary Priest" through the slogans he popularized: *The family that prays together stays together*, and *A world at prayer is a world at peace.* His work is carried on today under the sponsorship of the Congregation of the Holy Cross through the Holy Cross Family Ministries, which supports and promotes the spiritual well-being of the family. Faithful to Mary, the Mother of God, the Family Rosary and Family Rosary International encourage family prayer, especially the Rosary.

JESUS BEADS

"Lord Jesus Christ, Son of God, have mercy upon me, a sinner."

"Lord Jesus Christ, have mercy on me."

"Lord Jesus, have mercy."

"Jesus, Lamb of God, Who takes away the sins of the world, have mercy upon us."

Jesus Beads

The Jesus prayer takes many forms. Rooted in the Bible and accepted for centuries in the monastic life of Eastern Christianity, the Jesus prayer is a perfect prayer for modern Christians who want to follow St. Paul's advice to "pray constantly" (1 Thess. 5:17). Short and simple to repeat, this prayer is heavy with meaning.

The Jesus prayer is directed to the Son. No one has ever seen God, but God has revealed himself in Jesus Christ. In seeking for the heart of the Father, we find Him in and through the Son.

In biblical times, a person's name was not simply a way of identifying him. It was also a key to understanding the person — it had meaning. The meaning of the name Jesus is "one who saves." Christ is a Greek word, which means "the anointed one." During His lifetime on earth, Jesus was often referred to as "Rabbi" or "Teacher." After the Resurrection, he was most often called "Lord." Thus, in the Jesus prayer, we call on our Savior and King, acknowledging Him as Lord. In a spirit of humility, we recognize we are sinners and call on our King for mercy.

Prayer can be defined as the heart's conversation with God. With unceasing prayer, we can attain unity with Christ that displaces our own selves and allows for His indwelling in our hearts.

The Jesus prayer was prayed, in fact, while He still walked the earth. People began to call to Him for mercy when they acknowledged him as the Son of God. The blind beggar outside the city walls of Jericho called out, "Jesus, Son of David, have mercy on me!" (Mk. 10:47) The Canaanite woman cried out, "Have mercy on me, O Lord, Son of David" (Mt. 15:22). The ten lepers said, "Jesus, Master, have mercy on us" (Lk. 17:13).

From about the sixth century, the Jesus prayer was used in the monastery of St. Catherine on Mount Sinai. In the fourteenth century, Gregory of Sinai took the prayer to Mount Athos in Macedonia, where he instructed the people in this prayer, and soon the Holy Mount Athos became a center for the praying of the Jesus Prayer. Gradually a considerable literature on the use of this prayer developed. In the eighteenth century, many of these writings were collected and published in Venice under the title *Philokalia* — The Love of Good Things.

Although this is a common prayer in the Eastern Church, and the one prayed on the *chotki* (*chatky*), it was not until the middle of the twentieth century that this prayer made its way into the Western Church. Gregory of Sinai wrote little, but his teachings and practice of mental prayer, silence, and contemplation had great impact in the Orthodox and Eastern churches. He emphasized the importance of physical aids, such as rhythmical breathing, to perfect concentration in mental prayer. The Jesus beads are another aid to concentration and to unceasing prayer.

The Jesus beads consist of a string of 100 beads connected at the ends by a crucifix. No prayer is said on the crucifix, although making the Sign of the Cross is a good way to begin the beads. The person then, slowly and thoughtfully, repeats the Jesus prayer on each bead.

LITTLE CROWN OF THE INFANT JESUS OF PRAGUE

Devotion to the Child Jesus under the title "Infant Jesus of Prague" has spread worldwide through its promotion by the Carmelite Order (see entry under "Images").

Little Crown of the Infant Jesus

Venerable Sister Margaret of the Blessed Sacrament, a Sister of the Beaune Carmel (d. 1648), received a private revelation of Our Lord in which she was given a chaplet in honor of the Infant Jesus. The chaplet, known as the Little Crown, consists of fifteen beads. Three beads are in honor of the Holy Family: Jesus, Mary, and Joseph. On these the Lord's Prayer is recited. The other twelve beads are in honor of the Holy Childhood of Christ, and on them are recited twelve Hail Marys. Before each of the Lord's Prayers one says, "And the Word was made flesh." Before the first of the Hail Marys, one prays, "And the Word was made Flesh and dwelt among us." On the medal, one prays, "Divine Infant Jesus, I adore Thy Cross, and I accept all the crosses Thou wilt be pleased to send me. Adorable Trinity, I offer Thee for the glory of the Holy Name of God all the adorations of the Sacred Heart of the Holy Infant Jesus." In the revelations to Venerable Margaret, the Divine Infant promised special graces — above all, purity of heart and innocence — to all who carried the chaplet on their person and recited it in honor of the mysteries of His holy infancy.

ROSARY OF OUR LADY OF SORROWS (THE SERVITE ROSARY)

THE ROSARY OF THE SEVEN SORROWS

The sorrows of Mary, as described in the Gospel, are not just a private experience — they are part of the history of salvation. In devout recitation of the Rosary of Our Lady of Sorrows, one realizes the sufferings of the Blessed Virgin and sees their continuance in the Church today. Mary becomes the symbol of the compassion of the Church, called by God to stand with those who suffer. As the Constitutions of the Order of Friar Servants of Mary states, contemplation of the sorrows of Mary leads to an understanding share in human suffering as one stands "at the foot of those countless crosses where the Son of Man is still being crucified in His brothers and sisters in order to bring comfort and redemptive cooperation."

Devotion to the Sorrowful Mother began in the West about the twelfth century, promoted by such great saints as Anselm of Canterbury, Bernard of Clairvaux, and Bonaventure. The cultural climate of the time in which the Rosary of Our Lady of Sorrows developed was devoted to the Passion. Devotion to the Passion of Christ and the Sorrows of His Mother reached its pinnacle around the seventeenth century, although the Rosary of the Sorrowful Mother evolved gradually from the sixteenth through nineteenth centuries.

During the Middle Ages, the ordinary Catholic no longer spoke the language of the official prayer of the Church. Thus, many other prayer forms and devotions developed. Of these, the greatest was the Dominican Rosary. The Servite Rosary is an adaptation of this prayer form.

The Dominican Rosary, approved by papal bull of Sixtus IV in 1479, swiftly became popular among the laity. The origin of the Servite Rosary probably falls in the decade between 1607 and 1617 as, after the latter date, historians for the order have found many references to it. Presumably,

Servite Rosary of the Seven Sorrows

this devotion applied the structure of the Dominican Rosary — which also was used in churches of the order — to the custom of the daily meditation on the seven sorrows of the Blessed Virgin. From the year 1698 on, members of the order wore the Rosary on their belts; for all the Servants of Mary, priests, brothers, cloistered nuns, and sisters of congregations aggregated to the order, the beads became not only a part of the habit but also a sign of their esteem for this devotion.

The Servite Rosary is a meditation on the mystery-events of God's love for us, as reflected in the lives of Jesus and Mary. This Rosary, like the Dominican Rosary, is a biblical prayer. The events of sorrow and salvation contemplated in it are taken from the Gospels themselves, as well as the Church's interpretation of scriptural texts.

Through the years, the Rosary of Our Lady of Sorrows grew in esteem — not only of the Servites, but also of the laity associated with them — to such an extent that, in 1885, the Prior General of the Servants of Mary made a bold request of Pope Leo XIII: He asked for the favor of substituting the Servite Rosary for the Dominican Rosary, in churches proper to the order, whenever the Rosary was required in sacred functions. Additionally, he asked that, in this case, they might still enjoy all the indulgences and blessings granted to the use of the Dominican Rosary at such times. This request was granted.

Today, individuals often recite the Rosary of Our Lady of Sorrows as a private devotion. It is also recited by groups of people gathered in church, especially those churches affiliated in some way with the Servite order.

The chaplet consists of seven groups of seven beads, each septet separated by a medal of one of the sorrows. Each mystery is introduced by a meditation to guide reflection as the Our Father and seven Hail Marys are prayed. The Rosary is concluded with three Hail Marys as an added petition for true sorrow and a desire to model our lives on the example of the life and faith of Our

The seven sorrows as traditionally listed are:

1. Mary accepts in faith the prophecy of Simeon (Lk 2:34-35).
2. Mary flees into Egypt with Jesus and Joseph (Mt 2:73-74).
3. Mary seeks Jesus lost in Jerusalem (Lk 2:43-45).
4. Mary meets Jesus on the way to Calvary (Lk 23:26-27).
5. Mary stands near the cross of her Son (Jn 19:25-27).
6. Mary receives the body of Jesus taken down from the cross (Mt 27:57-59).
7. Mary places the body of Jesus in the tomb, awaiting the Resurrection (Jn 19:40-42).

A new alternative form has been written which lists the mysteries under the Biblical motif of rejection. This form is not intended to replace the traditional one, but to give an optional manner of saying the Rosary. The sorrows as listed for this new form are:

1. Jesus, the Son of God, is born in a cave: there was no room for his Mother at the inn (Lk. 2:1-7).
2. Jesus, Savior of humankind, is a sign of contradiction (Lk. 2:22-35).
3. Jesus, the newborn Messiah, is persecuted by Herod (Mt. 2:13-18).
4. Jesus, Brother of all, is rejected by His neighbors (Lk. 4:28-29).
5. Jesus, the Holy One of God, is arrested by the high priests and abandoned by His disciples (Mt. 26:47-56).
6. Jesus, the Just One, dies on the cross (Jn. 19:25-27).
7. Jesus, Master and Lord, is persecuted in His disciples (Acts 12:1-5).

Lady. At the end of the chaplet is a medal of Our Lady with her heart pierced with seven swords. A crucifixion scene is generally found on the reverse of this medal. When a group recites the Rosary in public, the structure includes other elements, often including the *Stabat Mater* or the Litany of Our Lady of Sorrows.

CORONA OF OUR MOTHER OF CONSOLATION
(AUGUSTINIAN ROSARY)

Augustinian Rosary of Consolation

Little is known of the origin of the corona of Our Lady of Consolation. Originally it was probably linked with the third order of St. Augustine. It does, however, have definite links with devotion to Mary under the title Our Mother of Consolation.

The tradition of asking the Mother of God for the gift of consolation dates back to the earliest centuries. The first written evidence of prayer to the *Theotokos*, Mother of God, is found on a scrap of Egyptian papyrus dating from between A.D. 300 and 450. In Greek is written: "Beneath the shelter of your tender compassion we fly for refuge, Mother of God. Do not overlook my supplications in adversity but deliver us out of danger."

The devotion to Mary under the title Mother of Consolation appears to come from two different sources. The first, treasured for centuries by the Order of St. Augustine, tells of St. Monica in the fourth century. Distraught with grief and anxiety for her wayward son, Augustine, Monica confided her trouble to the Mother of God, who appeared to her dressed in mourning clothes and wearing a shining cincture. Our Lady gave the cincture to St. Monica as a sign of her support and compassion, directing Monica to encourage others to wear it. Monica gave the cincture to Augustine, who later gave it to his community, thus instituting the order's wearing of the cincture as a token of fidelity to Our Mother of Consolation.

A second tradition, seemingly separate, dates from the fourteenth century and tells of a Roman nobleman in the Capitoline prison awaiting death. Reflecting on his approaching last moments, he dictated in his will that his son was to have a Madonna and Child painted and placed near the gallows for the consolation of all who would die in that place in the future. The son followed his father's wishes; when, in 1470, a youth who had been unjustly convicted was miraculously saved from the hangman's noose as his mother prayed before the picture, the place became a popular shrine.

More miracles followed and a church was built. The painting was given the title Mother of Consolation. Because of the large number of pilgrims, the devotion spread rapidly over Europe.

Our Mother of Consolation

Later, confraternities were established, but they ended in the nineteenth century because of political stress in Italy. The painting and the church remain under the care of the Capuchin Fathers.

The corona expresses our faith as we find it written in the Apostles' Creed. The chaplet consists of thirteen pairs of beads. Two additional beads and a medal of Our Lady of Consolation are attached to the body of the corona. The corona begins by calling to mind the scene in the Cenacle when the Apostles devoted themselves to constant prayer. There were some women in their company, and Mary the mother of Jesus, and his brothers (Acts 1:14). The leader begins by making the Sign of the Cross, when reciting in public; after the announcement of each of the twelve articles of the Apostles' Creed, a brief reading is taken from the writings of St. Augustine or other writings of the Augustinian traditions on the articles of faith. After the reading there follows a silence, then the Lord's Prayer and the Hail

Mary are prayed. When praying this corona in private, the readings may be omitted. The final Our Father and Hail Mary are said for the intentions of the Pope. The chaplet is ended by a recitation of the Hail, Holy Queen.

PASSIONIST CHAPLET OF THE FIVE WOUNDS

"He was wounded for our transgressions; he was bruised for our iniquities; upon him was the chastisement that made us whole, and with his stripes we are healed" (Is. 53:5).

Passionist Chaplet of the Five Wounds

Traditionally, it was to Blessed Angela of Foligno that Jesus revealed nothing would please Him more than devotion to His holy wounds. Speaking to St. Gemma Galgani, Our Lord showed her His wounds and said, "These are works of love, of infinite love! They show to what extent I have loved you."

The Most Reverend Father Paul Aloysius, C.P., the sixth superior general of the congregation, originated the Passionist chaplet of the Five Wounds in order to stimulate devotion to the Passion of Christ, through remembrance of the five holy wounds of Jesus, in a simple way. This devotion also honors the mystery of the risen Christ, who kept the marks of the five wounds in His glorified body. Father Paul Aloysius presented the idea for the chaplet to Pope Leo XII, who approved it in 1823. Additionally, he transferred to the Passionist format the indulgences previously attached to an older chaplet which was introduced in Rome by the Jesuits at the beginning of the seventeenth century.

The chaplet consists of five divisions of five beads each, on which are said the Glory Be to the Father. Customarily, the sections are divided by medallions, which represent the five wounds of Jesus in order — the wound in the left foot, the wound in the right foot, the wound in the left hand, the wound in the right hand and, finally, the wound in the sacred side. At the end of each section of beads, a Hail Mary in honor of the sorrows of Mary is said. At the end of the chaplet, three additional Hail Marys are said in honor of Our Lady's tears. The medallion at the end of the final three beads shows an image of Our Mother of Sorrows.

THE GARLAND OF THE HOLY CHILD MARY

Sister Mary Lawrence Scanlan, a member of the Franciscan Sisters of Allegany, has always had a strong devotion to the childhood of Mary. In the late 1950s, after being appointed vocation director of her Order, she was inspired to write a little chaplet in the virgin's honor. She called this the Garland of the Holy Child Mary.

Holy Virgin Mary, Lily of the Blessed Trinity, honoring your Immaculate Conception, we pray, through the merits of your childhood, that all youth may give glory to God by the purity and holiness of their lives.

[Three Hail Marys and a Glory Be]

Garland of the Holy Child Mary

Holy Virgin Mary, Morning Star, honoring your birth, we pray, through the merits of your childhood, that parents may foster religious vocations in their children, by their own noble and saintly lives.

[Three Hail Marys and a Glory Be]

Holy Virgin Mary, Cause of our Joy, honoring your sweet name, we pray, through the merits of your childhood for the sanctification of priests and religious.

[Three Hail Marys and a Glory Be]

Holy Virgin Mary, Seat of Wisdom, honoring your presentation in the Temple, we pray, through the merits of your childhood, for vocations to the priesthood and the religious life.

[Three Hail Marys and a Glory Be]

Let us pray:

Holy Virgin Mary, Model of Perfection, through the merits of your childhood, obtain for God's Church on earth fervent priests and religious and a truly apostolic laity that by their love and devoted service all may be united with Him forever in heaven. Amen.

Soon, her Community began to disseminate leaflets of the Garland, for the intention of obtaining vocations to the priesthood and the religious life. The chaplet was given the imprimatur by Justin J. McCarthy, Bishop of Camden, on March 24, 1958. Although a set of beads was made to use while praying the chaplet, they are not essential to the devotion.

CHAPLET OF MERCY OF THE HOLY WOUNDS OF JESUS

Sister Mary Martha Chambon, a humble lay sister of the Visitation Convent of Chambéry, France, was given many graces by Our Lord. In private revelations and in visions, Our Lord presented His wounds as a source of grace for sinners, telling her He had suffered as much for a single soul as for all souls together. He told her that it was His constant desire for mankind to profit by the Redemption by corresponding to His graces. He instructed

---

The Chaplet of Mercy in honor of the Holy Wounds may be said using the beads of a standard Rosary. On the cross and the first three beads is said the beautiful prayer inspired to a Roman priest:

"O Jesus, divine Redeemer, be merciful to us and to the whole world. Amen.

"Strong God, Holy God, immortal God, have mercy on us and on the whole world. Amen.

"Grace and mercy, oh my Jesus, during present dangers; cover us with Thy precious Blood. Amen.

"Eternal Father, grant us mercy through the Blood of Jesus Christ, Thy only Son; grant us mercy, we beseech Thee. Amen. Amen. Amen."

On the small beads, say: "My Jesus, pardon and mercy, by the merits of Thy Holy Wounds." On the large beads, say: "Eternal Father, I offer Thee the Wounds of our Lord Jesus Christ to heal those of our souls."

---

her to offer His wounds to God for the salvation of souls, especially those in Purgatory. Additionally, he asked for a Chaplet of Mercy in honor of His wounds, teaching her the aspirations that should be said. This chaplet was approved in favor of the Institute of the Visitation in 1912; by indult of the Sacred Penitentiary, it was extended to all the faithful in 1924.

THE CHAPLET OF DIVINE MERCY

The message of divine mercy is not new. The patriarchs and prophets proclaimed the mercy of God in the Old Testament. During His time on earth, Jesus Christ emphasized God's mercy and the covenant of love. From the time of Christ, the Church and holy men and women have reaffirmed the love and mercy of God.

In our own century, God revealed His mercy to a humble Polish sister, St. Faustina Kowalska, whom he called His secretary and Apostle of Mercy. In numerous interior communications, she received the mystery of God's mercy and the obligation on our part to respond to it with a fullness of trust in Him. Our Lord gave, through Sister Faustina, special means of drawing on His mercy: an image of the Divine Mercy, a chaplet, a novena, a prayer at the hour commemorating His death, and the request for a Feast of Mercy.

From 1959 to 1976, due largely to a mistranslation of some of Sister Faustina's writings, her form of this devotion was banned; however, it has all since been approved, and the ban removed, in the process of her beatification and canonization.

Helen Kowalska was born in 1905 in the village of Glogowiec, Poland. At the age of twenty, she entered the Congregation of the Sisters of Our Lady of Mercy, popularly called the Magdalene Sisters, whose major work is the education and training of girls who are morally and financially impoverished. She was accepted in the "second choir", and made perpetual vows in 1933, taking the name Sister Mary Faustina. She died October 5, 1938, of multiple tuberculosis, at the age of thirty-three.

Our Lord gave Sister Faustina a prayer for mercy. This chaplet is said on an ordinary set of Rosary beads of five decades. It begins with the Our Father, the Hail Mary, and the Creed. Then, on the large beads, pray "Eternal Father I offer you the Body and Blood, Soul and Divinity of Your Dearly Beloved Son, Our Lord Jesus Christ, in atonement for our sins and those of the whole world." On the small beads, pray: "For the sake of His sorrowful Passion, have mercy on us and on the whole world." At the end, pray three times: "Holy God, Holy Mighty One, Holy Immortal One, have mercy on us and on the whole world."

As a religious, St. Faustina was conscientious in following her rule and in the performance of her duties. Few, even among those she lived with, realized the interior graces she received and the work to which God called her. In 1934, in obedience to her spiritual director, St. Faustina began keeping a personal diary, which she titled *Divine Mercy in My Soul*. This diary contains a detailed account of her profound revelations and extraordinary spiritual experiences. The most fundamental element of the devotion to the divine mercy is complete confidence, or trust, in Jesus. In 1931, St. Faustina received the first apparition of Jesus as The Merciful One.

CHAPLET OF THE PRECIOUS BLOOD

In the early 1800s, St. Gaspar del Bufalo, with a deep personal appreciation of what Jesus did for us in His Passion and death, and seeing the need for positive actions in compassion to our neighbors in need, began to preach and widely spread the devotion to the Precious Blood. He did not consider worship of the Precious Blood simply another devotion, but as the summary of all religion. He said, "All the mysteries are summed up in the infinite price of

Chaplet of the Precious Blood

Redemption, as the lines of a circle to the center which they have in common!" This apostle of the Precious Blood founded an order of missionary preachers, dedicated to this ideal, known as the Society of the Precious Blood.

Under St. Gaspar's influence, Blessed Maria de Mattias founded an apostolic order of sisters under the title of Adorers of the Blood of Christ. The spirit of the Congregation is based on Maria's words, "How beautiful is the Cross when it is carried in the heart with love." Since that time, thirteen more Institutes have

The Chaplet of the Precious Blood is divided into seven groups containing thirty-three "Our Fathers." These prayers are in honor of the thirty-three years of Christ's life on earth, when His blood flowed in human veins before it was poured out in reparation for our sins. After each group, the "Glory be to the Father" is said in thanksgiving for the gift of the Precious Blood. While reciting each group, the petitioner is to meditate on the seven bloodsheddings of Jesus. The seven mysteries are when Jesus shed His Blood in (1) the circumcision, (2) the agony in the garden, (3) the scourging, (4) the crowning with thorns, (5) the carrying of the cross, (6) the crucifixion, and (7) when His side was pierced.

Canon Francesco Albertini (1770-1819) is the author of the chaplet of the Precious Blood. It was composed in 1808 as a meditation for the newly formed Confraternity of the Previous Blood, and approved in 1809 by Pope Pius VII. In 1843, Pope Gregory XVI approved and indulgenced a short form of the chaplet, which was shortened again by the Precious Blood Fathers who recited only a single Our Father for each mystery.

been established in the Church under the title of the Most Precious Blood of Jesus.

In 1960, Pope John XXIII approved the Litany of the Precious Blood, and through special indulgences encouraged its public and private recitation.Before announcing the opening of the Second Vatican Council, he went to pray at the tomb of St. Gaspar, calling upon him to intercede for the success of the council, and calling devotion to the Precious Blood of Jesus the "Devotion of Our Times."

Mother Catherine Aurelie, a Canadian mystic, founded the Institute of the Sisters Adorers of the Most Precious Blood, a cloistered, contemplative order, dedicated to love, immolation, and reparation. Mother Catherine especially recommended to her sisters the recitation of the chaplet of the Precious Blood.

The exact history of when the beads for the chaplet began to be used with the prayers is not clear; the beads were in existence, however, by 1893.

CHAPLET OF ST. ANTHONY

The marvelous power of miracles conferred on St. Anthony by God has won for the saint the title of Wonder-Worker, or *thaumaturge*. In the ancient responsory of the Church, it is said, "If then you ask for miracles, go to St. Anthony."

Since his death in 1231 at the age of thirty-six, this humble Franciscan of Padua has become one of the most popular saints of the Church throughout the world. A gifted preacher, during life he was called the "Hammer of Heretics." He attracted large crowds wherever he went, and numerous miraculous events occurred during his lifetime. He was

Chaplet of St. Anthony

The devotion known as the chaplet or beads of St. Anthony is practiced in honor of the thirteen miracles listed in the Miraculous Responsory. The chaplet is composed of thirteen groups of three beads each. On the first bead of each decade is said the Our Father, on the second the Hail Mary, and on the third, the Glory Be to the Father. At the end, the Miraculous Responsory is recited.

In one version, the person praying meditates on thirteen virtues of the saint. In another, he meditates on thirteen petitions that go along with the thirteen miracles in the Responsory.

canonized less than a year after his death by Pope Gregory IX and is named as one of the Doctors of the Church.

In 1263, the tomb of the saint was opened in order to transfer the remains to a new sanctuary built in his honor. Although the body had fallen to dust, his tongue remained incorrupt. At this occasion, St. Bonaventure, then Minister General of the Franciscan Order, took the tongue in his hands and said, "O blessed tongue that never ceased to praise God and always taught others to bless Him, now we plainly see how precious thou art in His sight." These words of St. Bonaventure now constitute the antiphon preceding the miraculous responsory, also authored by Bonaventure.

THE MIRACULOUS RESPONSORY
(BY ST. BONAVENTURE)

If miracles thou vain would see;
Lo, error, death, calamity.
The leprous stain, the demon flies,
From beds of pain the sick arise.
The hungry seas forgo their prey,
The prisoner's cruel chains give way;

While palsied limbs and chattels lost
Both young and old recovered boast.
And perils perish, plenty's hoard,
Is heaped on hunger's famished board;
Let those relate who know it well,
Let Padua of her patron tell.
The hungry seas forgo their prey,
The prisoner's cruel chains give way;
While palsied limbs and chattels lost
Both young and old recovered boast.

Glory be the Father, and to the Son, and to the Holy Spirit.
The hungry seas forgo their prey,
The prisoner's cruel chains give way;
While palsied limbs and chattels lost
Both young and old recovered boast.

V/. Pray for us, blessed Anthony,
R/. That we may be made worthy of the promises of Christ.

Let us pray.
O God, let the notive commemoration of Blessed Anthony,
Thy confessor, be a source of joy in Thy Church, that she
may always be fortified with spiritual assistance, and may
deserve to possess eternal joy. Through Christ our Lord.
Amen.

THE ROSARY FOR THE DEAD

"My friends, let us pray much and let us obtain many prayers
from others for the poor dead. The good God will return to us a
hundredfold the good we do them. Ah! If every one knew how
useful to those who practice it is this devotion to the holy souls
in Purgatory, they would not be so often forgotten; the good God
regards all we do for them as if it were done for Himself" (St.
John Vianney, Curé d'Ars).

In the mid-nineteenth century, Abbé Serre of the Chapel of the Hôtel Dieu at Nismes, France, composed the Rosary for the Dead for the benefit of the poor suffering souls in Purgatory. The Archconfraternity of Notre Dame du Suffrage promoted the chaplet.

The chaplet consists of four decades of ten beads each. In its original form, the chaplet had a medal of the Archconfraternity, representing the souls in Purgatory. The chaplet may also have five introductory beads, as found on the Dominican Rosary.

Rosary for the Dead

The *De Profundis* (Psalm 130) is said upon the cross, at the beginning and the ending of the chaplet. Anyone who is not familiar with that prayer may substitute an Our Father and a Hail Mary. The *Requiem Eternam* ("Eternal rest grant unto them, etc.") and the Acts of Faith, Hope, and Charity are said on the large beads, and on the small beads is said, "Sweet Heart of Mary, be my salvation."

Since the first edition of this book, this sacramental has generated more letters of inquiry than any other. People seem to find it a beautiful devotion by which to remember, especially, their beloved dead as well as the other souls in Purgatory. Today, many variations of the chaplet are available for purchase in religious goods stores, made of a variety of materials.

FRANCISCAN CROWN ROSARY (SERAPHIC ROSARY)

ROSARY OF THE SEVEN JOYS OF THE BLESSED VIRGIN MARY

The Franciscan Crown, or the Rosary of the Seven Joys of the Blessed Virgin Mary, is an ancient sacramental treasured by the Franciscan order. Father Luke Wadding, a well-known Franciscan historian, dates the inception of this chaplet to 1422, the entrance date into the novitiate of the order of an unnamed pious young man. Before his entrance, this young devotee of Mary had been accustomed to decorating a statue of the Virgin with crowns of fresh flowers. This practice was forbidden to him in the novitiate, and fearing a lack of devotion to his Queen, he determined to leave the order.

Franciscan Crown Rosary

In a vision, however, Our Lady appeared to him and told him, "Do not be sad and cast down, my son, because you are no longer permitted to place wreaths of flowers on my statue. I will teach you to change this pious practice into one that will be far more pleasing to me and far more meritorious to your soul. In place of the flowers that soon wither and cannot always be found, you can weave for me a crown from the flowers of your prayers that will always remain fresh."

With that, Our Lady requested the young friar say one Our Father and ten Hail Marys in honor of seven joyous occasions in her life: (1) the Annunciation, (2) the Visitation, (3) the birth of Christ, (4) the adoration of the Magi, (5) the finding of Jesus in the Temple, (6) the resurrection of Our Lord, and (7) the Assumption of the Blessed Virgin into Heaven.

As the vision faded, the overjoyed novice began to recite the prayers as she had instructed him to do. While he was devoutly praying, the novice master passed by and saw an angel weaving a wreath of roses. After every tenth rose, he inserted a golden lily. When the wreath was finished, the angel placed it on the head of the praying novice.

The novice master demanded, under holy obedience, that the novice explain to him the meaning of the vision. The novice complied, and the novice master was so impressed with what he had heard that he immediately told his brother friars. The practice of reciting the Crown of the Seven Joys soon spread to the entire Order.

In later years, two Hail Marys were added to make the total of the Hail Marys equal to 72, the number of years some people believe Our Lady lived on earth (although opinions differ on this number — see p. 278). A final Hail Mary and Our Father were added for the intention of the Pope. In the twentieth century, it has become customary to add a profession of faith such as the Apostles' Creed to the recitation of this crown. Additionally, since 1968 it has become customary to combine the former third and fourth mysteries and to add two other combined mysteries as the meditation for the fourth decade — the presentation of Jesus in the Temple and the purification of the Blessed Virgin.

KATERI INDIAN ROSARY

Kateri Indian Rosary

Blessed Kateri Tekakwitha, the "Lily of the Mohawks," was born in 1656 at Ossernenon, near Auriesville, New York, a land watered by the blood of the martyred St. Isaac Jogues and his Jesuit companions. Her mother was a Christian Algonquin, her father the Iroquois chief of the Turtle tribe. When Tekakwitha was only four, her parents and younger brother died in a smallpox epidemic. The disease left Kateri with weak eyesight and marked with scars. Her pagan uncle then became Turtle chief and adopted Tekakwitha into his lodge.

Tekakwitha grew up innocent and industrious. Long before she knew Him through the teaching of the blackrobes, she learned to love *Ra-wen-ni-io*, God the Creator.

At age eighteen, she begged Father de Lamberville, a French missionary, for baptism. Convinced of her sincerity, he allowed Tekakwitha to "take the Prayer" in 1676. It was then she was given the Christian name Kateri (Catherine).

From the time she became a Christian, Kateri was treated with contempt by her relatives and tribesmen. She bore all insults smilingly, with great patience. In 1677, through the intervention of her brother-in-law, Kateri fled to the Christian mission of Caughnawaga in Canada. Here she made her First Communion (1677) and took a long-cherished vow of perpetual virginity (1679), becoming the first of her people to make such a vow. She had hoped to form an Iroquois sisterhood in imitation of the French nuns, but fell ill and died in 1680, with the name of Jesus on her lips. Her cause for canonization was opened in 1939, and Pope John Paul II beatified her in 1980.

A chaplet has been composed by a member of the Tekakwitha League, in honor of Blessed Kateri.

The chaplet may be used as a private devotion to ask God to make Kateri a saint and to ask Kateri for her intercession for one's personal needs. The chaplet, rich in symbolism, calls to mind Blessed Kateri's love for God's beautiful earth and all its creatures. The chaplet is made in two patterns; one begins with a cross, one with a medal of Blessed Kateri and three beads.

The cross is made of staurolite, a crystal mineral naturally formed in the shape of a cross. According to one Native American legend, on the day Christ died, the woodland animals wept; their tiny tears, falling upon the earth, crystallized into these small crosses.

Chaplet of Blessed Kateri Tekakwitha

The chaplet begins with making the Sign of the Cross and asking God to make Kateri a saint. The 24 beads of the main Rosary represent the 24 years Kateri lived on earth. The chaplet has three colors — crystal clear, red, and brownish gold.

Many Native Americans believe the crystal-clear lakes and rivers are the tears of the Great Spirit. The Glory Be is recited on each of the crystal beads. We pray that the Holy Trinity, through the prayers of Kateri, whose name means "putting all things in order" and "moving all things before her," will restore the beauty of our waters, skies, forests, and air — the ecology of our entire world.

An Our Father is said on each of the brown or gold beads. Earth colors were popular with the Native Americans, and golden brown is the predominant color of the earth. God, Our Father, gave us the world in perfect order. Ask Blessed Kateri's intercession to set the earth, our minds, our bodies, and all our problems in order.

A Hail Mary is said on the red beads. Red, the traditional color of love, is also the color of the blood that flows in all mankind, transcending race and color. Red symbolizes the kind

Chaplet of St. Thérèse

of love we must have for all mankind, accepting each person as our brother or sister, and the great love Kateri had for Our Blessed Mother.

CHAPLET OF ST. THÉRÈSE

One of the greatest apostles of St. Thérèse Lisieux in the New World was Father Albert Dolan. Gifted as both a preacher and a writer, he introduced St. Thérèse and her "little way of spiritual childhood" to millions. He founded the Society of the Little Flower in 1923.

The chaplet of St. Thérèse stems from, and is promoted by, the Society. A private devotion that both honors the saint and invokes her intercession, it contains 24 beads in honor of the 24 years of her life. One additional bead and a medal of the saint complete the chaplet. On the single bead, an invocation to St. Thérèse as Patroness of the Missions is said: "St. Thérèse of the Child Jesus, Patroness of Missions, pray for us." A Glory Be is recited on each of the 24 beads in thanksgiving to the Holy Trinity for having given us the young saint and her "little way." It is customary to recite the chaplet for a period of either nine or twenty-fourdays.

THE LITTLE CROWN OF THE BLESSED VIRGIN

In a vision, St. John, the beloved disciple, saw a wonderful sign in the heavens. Scripture commentators interpret this as symbolic of Mary, with her virtues and privileges.

From this grew the devotion known as the Little Crown of Twelve Stars. A young Jesuit, St. John Berchmanns, and many other devotees of the Blessed Virgin made this devotion their daily favorite. St. Louis Mary de Montfort embellished the Little Crown by adding to each Hail Mary an invocation in praise of Mary's excellence, power, and goodness, ending with "Rejoice, O Virgin Mary! Rejoice a thousand times." St. Louis gave the Little Crown as a morn-

Little Crown of the Blessed Virgin

ing prayer to both of the religious families he started, the Montlort Fathers and the Daughters of Wisdom. It is one of the favorite devotions of the Confraternity of Mary, Queen of All Hearts.

This chaplet may be said with or without the use of the sacramental beads. The beads are arranged in three sets of four with a single bead before each group. The chaplet ends with a medal of Our Lady, Queen of All Hearts.

After an introductory prayer and an Our Father, four Hail Marys are recited in honor of Our Lady's crown of excellence. The invocations of this crown honor the divine maternity of the Blessed Virgin, her virginity, her purity, and her innumerable virtues. After the second Our Father is prayed, four Hail Marys are said in honor of the crown of power, honoring the royalty of the Blessed Virgin, her magnificence, her universal mediation,

Little Rosary of St. Anne

and the strength of her rule as Queen of Heaven. After the third and final Our Father, four Hail Marys are prayed with invocations that honor her crown of goodness: her mercy toward sinners, the poor, the just, and the dying. The chaplet ends with a Glory Be to the Father and a final prayer.

THE LITTLE ROSARY OF ST. ANNE

The Chaplet (or Little Rosary) of St. Anne originated in the last quarter of the nineteenth century. It is a pious invention of one of her devout clients. The chaplet consists of three Our Fathers and fifteen Hail Marys. The chaplet is begun by making the Sign of the Cross and devoutly kissing the medal of St. Anne, praying "Jesus, Mary, Anne." The first section is recited to thank Jesus for His favors, to ask His pardon for sins, and to implore His future favor. The second part is recited in praise of Mary with a request that she present the current petition to St. Anne. The final set of prayers presents the petition to the good St. Anne. After each Hail Mary, the petitioner prays: "Jesus, Mary,

Anne, grant me the favor I ask." At the end of each section, a Glory Be is recited as an act of praise to the Blessed Trinity.

Chaplet of the Sacred Heart

CHAPLET OF THE SACRED HEART

The Sacred Heart Society began in 1980 when a group of people — priests, religious, and laity together — determined to strive by common effort to foster public worship of the Sacred Heart and to exercise works of piety and charity in the name of this same loving Heart of Jesus. Originally the group chose the name Heralds of Christ for M. III, as their work was directed to preparing the world for Christ's 2000th birthday and ushering in the third millennium. In the Encyclical *Redeemer of Man*, which Pope John Paul II issued in 1979, he asked all to prepare for the year 2000. His words called for a reawakening in us of the awareness of the key truth of faith as expressed in the Gospel: "The Word became flesh and dwelt among us." He asked the people of God to prepare for a great Jubilee. Thus, this private association of the Christian faithful (Canon Law, rev. 1983, canons 298 ff.) began to direct their efforts toward this goal of bringing Christ and the love of His Sacred Heart to the world.

As a means to promote interest in Christ's love, and to give people a practical aid to promote trust in His Love, they devised a Rosary or chaplet in honor of the Sacred Heart, expressing to Jesus Christ our confidence in His love for us. It is made up of thirty-three beads, in honor of Christ's earthly life, and a Sacred Heart medal or emblem. On each bead, one prayerfully recites, "Sacred Heart of Jesus, I trust in Your love"(or any other short prayer of trust). The prayer is made especially for peace among peoples of the world, the needs of the Church, our families, all lovers of Christ, and the intentions of the Sacred Heart Society.

Anyone may copy and distribute this Rosary, using any color or style of beads available, but the chaplet should end with a medal or representation of the Sacred Heart. The faithful who make and use this Rosary should remember to have it blessed by a priest. Because of its simple design, the Rosary is often strung on cord rather than having the beads separated.

CHAPLET OF ST. PAUL

In the early days of this century, Rev. James Alberione, taking St. Paul as his mentor and example, began a great work of using modern communications to spread the Word of God. The member congregations of the Pauline family acknowledge him as founder, and carry out his ideas today in all parts of the globe, using cutting-edge communications as the means to reach souls.

Father Alberione composed this chaplet to St. Paul. The chaplet has five petitions, each followed by a prayerful refrain.

1. I bless You, O Jesus, for the great mercy granted to St. Paul in changing him from a bold persecutor to an ardent apostle of the Church. And you, O great Saint, obtain for me a heart docile to grace, conversion from my principal defect and total configuration with Jesus Christ.

   Refrain:

   Jesus Master, Way, Truth and Life, have mercy on us.
   Queen of Apostles, pray for us.
   St. Paul the Apostle, pray for us.

2. I bless You, O Jesus, for having elected the Apostle Paul as a model and preacher of holy virginity. And you, O St. Paul, my dear father, guard my mind, my heart and my senses in order that I may know, love and serve only Jesus and employ all my energies for His glory.

(Refrain)

3. I bless You, O Jesus, for having given through St. Paul examples and teachings of perfect obedience. And you, O great Saint, obtain for me a humble docility to all my superiors, for I am sure that in obedience I shall be victorious over my enemies.

(Refrain)

4. I bless You, O Jesus, for having taught me, by the deeds and by the words of St. Paul, the true spirit of poverty. And you, O great Saint, obtain for me the evangelical spirit of poverty, so that after having imitated you in life I may be your companion in heavenly glory.

(Refrain)

5. I bless You, O Jesus, for having given to St. Paul a heart so full of love for God and for the Church and for having saved so many souls through his meal. And you, our friend, obtain for me an ardent desire to carry out the apostolate of the media of social communication, of prayer, of example, of activity and of word so that I may merit the reward promised to good apostles.

(Refrain)

CHAPLET OF ST. MICHAEL

St. Michael the Archangel is one of three angels named in Holy Scripture. Christian tradition assigns four offices to him: (1) to fight against Satan; (2) to rescue the souls of the faithful from the power of the devil, especially at the hour of death; (3) to be the champion of God's people; and (4) to call away from earth and bring men's souls to judgment. He was venerated from earliest Christian times as an angelic healer.

Chaplet of St. Michael

The chaplet of St. Michael honors not only the great Archangel, but all the heavenly spirits. This chaplet originated in 1751, when St. Michael appeared to a devout Portuguese Carmelite, Antonia d'Astonac. He requested her to publish in his honor a chaplet of nine salutations, each one of which corresponds to one of the nine choirs of angels. One Our Father and three Hail Marys are said in conjunction with each of the salutations. The chaplet concludes with four Our Fathers honoring Sts. Michael, Gabriel, Raphael, and the Guardian Angel. He promised those who practiced the devotion faithfully that he would send an angel from each choir to accompany them when they received Holy Communion. He promised his assistance and that of all the holy angels during life to those who daily recited the chaplet, and to those faithful he also promised deliverance from the pains of Purgatory for themselves and the souls of their relatives. A group of Carmelite nuns who had experienced the spiritual benefits of this chaplet requested approval from Pope Pius IX, who indulgenced the chaplet in 1851.

The beads of this chaplet may be of a single color, usually black or white, or may be multicolored. One group of nuns made a nine-color chaplet based on the revelations of a German mystic. In the United States, the Oblates of St. Benedict distribute the chaplet, also made in nine colors, simply to separate the decades (the colors not having any special significance).

The chaplet is begun with an act of contrition and the recitation of the following invocation: "O God, come to my assistance. O Lord, make haste to help me. Glory be to the Father, etc."

The nine salutations are as follows:

"1. By the intercession of St. Michael and the celestial choir of Seraphim, may the Lord make us worthy to burn with the file of perfect charity.

"2. By the intercession of St. Michael and the celestial choir of Cherubim, may the Lord vouchsafe to grant us grace to leave the ways of wickedness to run in the paths of Christian perfection.

"3. By the intercession of St. Michael and the celestial choir of Thrones, may the Lord infuse into our hearts a true and sincere spirit of humility.

"4. By the intercession of St. Michael and the celestial choir of Dominions, may the Lord give us grace to govern our senses and subdue our unruly passions.

"5. By the intercession of St. Michael and the celestial choir of Powers, may the Lord vouchsafe to protect our souls against the snares and temptations of the devil.

"6. By the intercession of St. Michael and the celestial choir of Virtues may the Lord preserve us from evil and suffer us not to fall into temptation.

"7. By the intercession of St. Michael and the celestial choir of Principalities, may God fill our souls with a true spirit of obedience.

"8. By the intercession of St. Michael and the celestial choir of Archangels, may the Lord give us perseverance in faith and in all good works, in order that we may gain the glory of Paradise.

"9. By the intercession of St. Michael and the celestial choir of Angels, may the Lord grant us to be protected by them in this mortal life and conducted hereafter to eternal glory."

The chaplet is concluded with the following prayer: "O glorious Prince St. Michael, chief and commander of the heavenly hosts, guardian of souls, vanquisher of rebel spirits, servant in the house of the Divine King, and our admirable conductor, thou who dost shine with excellence and superhuman virtue, vouchsafe to deliver us from all evil, who turn to thee with confidence and enable us by thy gracious protection to serve God more and more faithfully every day. Pray for us, O glorious St. Michael, Prince of the Church of Jesus Christ, that we may be made worthy of His promises."

THE ROSARY OR CROWN OF OUR LORD (CAMALDOLESE)

Blessed Michael Pini was born in Florence about 1440. As a young man he was a cupbearer at the court of Lorenzo de' Medici. His virtues were so outstanding that de' Medici had him ordained a priest. On a visit to the Sacred Hermitage of Camaldoli, he was so impressed by the sanctity of life he found there that he resolved to stay and take the habit of St. Romuald.

After the ancient custom of the Camaldolese, Blessed Michael eventually was granted a more solitary life, staying by himself in a cell at first for a year and later for the rest of his life. In his meditations, he often thought of the petitions of the Our Father. He asked himself how the faithful could best obtain spiritual benefits from this prayer. As he studied the prayer, through divine inspiration he wrote a chaplet in honor of Our Lord. He made a set of beads that he presented to his Superior. The chaplet was presented to Pope Leo X and received his approbation in a papal bull of 1516.

The Rosary of Our Lord instituted by Blessed Michael commemorates the thirty-three years Jesus spent on earth for our salvation. Thus, thirty-three Our Fathers are recited. Five Hail Marys are said in honor of the five wounds of the Redeemer and to remind us of Mary, our Co-Redemptrix.

The Rosary of Our Lord is divided into four parts commemorating His birth and hidden life, His public life, His passion and death, and His glorification. In order to keep the mind more recollected, a mystery is assigned as a meditation during the recitation of each of the prayers. When the Rosary is recited in common, a preparatory prayer is recited, and the leader reads the mystery. When reciting privately, one can begin with any suitable mental or oral prayer. The Glory Be is said at the end of each decade, unless the Rosary is being said for the dead, in which case one would pray, "Eternal rest grant unto them," etc.

Unlike most other chaplets, which have a meditation for each decade or set of prayers, the Rosary of Our Lord has a meditation for each bead.

The four parts of the chaplet, as listed above, are the most standard way of reciting this devotion. However, an alternate set of mysteries may also be used with this chaplet. This second set focuses primarily on the passion of Our Lord, and when recited with these mysteries, is often called the Rosary of the Passion of Our Lord.

Finally, a short form of this chaplet — in place of a mystery or meditation for each prayer — presents a consideration for meditation before each decade.

The scope of this book does not allow for the printing of all of the mysteries of this beautiful chaplet. The reader who wishes to adopt this devotion should contact the Camaldolese hermits.

BRIGITTINE ROSARY

The chaplet of St. Bridget was instituted, and its propagation begun, by St. Bridget of Sweden (1304-1373). St. Bridget was a widow and a mystic, favored with numerous remarkable visions and revelations.

Brigittine Rosary

The chaplet consists of six decades of Hail Marys, each preceded by an Our Father and ended by a Credo. After the six decades, an Our Father and three Hail Marys are added.

The chaplet therefore includes seven Our Fathers, 63 Hail Marys, and six Credos. The recitation of it is intended to honor, by the seven Our Fathers, the seven sorrows and the seven joys of the Most Blessed Virgin; by the 63 Aves, the 63 years which, — according to yet another common custom, the Blessed Mother lived on earth (customs vary on this number; see p. 266).

Fifteen of the mysteries of this chaplet are the same as the Dominican Rosary, while the Brigittine chaplet adds a sixth mystery to each of the divisions. Added to the Joyful Mysteries is the Immaculate Conception; to the Sorrowful Mysteries, the Dead Jesus in the arms of His Mother; and to the Glorious Mysteries, the Patronage of Mary.

This chaplet was a favorite devotion of a number of religious orders, among them the Brothers of the Christian Schools.

THE *CHATKY (CHOTKI)*

The *chatky* is one of the major sacramentals of the Byzantine rite. (In Greek, it is also known as the *konboskienon* or the *kon-*

bologion; in Russian, *chotki*.) Its use began with the desert fathers in Egypt about the fourth century; it became a part of the monastic habit, likened to the "sword of the spirit," blessed and presented to a monk when he was tonsured.

From the beginning, the *chatky* was adopted by the devout laity. It found its way to the West through the Russian émigrés who fled the Communist Revolution. The sacramental is worn about the

Chatky

neck among the Byzantines, and the Orthodox generally wear it on their belts.

The *chatky* is generally made of wool (although some are made of wooden beads), consisting of a varied number of knots. The shorter (and more common) have 100, while some of the longer ones, 300. The knots are hand-tied, each made up of seven crosses, one tied atop the other. A cross, tied with similar knots, ends the *chatky*. On a new *chatky*, the bead-shaped knots are tight and close together. With use, the *chatky* lengthens considerably.

A single prayer is recited on the *chatky* — the Jesus Prayer: "Lord Jesus Christ, Son of God, be merciful to me, a sinner." Prayers on the *chatky* are the most common penance in the Byzantine rite, and it is customary to recite it and accompany the prayers with prostration.

CHAPLET OF THE HOLY SPIRIT (1)

Among the myriad devotions brought to the Catholic Church by the spiritual children of St. Francis of Assisi is the Chaplet of the Holy Spirit. It was composed and promoted by John Mary Finigan of King's Lynn (1857-1931), a Franciscan

Chaplet of the Holy Spirit

Capuchin of the Great Britain province. This "apostle of the Holy Spirit" composed the chaplet in order to give the faithful an easy means of honoring the Holy Spirit. The Vatican approved the chaplet in 1900.

There are five mysteries of this chaplet. Each mystery is outlined with a scriptural meditation and a suggested practice for drawing grace into our own life. The chaplet begins with the Sign of the Cross, an Act of Contrition and the reciting of the prayer-hymn "Come Holy Ghost, Creator Blest." On the first two beads of the mystery the Our Father and the Hail Mary are recited. Then, seven Glory Be to the Fathers are recited. These prayers should be recited after reading the Scripture extract and meditating prayerfully on the suggested practice. The mysteries are as follows:

1. Jesus is conceived by the Holy Spirit of the Virgin Mary.
2. The Spirit of the Lord rests upon Jesus.
3. Jesus is led by the Spirit into the desert.
4. The Holy Spirit in the Church.
5. The Holy Spirit in the souls of the just.

The chaplet concludes with the Apostles' Creed followed by one Our Father and Hail Mary for the intentions of the Holy Father.

CHAPLET OF THE HOLY SPIRIT (2)

Father Mateo Crawley-Boevey, SS.CC., called the "Modern Apostle of the Sacred Heart" by Pope Paul VI, composed this chaplet as a prayer of adoration to the Paraclete in honor of His Seven Gifts. He proposed the chaplet as a means to grow in love for the Paraclete, Consoler, and Advocate, and to help draw down the sevenfold gifts of wisdom, understanding, knowledge, counsel, fortitude, piety, and fear of the Lord.

The Chaplet of the Holy Spirit is said using a set of regular Rosary beads. Begin by saying the Apostles' Creed, the Glory Be to the Father, and an Our Father. Then the prayer is said, "Father, Father, send us the promised Paraclete, through Jesus Christ, Our Lord, Amen." On the ten small beads, say, "Come, Holy Spirit, fill the hearts of Your faithful and kindle in them the fire of Your love." After the tenth bead say, "Send forth Your Spirit and they shall be created, and You shall renew the face of the earth." The other decades follow in the same manner, beginning with the Our

Father. After the seventh and last decade, recite the Hail Holy Queen in honor of the Blessed Virgin, our Heavenly Queen, who presided in the Cenacle on the great Sunday of Pentecost.

Meditations for this chaplet may be made on seven glorious mysteries relating to seven wonderful operations of the Paraclete. These should be made briefly between the decades:

1. Let us honor the Holy Spirit and adore Him who is Love Substantial, proceeding from the Father and the Son, and uniting Them in an infinite and eternal love.

2. Let us honor the operation of the Holy Spirit and adore Him in the Immaculate Conception of Mary, sanctifying her from the first moment with the plenitude of grace.

3. Let us honor the operation of the Holy Spirit and adore Him in the Incarnation of the Word, in the womb of the Virgin Mary, the Son of God by His divine nature and the Son of the Virgin by the flesh.

4. Let us honor the operation of the Holy Spirit and adore Him proclaiming the Church on the glorious day of Pentecost.

5. Let us honor the operation of the Holy Spirit and adore Him dwelling in the Church and assisting her faithfully according to the divine promise even to the consummation of the world.

6. Let us honor the wonderful operation of the Holy Spirit creating within the Church that other Christ, the priest, and conferring the plenitude of the priesthood on the bishops.

7. Let us honor the operation of the Holy Spirit and adore Him in the heroic virtues of the saints in the Church, that hidden and marvelous work of the "Adorable Sanctifier."

In recent years, a special chaplet has been made. In this version, the prayer on the small beads is said only seven times, as each decade has only seven beads rather than the ten beads of a standard Rosary.

CHAPLET OF MARY, MODEL FOR MOTHERS

This chaplet was written by the author of this book to honor Mary as model for mothers and to thank her for her daily assistance in the most difficult, important, and rewarding job any woman could have. No special beads are needed for the chaplet — ten fingers can serve as a reminder if needed. A single Hail Mary follows each mystery, and the entire chaplet is concluded with the Memorare of St. Bernard.

1. Annunciation — Mary, you were only about fifteen when the angel came to ask you to be the Mother of God. Alone and unmarried, you must have been frightened. Be with all those who today have found out that they are pregnant. For those who are not glad of the news, assist them to say 'yes' to the new life growing within them. Hail Mary . . .

2. Visitation — Mary, you hastened to your cousin to help her out during her pregnancy. Her preborn child recognized yours and leapt in his mother's womb. Take the preborn children who today will be pulled from their mothers' wombs by abortion into your tender and immaculate heart. Hail Mary . . .

3. Presentation — You followed the law and presented your Child in the Temple. Simeon told you that a sword would pierce your loving heart. In Baptism, I, too, have presented my children according to the law. I realize that I, too, will have swords of sorrow in my heart. Give me the strength to bear what is the difficult part of what is to come for my children. Hail Mary . . .

4. Finding in the Temple — How terrified you must have been, how worried, when you found Jesus was not where He was supposed to be. How overjoyed your heart felt when you found Him in the Temple! How proud you must have been to hear His words to the learned teachers, and how gratified that He went and was subject to you. Help me to trust that my children will be safe, yet understand my motherly worries and terrors. Help my children to be wise, and to be subject to me only in so far as I am subject to your Divine Child. Hail Mary . . .

5. The Wedding at Cana — His time was not come, He said; yet with the compassionate heart of a mother you understood the family's disgrace and made your request in perfect faith. May I live each day in perfect faith in the help of your Son. Hail Mary . . .

6. The Scourging — How did you bear to see your innocent Child broken and bloody? Help me to bear the hurts, the fears, the illnesses, and the anguish of my children. Help me to water their growth and comfort them with my prayers and my tears. Hail Mary . . .

7. The Road to Calvary — Jesus walked alone, dragging His heavy cross. You could not carry it for Him, although you gladly would have done so. How grateful you must have been to the Cyrenian for his assistance, and for the woman who compassionately wiped the face of Jesus. Help me to realize that I cannot carry my children's crosses for them, but that my love can be a support for them. Inspire me with gratitude for all those who assist my children — relatives, teachers, friends. Remind me to extend my love outward daily. Hail Mary . . .

8. The Crucifixion — Only a mother who has watched her child suffering and dying can begin to really comprehend your anguish at this dark hour. The pain must have felt as if your very heart were being wrenched from your breast. Remind me daily of all the suffering children of the world — from the starving child in the fourth world to the drug addict and the AIDS victim and the homeless in my own town — and of their sorrowful mothers. Hail Mary . . .

9. The Resurrection — Your faith was rewarded, and your Child returned from death. Before your heart was bursting with Sorrow; now it seems to burst with relief and joy in the glorious miracle of renewed life. Fill my heart with the glorious mystery of the Resurrection, and admit me to the company of the Easter People. Hail Mary . . .

10. The Crowning as Queen of Heaven — Mary, you said "yes" to God. Throughout your life, in sunshine and in shadow, you were His faithful servant. After your falling asleep, you were taken to your Son, your Divine Master. Jesus said, 'Let not your hearts be troubled; believe in God, believe also in me. In my Father's house are many rooms; if it were not so, would I have told you that I go to prepare a place for you? And when I go and prepare a place for you, I will come again and will take you to myself, that where I am you may be also. And you know the way where I am going' (Jn 14:1-4). Dearest Queen, help me to say 'yes' daily to all that God asks of me in order that I may one day go to the place that He has prepared for me. Hail Mary . . .

THE *MEMORARE*

Remember, O most gracious Virgin Mary, that never was it known that anyone who fled to thy protection, implored thy help, or sought thy intercession was left unaided. Inspired by this confidence, I fly unto thee, O Virgin of Virgins, My Mother. To thee I come, before thee I stand, sinful and sorrowful. O Mother of the Word Incarnate, despise not my petitions, but in thy mercy hear and answer me.

CHAPLET OF BLESSED MIGUEL PRO, S.J.

This chaplet honors the well-known hero of the persecution of the Catholic Church in Mexico in the 1920s and 1930s, Blessed Miguel Agustin Pro, S.J. Pro was executed for the Faith in 1927. The chaplet was given the imprimatur by Joseph Fiorenza, Bishop of Galveston-Houston, on August 13, 1995.

The chaplet consists of a crucifix or medal of Blessed Miguel, followed by six white beads to symbolize his purity and eleven red beads that symbolize his martyrdom. On the first beads, traditional prayers in honor of the Trinity, the Holy Spirit, Our Father, Our Lady, the angels, and the saints are prayed. The eleven following beads recall highlights in Blessed Pro's life and his connection to us and are followed with the response *"Viva Cristo Rey"* ("Long live Christ the King").

Blessed Miguel Pro Chaplet

CHAPLET OF THE TEN EVANGELICAL VIRTUES OF THE MOST BLESSED VIRGIN MARY

In 1501, St. Joanne de Valois (1464-1505) and Blessed Gilbert-Nicolas, OFM (1463-1532) co-founded the Sisters of the Annunciation of the Blessed Virgin Mary (Annunciades). Blessed Gilbert wrote the Rule of the Ten Virtues of the Most Blessed Virgin Mary, and St. Joanne then composed the Chaplet of the Ten Evangelical Virtues of the Most Blessed Virgin Mary.

Later, a men's order, The Marians (The Marians of the Immaculate Conception), received the rule in 1699. Until the renovation of the Order in 1910, Marian priests and brothers professed their solemn vows based on the Rule of the Ten Virtues written by Blessed Gilbert. Before the renovation, each Marian would hang his chaplet beads from the sash of his white habit. Called a *decima* ("ten" in Latin), the chaplet is comprised of ten black beads with a crucifix on one end and a medal with an image of Mary Immaculate on the other. This chaplet was given to each White Marian on the first day of his religious life, when he was vested in his habit.

The White Marians (the common name for the order before the renovation, when the white habit was abolished) carried their chaplet, or *decimal,* with them all their lives and were buried holding it in their hands.

The Chaplet of the Ten Evangelical Virtues of the Most Blessed Virgin Mary was the Marians' everyday prayer for almost two and a half centuries. In fact, in Marian iconography, paintings of our Marian Founder, Fr. Stanislaus Papczynski, and Ven. Fr. Casimir Wyszynski, typically depict them holding their chaplet beads.

The chaplet is prayed as the Rosary, on a standard set of Rosary beads. The Sign of the Cross begins the chaplet. On each decade, the Our Father is prayed first. Then, ten Hail Marys, with an addition in each: after the phrase, "Holy Mary, Mother of God," one virtue is added to the prayer, in the order in which they are shown below — Most Pure to Most Sorrowful — after which the Ave is finished the usual way, with "Pray for us sinners now and at the hour of our death. Amen."

Holy Mary, Mother of God, most pure . . .
. . . most prudent
. . . most humble
. . . most faithful
. . . most devout
. . . most obedient
. . . most poor
. . . most patient
. . . most merciful
. . . most sorrowful

WORLD MISSION ROSARY

Archbishop Fulton J. Sheen introduced this Rosary in the mid-twentieth century to encourage prayers for the missions and missionaries. It is a standard Dominican Rosary of five decades, with each decade a different color to symbolize the continents: green for Africa, red for the Americas, white for Europe, blue for Oceania, and yellow for Asia.

As the beads are prayed, the supplicant is encouraged to offer those prayers for the missionary efforts of the Church in each continent.

CROWN OF OUR LADY OF TEARS

The Crown of Our Lady of Tears is a chaplet promoted by the Institute of the Missionaries of the Scourged Jesus since 1930, based on visions of Mary reported by the institute's co-founder, Sister Amelia of Jesus Crucified.

The chaplet has 49 white beads, divided into seven parts by seven larger beads of the same color, similar to the Rosary of the Seven Sorrows of Mary. At the end, there are three more small beads and a medal of Our Lady of Tears.

Crown of Our Lady of Tears

The prepatory prayer is:

O crucified Jesus, we fall at Your feet and offer You the tears of the one who with deep compassionate love accompanied You on Your sorrowful way of the Cross. O good Master, grant that we take to heart the lessons which the tears of Your most holy Mother teach us, so that we may fulfill Your holy will on earth, that we may be worthy to praise and exalt You in Heaven for all eternity. Amen.

On the large beads and the final three beads, the supplicant prays:

O Jesus, look upon the tears of the one who loved You most on earth and loves You most ardently in heaven. On the small beads, pray: O Jesus, listen to our prayers, for the sake of the tears of Your most Holy Mother. On the medal, pray: O Mary, Mother of Love, Sorrow, and Mercy, we beseech you to unite your prayers with ours so that Jesus, your Divine Son, to whom we turn, may hear our petitions in the name of your maternal tears, and grant us, not only the favors we now ask, but the crown of everlasting life. Amen.

NATURE'S SACRAMENTALS

Throughout Christian history, plants, flowers, and other objects from nature have been used sacramentally. From the earliest times, Christians began to recognize God's bounty as precious gifts, and used them to draw closer to their Creator.

HERBAL LORE IN CHRISTIAN TRADITION

Despite the chaos of the Dark Ages, the Christian Church grew steadily; in the fourth century, monasteries were founded and became storehouses of learning. Throughout the Middle Ages, the monks preserved knowledge of plants and herbal lore, and each monastery had several gardens. Christian laymen considered flowers to be pagan, associating them with the wreathed Romans and their orgies; by contrast, however, the monks used flowers to decorate the altars and to make wreaths that priests wore on feast days. In this way, the monks "Christianized" the flowers and herbs, associating them with Christ, Our Lady, and the saints.

Many popular legends became associated with plants familiar to today's gardeners.

- Legend tells that St. Helen found the True Cross in a patch of basil.
- The ancient plant flax was used to make the linen of the shroud of Our Lord.
- Garlic was a protection against plague, and legend holds that it grew at Calvary.
- Lavender represented the Virgin's purity and virtue and was burned on St. John's Eve to drive away evil spirits.

- On St. Luke's Day, single women anointed themselves with a marjoram mixture and prayed to St. Luke to dream of their future husband.
- A good growth of parsley on a grave meant the soul of the person there was at rest.
- The legend of rosemary says it sheltered the Virgin on her flight to Egypt. She dried her cloak on the plant, imparting the blue color to the flowers.
- Spearmint was dedicated to the Virgin and was called *Erba Santa Maria* or "Menthe de Notre Dame."
- Legend holds that the Virgin accompanies children when they pick strawberries on St. John's Day.
- Thyme, by ancient tradition, was one of the herbs that formed the bed of the Virgin. It was a symbol of courage and energy to the knights of the Crusades.
- Roses and lilies are also associated with the Virgin. The red rose with its thorns symbolized the crucifixion.
- Wood sorrel (*oxalis*) was nicknamed "alleluia" because it bloomed after Easter, when the Gospel response was "alleluia."

Hundreds of other legends were associated with plants and herbs during this time.

HOLY HERBS

Christians also adapted and used the ancient practice of using herbs for medicinal purposes. Medieval monastic communities both preserved and applied early Greek and Roman knowledge of the medicinal use of plants. Common recommended practices (prescriptions) were written in books called "herbals." In the twelfth century, the German abbess Hildegard of Bingen wrote the *Book of Healing Herbs*, which described a wide range of plants and their uses, and the treatment of human illness became an extension of Church teaching. Christian healers followed the example of St. Basil, Bishop of Caesarea, in proving care and shelter for the sick, for lepers, and for travelers.

In the eighth century, Charlemagne, King of the Franks and the First Holy Roman Emperor, designated a group of useful plants to be grown in his domain. In the ninth century, the patriarch of Jerusalem sent prescriptions from the East to Alfred the Great, King of the West Saxons.

As many plants became associated with Christian saints and martyrs — and so lost previous pagan symbolism — Christian missionaries used them as teaching tools. The largely uneducated population could not read, but, as farmers, were familiar with the native plants, so missionaries turned many into lessons. One famous example of this practice was St. Patrick's use of the shamrock as a symbol of the Holy Trinity.

Plants were sometimes even used as calendars. Those who could not read a calendar could remember that Michaelmas daisies flowered near time for the Feast of St. Michael. The wood sorrel was nicknamed "alleluia" because it bloomed when the Gospel response was alleluia, between Easter and Whitsuntide. St. John's Wort received its name because it bloomed near the Feast of St. John the Baptist. Dedicated to the saint, the Christians continued to hang the plant in doorways to repel evil spirits, just as they did in previous, pagan times. The priests and monks collected the newly "holy" herb to use in casting out devils.

European immigrants took their folk medicine to America, where it blended with that practiced by native Americans for centuries. Even after the advent of modern, laboratory-manufactured pharmaceuticals, botanical medicines and folk healers remained popular among the common people, particularly in rural areas of the Ozark and Appalachian mountains. And, in the American Southwest, *curanderos* and Native American medicine men do a brisk business in herbal remedies to this day. Some famous *curanderos* — notably Don Pedrito Jaramillo and Nino Fidencia —

have been acclaimed as folk saints by the people, who believe it is only a matter of time before the Church canonizes them.

Medical science has proved the truth of many "old wives' tales" of herbal folk medicine. The useful properties of plants such as aloe vera, garlic, mint, and peppers, for example, have been known and used for centuries; today, scientists analyze the chemicals in these plants to explain how and why they work.

MARY GARDENS

One lovely medieval custom is what is called a "Mary Garden," a small portion of a larger garden, set aside in honor of the Virgin and featuring some of the hundreds of flowers and herbs associated by legend with Mary. This tradition returned to popularity in Europe and the United States in the mid-twentieth century.

The first Mary Garden in the United States is believed to be that at St. Joseph's Church in Woods Hole, Massachusetts. In 1932, Mrs. Frances Crane Lillie, a summer resident of Woods Hole, researched herbs and plants with old religious names that symbolized the Virgin Mary. She planted a selection of these in a garden at St. Joseph's Church. After the first year of Mrs. Lillie's

Mary Gardens

"Garden of Our Lady," revisions were made and, in 1933, it was replenished with 48 specimens planted around a commissioned statue of the Virgin Mary in a cross-shaped bed.

After twice being destroyed by hurricanes, the garden has been restored to its original planting plan. The restoration was prompted by the rediscovery of the garden's historical uniqueness and significance by the parishioners in the course of the research undertaken for the writing of a commemorative history for the centennial of the parish.

The Woods Hole garden was the inspiration for the foundation of an organization called Mary's Gardens, begun in Philadelphia in 1951 by two young businessmen, Edward A.G. McTague and John S. Stokes, Jr. The aim of this nonprofit group is to revive the medieval practice of cultivating gardens of herbs and flowers with Marian names, and to research the hundreds of plants symbolic of the life, mysteries, and privileges of the Blessed Virgin Mary. The founders hope that people will plant Mary Gardens as a prayerful, religious work of stewardship for God's flower riches and artistry with devotion, praise, meditation, and commitment. Research by this foundation has resulted in a list of over a thousand herb, flower, shrub, and tree names symbolic of Mary. Proposed initially for home gardens, Mary Gardens soon became established also at schools, parishes, burial plots, institutions, and shrines. In 1983, a Mary Garden was even established inside prison walls, at the Idaho State Penitentiary. A prisoner-artist painted the traditional image of Our Lady of Guadalupe, and a shrine was built around it made of rocks dug from the prison yard, flowers, and grass.

Some of the better-known Mary Gardens today are those at Our Lady's national shrines at Knock, Ireland, and Akita, Japan; at the Artane Oratory of the Resurrection in Dublin; and in the cloister planting of Lincoln Cathedral in England. In the United States, a beautiful Mary Garden can be found at St. Mary's Parish, Annapolis, Maryland, adjacent to the historic Carroll House.

Today, an informal association of committed persons in Pennsylvania, Massachusetts, Maryland, Ohio, and Dublin, Ireland continues the work of Mary's Gardens. In 1995, the organization opened an Internet Web site to make their literature available in electronic form.

CHRISTMAS PLANTS AND FLOWERS

The custom of decorating homes at festive times is worldwide and ancient. After the time of the persecutions, the Church soon approved the custom of decorating both church and home with plants and flowers at the Christmas season. Pope St. Gregory I (604), in a letter to St. Augustine of Canterbury, advised him to permit, and even encourage, harmless popular customs which in themselves were not pagan and could be given Christian interpretations.

Most of the plants traditionally used at Christmas are evergreens for two reasons: 1) they were usually the only ones available in winter and 2) from ancient times, evergreens have been symbolic of eternal life.

Mistletoe was a sacred plant in the pagan religion of the Druids of Britain, who believed it had all sorts of miraculous qualities. It was considered so sacred that even enemies who met beneath mistletoe in the forest would lay down their arms and keep a truce until the following day. From this practice came the modern practice of suspending mistletoe over a doorway as a token of goodwill and peace. A kiss under mistletoe was interpreted as a pledge of love and a promise of marriage, an omen of happiness and good fortune to the lovers who scaled their engagement by a kiss beneath the sacred plant.

After Britain was converted to Christianity, the bishops did not allow mistletoe to be used in churches because it had been the main symbol of a pagan religion. To this day, it is rarely used as a decoration for altars. However, the Cathedral of York was an exception, and at a period before the Reformation, a large bundle of mistletoe was annually brought into the sanctuary at Christmas and solemnly placed on the altar by the priest. The plant that the Druids had called "All heal" was thus used as a symbol of the Divine Healer of nations, Christ.

Later, the English adopted the mistletoe as a decoration for their homes, and the pagan meaning was soon forgotten. It simply became a token of goodwill and friendship, and the kissing lost its solemn meaning.

Holly was a symbol, to early Christians of northern Europe, of the burning thorn bush of Moses and the flaming love of God that filled Mary's heart. The prickly points and red berries resembling blood also reminded them that the Divine Child would wear a crown of thorns. The appearance of holly in the homes of old England opened the season of feasting and good cheer. Today its green leaves and red berries have become a symbol of Christmas, decorating not only homes and churches but also cards, wrapping paper, and other Christmas items.

In the medieval age, superstition endowed holly with power against witchcraft, and unmarried women were advised to fasten holly to their beds at Christmas to guard them from being turned into witches by the Evil One. In Germany, branches of holly which had been used in church were brought home as a protection against lightning. Holly was supposed to be lucky for men, as ivy was for women.

Ivy, in pagan Rome, was the badge of the wine god Bacchus, displayed to symbolize drinking and feasting. Later, for this reason, it was banished from Christian homes. In England, it was banned from the inside of homes and allowed to grow only on the outside. Thus, its use as a Christmas decoration was not common during medieval times. The symbolism of human weakness clinging to divine strength was frequently ascribed to ivy, however, and some poets in old England defended its use as a decoration. Later, the delicate ground ivy became a favorite plant of the English home; it traveled to the New World with the pioneer settlers.

The *bay laurel* is an ancient symbol of triumph, used at Christmas to proclaim the victory over death and sin signified by the birth of Christ.

Bay Laurel

It was probably the first plant used as a Christmas decoration: early Christians at Rome adorn their homes with it at the Nativity. The wreath was a Roman symbol of victory, and it is from Rome that the modern custom derives of hanging laurel wreaths on the outside of doors as a friendly greeting to our fellowmen. Immigrants introduced it to the United States from England and Ireland, gradually becoming part of American culture — although today, evergreen wreaths are as common, if not more so, than laurel wreaths.

According to an old legend, God honored the delicate *rosemary* in reward for its humble service to Mary and her Child on the flight into Egypt. On the way, Mary washed the tiny garments of the Christ Child and spread them over a rosemary bush to dry. In other medieval legends, this plant is pictured as a great protection and help against evil spirits, especially if it has been used in church on Christmas Day.

It is a custom in some parts of central Europe to break off a branch of the *cherry tree* on St. Barbara's Day (December 4), place it in a pot of water in the kitchen, and wait for the twig to blossom at Christmastime. Such cherry branches flowering at Christmas were considered omens of good luck.

A native of Central America, the *poinsettia* is widely used in churches and homes at Christmas because the flaming star of its red bracts resembles the star of Bethlehem. Dr. Joel Roberts Poinsett (1851), the U.S. ambassador to Mexico, brought this flower with him back to his home in South Carolina. In Mexico, the flower is called the "Flower of Holy Night." Its origin is explained by a charming Mexican legend. A poor little boy went to church on Christmas Eve in sadness because he had no gift to bring to the Holy Child. He knelt humbly outside the church and prayed fervently in tears, assuring Our Lord how much he wished to offer Him a lovely present, telling Him that he was poor and afraid to approach with empty hands. When the child rose from his knees, he saw a green plant with gorgeous blooms spring up at his feet. The Poinsettia is a prolific bloomer and has spread throughout the United States.

EASTER LILY

Lilies have traditionally been symbols of beauty, perfection, and goodness. Both in the Old and New Testaments, the Scriptures often make use of this symbolism. Our Lord Himself pointed the lily out to His Apostles, saying that "even Solomon in all his glory was not arrayed like one of these" (Mt. 6:28).

The Easter lily did not directly originate from religious symbolism; it has, instead, acquired religious symbolism. This large white lily was introduced in Bermuda from Japan at the middle of the nineteenth century. The florist W.K. Harris brought it to the United States in 1882 and spread its use here. In America, it flowers first around Easter time, and soon came to be called the "Easter lily." The American public quickly made it a symbolic feature of the Easter celebration. Churches began using it as a decoration for Easter Day, and people made it a favorite in their homes for the Easter season.

ROSE

This flower was long associated with Greek and Egyptian gods; during the Middle Ages, the Church began using it as a symbol for the Blessed Mother. A number of pious legends connecting Our Lady with roses date back to medieval times.

Our Lady of Guadalupe placed rare Castilian roses in St. Juan Diego's cloak as a sign of the truth of her presence. At Lourdes, France, St. Bernadette reported that Our Lady appeared to her standing on a rosebush, and with golden roses on her feet. Visionaries at LaSalette said Our Lady wore roses.

Roses and rose petals have often been blessed as sacramentals in Dominican churches on the Feast of the Holy Rosary. Roses are also associated with St. Thérèse of Lisieux, the Little Flower, because of her promise to send a "shower of roses" from heaven. They are also associated with St. Rita of Cascia and St. Dorothy.

BLESSED ROSES

A pious custom in Dominican (and some other) churches on the Feast of the Holy Rosary is the blessing of roses, because the rose is seen as a figure of the Rosary and its mysteries. The green leaves represent the Joyful Mysteries; the thorns of the bush stand for the Sorrowful Mysteries; and the Glorious Mysteries are seen in the flowers.

The formula in the Roman Ritual for the blessing of the roses reads:

> O God, Creator and Preserver of mankind, deign to pour out Thy heavenly benediction upon these roses, which we offer to Thee through devotion and reverence for Our Lady of the Rosary. Grant that these roses, which are made by Thy Providence to yield an agreeable perfume for the use of men and women, may receive such a blessing by the sign of Thy holy cross that all the sick on whom they shall be laid and all who shall keep them in their houses may be cured of their ills; and that the devils may fly in terror from these dwellings, not daring to disturb Thy servants.

One of the most famous oil wells in Texas is the Santa Rita No. 1. This well, drilled on state-owned lands, opened the field that pumped riches into the University of Texas, where the original pump is displayed today in Austin. The name originated with a group of Catholic women from New York, who had invested in stock sold by the driller. They asked that the well be named for St. Rita, as patron of the impossible. After the driller completed the derrick over the well, he climbed to the top, sprinkled dried rose petals blessed in the saint's name and given him by the investors, and christened the well.

Other natural things used sacramentally or symbolically are:

BLESSED MAGNOLIA LEAF

The blessing of magnolia leaves is a pious custom among those of French descent in Louisiana. A blessed magnolia leaf, two blessed candles, and holy water are kept on a shelf near the family shrine where night prayers are said.

PANSY

This tricolor plant has traditionally been referred to as "the Trinity flower" in parts of Europe and used as symbol for the Trinity.

Since medieval times, there have been many imaginative and symbolic ways to indicate the great mystery of the Holy Trinity. The Church has not officially accepted any of them, but has tolerated some and forbidden others. Three plants — the shamrock, the pansy (viola tricolor), and, in Puerto Rico, a delicately perfumed white flower with three petals, named Trinitaria — have traditionally been seen as symbols of the Trinity.

LILY

Native to warmer regions, lilies began to appear in the gardens of Europe by the fourteenth century, and soon were symbolically associated with the purity of Mary, St. Joseph, and other saints.

In early paintings of the Annunciation, St. Gabriel originally carried a scepter or a spray of olive leaves; later, the lily replaced these in artistic representations of the occasion, as the white of the *Lilium candidum* (Madonna lily) came to symbolize the Virgin's purity. Even today, this flower is traditionally used in Europe in the celebrations of the Visitation.

Lilies are also blessed on the Feast of St. Anthony of Padua. As part of the ritual blessing, the priest prays:

> You [God] in your great kindness have given them to man, and endowed them with a sweet fragrance to lighten the burden of the sick. Therefore, let them be filled with such power that whether they are used by the sick, or kept in homes or other places, or devoutly carried on one's person, they may serve to drive out evil spirits, safeguard holy chastity, and turn away illness … all this through the prayers of St. Anthony … and finally impart to your servants grace and peace through Christ our Lord.

St. Joseph is often represented in art holding lilies, to symbolize the blooming branch he took to the temple; also, to symbolize his purity and virtue.

LILY OF THE VALLEY

This plant is not only a flower, but also one of the titles for Christ.

Anna Maria Taigi, a housewife, mother, and mystic now counted among the Beati of the Church, was in church one day when Our Lord appeared to her in the Eucharist. She saw within the Host a beautiful lily in full bloom. Upon this flower, as though it were a throne, appeared the Lord in supernatural beauty. While admiring this vision, she heard a voice saying, "I am the flower of the field, the lily of the valley."

St. Francis of Assisi gave orders to the brother gardener not to plant the entire garden in pot herbs (useful herbs and food), but to leave part to produce flowers "for the love of Him Who is called the flower of the field and the lily of the valley."

Another name for the Lily of the Valley is "Mary's tears." It was a popular flower for the garlands used on Whitsunday in England.

YEW

The yew, an ancient symbol of death, is often found in European churchyards, especially in the South of England. In Ireland, the yew was used as a substitute for palms on Passion Sunday.

ST. BENEDICT'S HERB

St. Benedict's herb, Avens (*Geum urbanum*), is also known as city avens, colewort, clove root, goldy star, herb bennet, way bennet, and wild rye. It was called the "blessed herb" in the Middle Ages, when it was worn as an amulet believed to stave off evil spirits.

A publication on herbals in 1491 states that "where the root is in the house, Satan can do nothing and flees." The name "St. Benedict's herb" comes from the legend that an evil monk once presented the saint with a goblet of poisoned wine, the saint blessed the wine, and the goblet shattered. In medieval times, the plant's graceful trefoil leaves and the five petals of its yellow bloom symbolized the Holy Trinity and the five wounds of Our Lord.

OLIVE

Branches from the olive tree have traditionally been used as a symbol of peace. A plant grown prolifically in the Holy Land, its wood is often used in making crosses, holy images, and other sacramentals.

ST. PETER'S PLANT

This name is given to any flower or herb traditionally associated with St. Peter, including *primula hirsuta*, which was used as a medicinal tea, especially as a remedy for snake or dog bite.

WREATH

Originally a common symbol of victory, the Church adopted wreaths early for popular use.

Circular wreaths, woven of flowers and greenery, have been popular since pre-Christian times. Wreaths of bay laurel were awarded to the victors in the Olympic Games and to heroes returning from war, and are still today known as a symbol for victory.

A number of pagan groups, especially the worshipers of Baal, used wreaths of marsh marigold to ward off evil spirits. Then, during the Middle Ages, the plant was "Christianized" and dedicated to the Virgin.

In Poland, young girls carried large wreaths made of the recently harvested rye or wheat, intertwined with poppies and bachelor button, for the annual *Dozynki,* or harvest walk and celebration. The fruit of the orchard — plums, apples, and pears — was tied to the wreaths with yellow, red, blue, and purple ribbons.

In France and many sections of central Europe, the Feast of Corpus Christi was known as the Day of Wreaths. Huge bouquets of flowers were borne on the top of wooden poles, and wreaths and bouquets of exquisite flowers in various colors were attached to flags and banners, houses, and green arches that spanned the streets. The men wore small wreaths on their left arms in the processions, and the girls wore them on their heads. The monstrance containing the Blessed Sacrament was adorned with a wreath of choice flowers. In Poland, the wreaths were blessed on the eve of the feast. After the feast, the people took them home. These wreaths were then hung on the walls, windows, and doors of the houses, and were put up on poles in the gardens, fields, and pastures with a prayer for protection and blessing upon the growing harvest. Evergreen wreaths, of course, are common at Christmas, and solemn wreaths are part of the funeral customs of many countries.

COCKLESHELL

The humble cockleshell is a symbol of a successful pilgrimage to St. James's shrine in Compostela, Spain. Traditionally, pilgrims walk to the nearby coast and pick up a shell as a memento. Some wear the shell on their coat or hat. The symbol became recognized as a symbol denoting a pilgrim and, today, is often used in Christian iconography.

Cockleshell

MISCELLANEOUS SACRAMENTALS

CANDLES

Candles have been used from classical times in worship and in rites for the dead. Like other items that became sacramentals for Christians, candles have a history that is secular or pagan in origin. Carrying tapers was one sign of respect for the high dignitaries of the Roman empire. The Church, from a very early period, took them into her service to enhance the splendor of religious ceremonials. These early candles were any kind of taper in which a wick, often made of a strip of papyrus, was encased in animal fat or wax.

Baptismal Candle

The use of a multitude of candles and lamps was a prominent feature of the celebration of the Easter vigil, which dates almost from apostolic times. Their use was not confined to the hours when artificial light was necessary. St. Jerome, about the end of the third century, declared that candles were lit at the reading of the Gospel not to put darkness to flight but as a sign of joy. The great Paschal candle represents Christ the true Light, and the smaller candles represent the Christians who strive to reproduce the light of Christ in their lives.

Besides their use at baptism and funerals, candles were used in a number of other ways. They were constantly used in the

Roman Ceremonial from the seventh century, and probably earlier. The candles were placed on the floor of the sanctuary and it was not until later that they were placed on the altar. Exactly when candles were moved to the altar has not been pinpointed, but the practice was well established by the twelfth century. Rubrics prescribe the number and use of candles for all Masses and other ceremonies.

The candles used for liturgical purposes are primarily made of beeswax. Historically the idea of the supposed virginity of bees was insisted on, and the wax thus was regarded as typifying in a most appropriate way the flesh of Jesus Christ born of a virgin mother. As a rule, liturgical candles are white, although some are made of unbleached wax and gilt, and paint may be added under some circumstances. It is fitting that these candles should be blessed, but that is not a regulation.

An elaborate blessing was performed on the Feast of the Purification, Candlemas Day, which was followed by a distribution of candles and a procession. When the Pope was resident and performed the blessing, a number of the candles were thrown to the crowd and some were sent as special presents to persons of note.

The first historical description of the feast of the Purification is given about 390, when the feast was held in Jerusalem. From here, it spread into the other churches of the Orient. It first appears in the liturgical books of the Western Church in the seventh century. Pope Sergius I (701) first prescribed the procession with candles for this feast and for the other three feasts of Mary then celebrated in Rome. The ceremony of blessing for the candles originated at the end of the eighth century in the Carolingian Empire, as did most of the other liturgical blessings.

Candles were and are commonly used to burn before shrines toward which the faithful wish to show a special devotion. The candles burning their life out in front of a statue are symbolic of prayer and sacrifice. The custom may have begun with the practice of

Distribution of candles by the Pope

burning lights at the tombs of the martyrs in the catacombs. Here, lights were kept burning for lengths of time as a sign of unity with the Christians who remained on earth. The candles kept a silent vigil before the graves, and thus came to be known as vigil lights. One curious medieval practice was to offer a candle or candles equal in height to the person for whom some favor was asked. This was called "measuring to" such and such a saint. This practice can be traced from the time of St. Radegund (d. 587) through the Middle Ages. It was especially common in England and the north of France in the twelfth and thirteenth centuries.

In the past, candles were required on the altar for the solemn recitation of the Divine Office, for the celebration of Mass, and for other services. Candles were lit in ritual order to show reverence for the crucifix or tabernacle. At Benediction, twelve candles were lit. During ordination to the priesthood, the candidate used to present a candle to the bishop. Candles are also used during the dedication of a church, at the blessing of a baptismal font, at the churching of a new mother, at the singing of the Gospel, and during liturgical processions, among other occasions. During medieval times, after a sentence of excommunication was read, a bell tolled while the ritual book was closed, and a lighted candle was thrown to the ground to indicate the person's fall from grace. Today candles are principally used on or near the altar for the celebration of Mass.

Before Mass on February 2, candles are blessed in the church. Wearing a purple stole, the celebrant blesses the candles with prayers, sprinkles them with holy water, and incenses them before distributing them to the clergy and people as the *Nunc Dimittis* is being sung. Then a procession is formed with lighted candles and antiphons sung.

In many Latin countries, the image of the child Jesus is taken from the Christmas crib and dressed in new clothes. It is taken to church on this day to be blessed by the priest and will be seated in a little chair on the family altar during the coming year.

On the Feast of St. Blaise, the throat of the person to be blessed is centered between two crossed white candles while the person stands or kneels before the altar. The priest prays, "May God deliver you from trouble of the throat and from every other evil through the intercession of St. Blaise, bishop and martyr."

In many cultures, the candles used at Baptism are decorated. After the ceremony, they are taken home and kept as a sacramental. In some parts of Eastern Europe, this candle was placed in the hands of the dead before burial.

We are most familiar with the term "hearse" in its death-related aspect. However, it is also a type of candelabrum that has been used since the seventh century for the Holy Week service of Tenebrae, during which the candles are extinguished ceremonially, one by one. Historically, this "hearse" is a triangular candlestick, which holds seven to 24 candles of unbleached wax. The usual number now, where Tenebrae has been revived (as it fell into disuse after Vatican Council II), is fifteen. The triangle itself represents the Blessed Trinity. The highest candle represents Christ, and the rest of the candles represent the twelve Apostles.

OILS

The use of oil for anointing far antedates Christianity. Historically, from the Hebrews to the primitive Church, it has stood for strength, sweetness, and spiritual activity. Pure olive oil is used for the Oil of Catechumens and of the Sick, and is an ingredient of holy Chrism. Olive oil is the prescribed oil for burning in sanctuary lamps, but other — preferably vegetable — oils may be substituted.

The Mass of the Chrism is solemnly celebrated in every cathedral on Holy Thursday. During this Mass, the bishop blesses the Oil of Catechumens and the Oil of the Sick, and consecrates the Chrism.

The Oil of Catechumens is used in the anointing prior to Baptism.

The Oil of the Sick is used in sacramental anointings of the sick. The use of this oil is based on the injunction of St. James in his epistle: "Is any among you sick? Let him call for the elders of the church, and let them pray over him, anointing him with oil in the name of the Lord to heal him. And the prayer of faith will save the sick man, and the Lord will raise him up; and if he has committed sins, he will be forgiven" (Jas. 5:14-15).

Chrism is a mixture of olive oil and balm (balsam). It is used in administering Baptism, Confirmation, Holy Orders, and in the consecration of churches. Anointing with chrism signifies the fullness and diffusion of grace. In the East, the consecration of the Chrism is a symbol of patriarchal authority. There, other ingredients including ginger, wine, and rose water are added.

Oil of the Saints is oil or other liquid that has exuded from the relics of certain saints, oil which has been poured over the relics of certain saints and collected as a sacramental, or oil blessed in honor of a certain saint. This oil is used for anointing, with prayer for the intercession of the saint and faith in God, for health of the soul and body.

Oil of St. Thérèse *(in container, lower right)*

The word "manna" is often used in place of the word "oil" when describing the liquids that exude from the relics of some saints. Possibly this is due to the fact that the formation of this oil is as mysterious as was the formation of the manna supplied to the Israelites during their wandering in the wilderness in Old Testament times. The oil that has been observed originating from the relics of saints generally takes the form of a colorless, odorless, tasteless fluid and has occurred in different countries with various atmospheric conditions and circumstances.

Three major saints with whose relics this phenomenon is associated are *St. Andrew,* who died in the first century; *St. Nicholas,* who died in the fourth; and *St. Walburga,* who died in the eighth. Medical science cannot explain why their bones secrete a liquid which collects even at times that would seem unfavorable for the formation of *any* liquid.

The relics of *St. Gerard Majella* exuded a fluid for a time, although this has not continued to the present, and the first miracle accepted for his beatification involved the cure of a dying man who applied this mysterious oil and was restored to complete health. Other saints whose relics or bodies gave off a fluid include *St. Agnes of Montepulciano, St. Camillus de Lellis, St. Paschal Baylon, St. Julia Billiart, St. Mary Magdalene dei Pazzi, Venerable Mother Maria of Jesus, Blessed Matthia Nazzarei of Matelica,* and, in our own times, *St. Sharbel Makhlouf.*

St. Sharbel died in 1898. After four months of observing a bright light over his grave, the monks he had lived with asked permission to exhume the body; it was found perfectly incorrupt. But a mysterious fluid appeared to be coming from the body, out of the pores, which seemed to be a mixture of blood and sweat. His body was reburied in the chapel and the fluid continued to exude for over half a century, leaking through the casket and the chapel wall. At the ritual exhumation before beatification in 1965, the body had decomposed and the fluid had stopped its flow. There are numerous well-documented incidents of this phenomenon, but no natural explanation has been found for it.

From the middle of the fifth century, it was a custom to pour oil or water over the relics of martyrs and to collect this liquid as a relic called *oleum martyris.* The custom was later extended, as well, to the relics of saints who were not martyrs. St. Paulinus of Nola and St. Martin of Tours are examples of saints whose relics have been thus treated.

In the fifth and sixth centuries, the tomb of the martyr St. Menas became a popular place of pilgrimage. As a souvenir, flasks of oil and water were given to the pilgrims. The water probably came from a well near the tomb; the oil was taken from that burned in lamps before the tomb. This practice has continued as a part of the cultus of a number of saints through modem times. A special prayer for the blessing of oil in honor of St. Serapion,

Martyr, was found in the Roman Ritual. Originally this blessing had been reserved to the Order of Our Lady of Ransom.

OIL OF ST. ANNE

This is blessed oil from St. Anne's shrine, based on the ancient custom of blessing oil for the sick at various pilgrimage sites. In earlier times, pilgrims took oil from the lamps burning at the shrine, had it blessed, and brought it home for the sick.

OIL OF ST. JOHN

A traditional medieval remedy made from plants collected on the Feast of the Nativity of St. John the Baptist.

On St. John's morning, the peasants of Piedmont and Lombardy went out to search the oak leaves for the "oil of St. John" which was supposed to heal all wounds made with cutting instruments. Originally, perhaps, this oil was simply mistletoe or a decoction made from it. In the French province of Bourbonnais, a popular remedy for epilepsy was a decoction of mistletoe that had been gathered on an oak on St. John's Day and boiled with rye flour.

AGNUS DEI (LAMB OF GOD)

"Lamb of God, who takes away the sin of the world, have mercy on us" (cf. Jn. 1:29).

In addition to the words spoken by St. John the Baptist to Our Lord, repeated as an invocation before communion in the Mass, *Agnus Dei* (Latin for "Lamb of God") is also the name of one of the oldest sacramentals of the Church. It is a small disc of wax stamped with a lamb, representing Our Lord as victim. Sometimes, the lamb is shown with a halo and cross or pennon (streamer). The wax is taken from Paschal candles or candles blessed by the Pope on Candlemas Day.

The *Agnus Deis* originated from the custom of using bits of the Paschal candle as articles of devotion. These sacramentals are often encased in silk or leather to protect the image and are often ornately embellished with embroidery, lace, or other fancy stitchery. They were generally made in convents. The Pope solemnly blessed them on the Wednesday of Holy Week in the first, and every subsequent seventh, year of his reign; the prayers included references to the dangers of fire, flood, storm, plague, and childbirth. When the discs of wax were brought to the Pope, he dipped them into a vessel of water

Agnus Dei

mixed with chrism and balsam while he recited the consecratory prayers. The distribution of the *Agnus Deis* took place on Easter Saturday when the Pope, after the *Agnus Dei* of the Mass, put a packet of the sacramentals into the inverted miter of each cardinal and bishop who came up to receive them.

This sacramental is sometimes worn about the neck, much as we would wear a medal, and is used as a reminder to seek God's protection in trouble. As in the case of the Paschal candle, the wax of the *Agnus Dei* symbolizes the virgin flesh of Christ; the cross, associated with the lamb, suggests the idea of the victim offered in sacrifice. As the blood of the paschal lamb of the Old Testament protected each household from the destroying angel, the purpose of these sacramentals is to protect those who use them from all malign influences. The efficacy of this sacramental is not, of course, from the wax, the balsam, or the chrism; the efficacy of the *Agnus Dei* is from the blessing of the Church and the merits of the "Lamb of God, who takes away the sins of the world."

VIA MATRIS (THE WAY OF THE SORROWFUL MOTHER)

In 1233, Our Blessed Lady appeared to seven noblemen of Florence and instructed them to establish a religious order, which would preach her sorrows to the world. In another apparition, she gave them instructions for a habit, a rule, and a name — Servants of Mary. The order became the last of the five mendicant orders of the Church.

The seven saints retreated to Monte Senario and built the first monastery of the new order. From here began a wave of devotion to Our Mother of Sorrows that spread throughout the civilized world. The *Via Matris* is among the many devotions that grew out of the fervent preaching of the Servites. One historical study indicates that the devotion existed as early as the fourteenth century in Flanders.

The stations of the *Via Matris* are as follows:

1. The Prophecy of Simeon

Simeon blessed them, and said to Mary his mother, "Behold, this child is set for the fall and the rising of many in Israel, and for a sign that is spoken against (and a sword will pierce through your own soul also), that thoughts out of many hearts may be revealed" (Lk. 2:34-35).

2. The Flight Into Egypt

Now when they [the wise men] had departed, behold, an angel of the Lord appeared to Joseph in a dream and said, "Rise, take the Child and His mother, and flee to Egypt, and remain there till I tell you; for Herod is about to search for the child, to destroy him." And he rose and took the child and his mother by night, and departed to Egypt, and remained there until the death of Herod (Mt. 2:13- 14).

---

3. The Loss of Jesus in the Temple

And when the feast was ended, as they were returning, the boy Jesus stayed behind in Jerusalem. His parents did not know it, but supposing him to be in the company they went a day's journey, and they sought him among their kinsfolk and acquaintance; and when they did not find him, they returned to Jerusalem, seeking him (Lk. 2:43-45).

4. Mary Meets Jesus on the Way to Calvary

And there followed him a great multitude of the people, and of women who bewailed and lamented him (Lk. 23:27).

5. Jesus Dies on the Cross

But standing by the cross of Jesus were his mother, and his mother's sister . . . When Jesus saw his mother, and the disciple whom he loved standing near, he said to his mother, "Woman, behold, your son." Then he said to the disciple, "Behold your mother" (Jn. 19:25-27).

6. Mary Receives the Dead Body of Jesus in Her Arms

Joseph of Arimathea, a respected member of the council . . . took courage and went to Pilate, and asked for the body of Jesus . . . and he bought a linen shroud, and taking him down, wrapped him in the linen shroud (Mk. 15:43-46).

7. Jesus Is Laid in the Tomb

Now in the place where he was crucified there was a garden, and in the garden a new tomb where no one had ever been laid. So because of the Jewish day of Preparation, as the tomb was close at hand, they laid Jesus there (Jn. 19:41-42).

Patterned on the Stations of the Cross, the *Via Matris* is a set of seven stations commemorating the seven sorrows of Our Lady. The stations are canonically erected in churches; although the blessing and erection of these stations used to be reserved to the Servite Order, since Vatican II any priest may perform the ritual. Pope Gregory XVI first indulgenced them.

NOVENAS

A "novena" is a prayer extended over a period of nine days, and said for some special petition. The word comes from the Latin word *novenus,* meaning a set of nine. Various reasons have been advanced for the choice of nine days, but basically the custom seems to have been taken over from Roman paganism. Originally, the novena was made for the repose of the soul of a dead person, and the term "novena" is still used for the series of Masses said after the death of a pope.

The first novena of the Church took place when the Apostles and disciples, along with our Blessed Lady, awaited the coming of the Holy Spirit. After the Ascension, the Apostles, Mary, and the disciples — men and women numbering about 120 persons —gathered in the Cenacle, the upper room in Jerusalem where the Last Supper had taken place. There they spent the time in prayer, awaiting the fulfillment of the Lord's promise: "Stay in the city, until you are clothed with power from on high" (Lk. 24:49).

Following the example of the Apostles, the faithful make novenas directly to God or to Him through one of the saints to obtain spiritual or temporal favors. Any suitable prayers may be used in making a novena, but it is preferable to hear Mass and receive Holy Communion daily as practices of the novena.

Public novenas are made in churches, often in preparation for a specific feast. Other elements of the novena services may include the Stations of the Cross or the *Via Matris;* litanies, hymns, and the novena prayers may be followed by Benediction. A perpetual novena is one held regularly on the same day, such as every Friday, in a church, like the popular novena to Our Lady of Perpetual Help. Attending the devotions nine times consecutively constitutes a novena. Novenas may be made privately by individuals also.

Many beautiful novena services have been composed through the years. Saints have composed some; at least one, that of the Queen of the Holy Rosary, was begun at the direction of Our Lady in a vision.

QUINCEAÑERA

The *Quinceañera* is a Catholic celebration familiar to those in the Southwestern United States and wherever those of Spanish descent reside. It is the traditional celebration when a young lady turns fifteen.

The service and Mass are quite beautiful. In it, the girl renews the promises made for her at baptism. The priest reminds her that she has become a woman, and is now the traditional age Our Blessed Mother was when she became the Mother of God. The girl promises to remain faithful to God and to follow His will for her life, whether as a married woman, a

At a *quince años* for twin sisters

single woman, or a religious. She asks that God's graces not be wasted in her. Then she asks Our Lady to present her offering to the Lord, and to be her model of a valiant woman, her strength, and her guide.

The girl is traditionally dressed in a long dress almost as elaborate as a wedding gown, but in her chosen colors. She wears a long lace mantilla. She has fifteen attendants representing her fif-

Quinceañera cake (*left*) and *Quinceañera* table (*right*)

teen years, and these range in age from about five years old to older girls who are usually the girl's best friends. During the ceremony, the priest blesses gifts for the girl such as a Bible, a Rosary, a cross, a medal, and the crown. The mantilla is removed, and the girl is crowned with a jeweled tiara.

After the Mass, a joyous fiesta is held, with mariachi musicians serenading the birthday girl. The refreshments are ample, including an elaborate cake. The girl celebrating her *quince años* begins the dancing by granting the first dance to her father or closest male relative. Then all, from youngest to oldest, join in the fun and festivities.

SACRED HEART AUTO EMBLEM

In 1954, Father Gregory Bezy, S.C.J., was inspired to initiate a league of "prayerful, careful, and reparative drivers." While praying in the Sacred Heart Church in Walls, Mississippi, Father Gregory recognized that thousands of people were being killed or maimed in automobile accidents yearly. He firmly believed that if he could convince people to turn the chore of driving into a prayerful activity, drivers would become more alert and avoid accidents. He also felt that driving could be a worthwhile time for people to make reparation for the lack of courtesy displayed by so many drivers on the roads.

The Sacred Heart Fathers and Brothers had been invited by the bishop to come to northern Mississippi to help in the evangelization of his diocese. The diocese was poor, and the congregation needed to support their mission work financially. Father Bezy had been appointed by the provincial superior to raise the funds needed for the missionary work, and he had already begun the Sacred Heart League and the Sacred Heart Southern Missions to solicit contributions for the work through direct mail.

To remind people that driving time could be prayer time, Father Gregory had a statue of the Sacred Heart designed which could be placed on the dashboard of cars and other vehicles. When dashboards were metal, a small magnet in the plastic statue was used to hold it in place. The statues were mailed to millions of people across the United States in an effort to get them to join the "apostolate of prayerful, careful, and reparative driving." Excess contributions collected were used to support the home-mission effort in northern Mississippi.

In the late '60s, Father Gregory and his assistant, Roger Courts, designed a symbol of the Auto League which was more appealing to post-Vatican II Catholics, a Sacred Heart dashboard medal. The medals were mailed out nationwide in an effort to continue and expand the Auto League and the other apostolic works of the Sacred Heart League and Southern Mission. As with any item that is mass-produced and widely distributed, the dashboard medal lost its popularity as had the statue. Therefore, the league currently distributes a membership key ring.

Highway death tolls have increased vastly since 1954 so, obviously, there is still a need for careful and prayerful driving. These small Sacred Heart auto emblems can and should serve as a valuable reminder to today's drivers. As in the past, excess funds collected are used in the home missions in northern Mississippi, providing health, education, and social services to thousands of residents. Additionally, the Apostolate of the Printed Word, a work of the Sacred Heart League begun in 1976, designs, publishes, and distributes religious and devotional materials to encourage and enhance the spiritual life of the recipients. These materials are distributed to friends and benefactors of the Sacred Heart League free of charge, and quantities of them are made available to bona fide ministries and institutions. Nearly two million Good News New Testaments have been distributed to date, along with other publications. This Apostolate of the Printed Word fulfills one of the main purposes of the Sacred Heart League — to promote devotion to the Sacred Heart of Jesus.

THE LITTLE SACHET (GOSPEL OF THE HOLY NAME)

"When JESUS was named — Satan was disarmed . . . He [Jesus] made me understand the glory it gives Him to celebrate His victory in those words, for they cause the demon to tremble with rage; and He promised to bless all who wear this Gospel, and

Little Sachet (Gospel of the Holy Name)

to defend them against the attacks of Satan."

Sister St. Pierre, a Nun of the Carmel in Tours France, in 1847 made known the devotion to this "little sachet" to all who came to her monastery seeking help, cures, and consolation. It consists of a leaflet on which are printed the Gospel passage from Luke which mentions the giving of the name of "Jesus" to our Savior, a picture of the Christ Jesus, the initials I.H.S., and some invocations to inspire confidence, together with the line "When Jesus was named, Satan was disarmed." The leaflet is folded into a small square, encased in a pouch, and carried or worn about the person as a reminder of the power of the Most Holy Name of Jesus.

The faithful are encouraged to recite the doxology (Glory be to the Father) five times, and say the ejaculation "Blessed be the Most Holy Name of Jesus without end" frequently, while wearing the sachet.

SPIRITUAL COMMUNION

Nothing can really compare with receiving Our Lord in Holy Communion. A spiritual communion, however, can be offered often. "To communicate spiritually . . . is extremely profitable," said St. Thérèse of Lisieux, "and afterwards you may practice inward recollection . . . for this impresses upon us a deep love of the Lord. If we prepare to receive Him, He never fails to give, and He gives in many ways that we cannot understand."

One suggested form of spiritual communion is as follows: "O Lord Jesus, since I am unable at this time to receive You in the Holy Sacrament of the Eucharist, I beg You to come spiritually into my heart in the spirit of Your holiness, in the truth of Your goodness, in the fullness of Your power, in the communion of Your mysteries, and in the perfection of Your ways. O Lord, I believe, I trust, I glorify You. I'm sorry for all my sins. O Sacrament most Holy, O Sacrament divine, all praise and all thanksgiving be every moment Thine."

MY TICKET TO HEAVEN

In 1982, Father Paul Thomas, a priest of the Altoona-Johnstown diocese (Pennsylvania), told his congregation, "I have been telling people how to get to heaven for 40 years. I am going to put it in a nutshell for you."

Father Paul then sat down and composed a meditation that begins, "Lord Jesus, Your holy will be done . . . first, last, and always. But it is Your holy will that I go to heaven when I die. Therefore, may this be my ticket to Heaven."

Father Paul then had his office girl mimeograph copies of the meditation, which he attached to his Sunday bulletin for the 300

My Ticket to Heaven Booklet

families of his parish. He never dreamed it would go outside his own congregation. A retired high school principal from a distant town attended Mass at Father Paul's parish that weekend and wrote him a letter commending him on the meditation, expressing the fact that many people needed the type of uplift that the meditation contained. Father Paul thought that perhaps he should make it available to others; accordingly, he had his local printer make five thousand copies. These were gone before he knew it, so he had them reprinted. By the early 1990s, nearly three million copies had been distributed all over the world.

Father Paul made no charge for the booklets, although many have sent donations to help in the cost of reprinting. The meditation, a straightforward presentation of the cardinal mysteries of the Christian faith, includes a number of biblical references. The booklet is not copyrighted; those who receive them have permission to reproduce them, or translate them into other languages.

The *My Ticket to Heaven* is a guide for life and a preparation for a good death. Father Paul prepared carefully for his own peaceful death; always considerate, he pre-addressed postcards to his friends and correspondents and gave them to his niece to mail after filling in the date of his death. These postcards — a final sermon to many of those who received them — read, in part: "I took off for home on January 6, 2002. A tiny prayer by you could help to make my flight non-stop. . . . I will be waiting for you."

Father Paul wanted his apostolate to continue after his death, so he had sought for, and found, a man in Kentucky who agreed to continue publishing the Tickets. The man — who prefers to remain anonymous — is simply known as "the publisher," and continues to distribute the Tickets at no charge, asking only for a self-addressed stamped envelope to hold down postage costs.

THIRTEEN COINS (*LAS ARRAS*)

Thirteen coins, known as *Las Arras*, are a traditional keepsake in a Mexican-American wedding. The groom presents the bride with the coins as a symbol of giving her everything he has and vowing to support her.

ST. JOSEPH'S ALTAR

St. Joseph's Altar

Sicilian immigrants brought the custom of St. Joseph's Altar to the United States. The custom is prevalent in America today wherever there are Italian-Americans.

The St. Joseph Altar originated in a region of Sicily many centuries ago, during a period of drought and famine. The people turned to St. Joseph, asking his help and intercession. Rains came, and their crops prospered. In thanksgiving, the community brought their prized food as an offering to their patron.

Originally, the tables or altars were family affairs, but as the Italian-American population grew, the celebrations became more public. Today, the altar is generally large, with three levels to represent the Holy Trinity. The statue of St. Joseph is given the most prominent place, although representations of the Holy Family and the Blessed Virgin are often also displayed. The altar is draped in white and adorned with flowers. The finest grains, fruits, vegetables, seafood, and wine are prepared, and all are invited to share in the prayers and festivity.

Reasons for erecting St. Joseph's Altars vary. For many, it is to fulfill a promise or give thanks for a favor. For others, the altar is a petition. For all, it is an opportunity to share with those less fortunate. Preparations begin weeks in advance of the feast, and much hard work is involved in this labor of love. Many hours are spent making the elaborate loaves of bread, cakes, and cookies that adorn the altar. Many of these are symbolic: shapes include the crown of thorns, hearts symbolizing the Sacred Hearts of Jesus and Mary, the cross, the chalice, a monstrance, St. Joseph's staff, fish, birds, flowers, and many more.

The meals served for the St. Joseph altar include fruits, vegetables, seafood, and pasta dishes. Often, children are dressed as members of the Holy Family, sometimes with angels or favorite saints accompanying them. The children are served first with a portion of each of the delicacies from the altar. This ritual is solemnly observed and accompanied by prayer and hymns. Guests are invited to dine after the "Holy Family" members have completed their meal.

Originally, in Sicily, the families would go out to the poor in the community and bring them into their houses. The master of the house and his family would bathe the feet of the poor, just as Christ had done to his disciples before the Last Supper. Then the visitors would be seated at the table. The poor would be served first, after which the family and invited guests would eat. At the end of the feast, the remains would be gathered and distributed to the poor.

When the Sicilian immigrants reached the United States, however, most could speak no English and felt awkward about choosing people who did not understand the language or their custom. Consequently, they selected children of the family and friends to represent the Holy Family or Christ and his Apostles. Instead of the foot-washing ceremony, the children would stand on benches or chairs and those present would kiss their hands and feet as an act of humility. Afterward, the host, his family, and friends would carry baskets of food to those in need.

St. Joseph's Altars often feature a bowl of green fava beans, from which guests take home a "lucky bean." This custom stems from one of the famines in Sicily. At that time, the fava bean was used as cattle fodder. In order to survive, the farmers cooked and ate them. Today, fava beans are considered a delicacy and used in numerous recipes. When dried, and blessed, it is used as a sacramental. An old Sicilian saying is that if you carry a blessed fava bean in your purse, your purse will never be empty. (And, of course, it is not. It always contains at least the bean.)

Another custom prevalent among Italian-Americans is to save blessed bread from the St. Joseph's Altar as a sacramental.

The saint is invoked in cases of danger from storms. Some people keep pieces of it in their cars to protect against harm from collisions.

St. Joseph's Bread *(foreground)*

ST. JOSEPH REALTY KIT

Traditionally, many of the faithful seek St. Joseph's intercession when buying or selling property. St. Joseph's role in selling real estate may have arisen from his being patron saint of carpenters, although the exact origin of this custom is clouded in history. Although the custom borders on superstition, many persons with true devotion to the saint have acted in good faith to request his aid.

- St. Brother André of Montreal appealed to St. Joseph repeatedly in matters of property.
- Herbert Cardinal Vaughn, Archbishop of Westminster, London, was trying to purchase property to begin his new religious community, the Millhill Josephites. Having been refused by the owner of the desired property, the cardinal asked the owner to keep a package for him and put it in a closet under the staircase. The owner complied with the request, little knowing the package contained a statue of St. Joseph. Soon after, the owner changed his mind and sold the property to the cardinal.
- Dorothy Day is another who had a great devotion to St. Joseph, and who asked his help in obtaining property. She buried a medal of the saint on the land she wished to acquire. No doubt from this tradition has come the popular, if somewhat bizarre, custom in the United States of burying a statue of St. Joseph in order to sell real estate. Religious goods stores all across the U.S. report high sales of inexpensive statues of the saint, which people then bury in the backyard — sometimes upside down — and pray for a speedy and successful sale of their property.

ST. TERESA'S BOOKMARK

The great Carmelite reformer and mystic, Teresa de Ahumada y Cepeda (1515-1582) (Teresa of Ávila), was known for her charming wit and common sense as much as for her mystical experiences. Teresa's spiritual maturity was recognized as her books and letters became known; today, her works are regarded as classics of spiritual literature. She combined a life of mystical contemplation with one of dazzling activity.

Teresa died in 1582 and was canonized in 1622 by Pope Gregory XV. She was declared a Doctor of the Church in 1970. Her feast day is October 15.

One of her maxims, commonly known as St. Teresa's Bookmark, reads:

Let nothing trouble you, let nothing frighten you.
All things are passing; God never changes.
Patience obtains all things.
He who possesses God lacks nothing: God alone suffices.

UMBRELLAS

The word "umbrella" is derived from the Latin word *umbra*, which means "shade." The first umbrellas were for protection from the sun and were possibly inspired from the canopy of a tree, which would offer a cool shade from the heat of the day. Umbrellas probably originated in China about the eleventh century B.C., although ancient sculptures from Neneveh, Persepolis, and Thebes have been found depicting their use, and evidence also indicates ancient use in India. These early forms of umbrella were probably a converted branch or leaf from a tree, or a hat on a stick.

The word "parasol" comes from the Latin words *papare* (to prepare), and *sol* (sun). Today we tend to use the word "parasol" for protection against the sun, and "umbrella" for that against rain. The original difference in terms was that the person *being* shaded carried an umbrella, while *others* would carry the parasol for him or her.

The first umbrellas (or, more correctly, parasols) were associated with rank and status. They were used in early pagan religious practice. The Coptic Church traditionally used parasols in some of their ceremonies, and continues to do so today.

The parasol or umbrella can symbolize the vault of heaven. In its symbolic and protective role, the umbrella can be compared to the *baldachin* (canopy) in many of its forms.

During the Middle Ages, an umbrella was used in ceremonial regalia for the pope. The custom may have originated from a parasol given to Pope Sylvester I by Constantine.

The striped canopy of an umbrella depicting the papal colors of red and gold, above the crossed keys of St. Peter, was once used on a papal badge. Known as an *ombrellino*, it is still worn by the *Cardinal Camerlengo* as acting head of the Catholic Church during an interregnum in the papacy.

Christians in India celebrate their festivals broadly on the pattern adopted worldwide. However some influence of local Indian tradition is evident among Syrian Christians, who use elephants, umbrellas, and traditional music as accessories to their festivities and celebrations.

JESSE TREE

This "tree" is actually a representation of the genealogy of Jesus Christ. Original images of it feature a reclining figure of Jesse from whose loins emerge a great trunk with branches holding figures of his royal descendants. The tree culminates with the figures of Mary and Jesus, frequently represented in a flower or bud.

More recently, it is a family Advent custom of decorating a Christmas tree with ornaments or objects representing Old Testament events from creation to the birth of Jesus. The Jesse Tree

The Jesse Tree and Advent symbols

Our Sunday Visitor art by Kevin Davidson

gets its name from the Book of Isaiah: "There shall come forth a shoot from the stump of Jesse, and a branch shall grow out of his roots" (11:1).

MILAGROS

The word is from the Spanish for "miracles."

Milagros are small metal images of hearts, people, animals, and body parts that are used as *ex voto* offerings in Hispanic countries. They are hung on the images of the saints in thanksgiving for favors. These are also known as *promesas* (promises).

Various *Milagros*

CONCLUSION —
THE SACRAMENTAL LIFE

When people enter your home today, do they know it is a Catholic home?

As Archbishop Miller so beautifully explained in the introduction to this book, sacramentals resemble the sacraments, but were instituted by the Church and can help prepare us to receive grace. These outward signs are beneficial to us who live with them, as well as those who visit, and truly express our incarnational-bodily Christianity.

From ancient times, the Church has pronounced her blessings over men and women, their activities, and the objects they use in everyday life. Our sacramentals are visible signs to remind us that God blesses every dimension of our life; used wisely, they enable us to experience the world through Catholic eyes and with a Catholic heart. As the great saint of Assisi, Francis Bernardone, reminded us, *all creation speaks to us of God*. Material objects and blessings enfold and permeate Catholic life as reminders of the mysteries of creation and redemption.

Children, especially, need these physical reminders of our loving and living God. With the proper use of sacramentals, our homes can have more than a "Better Homes and Gardens" look. They can have an atmosphere that encourages a truly better home, one where God is part of the family every day of the week, instead of only on Sunday.

The variety of sacramentals is endless and changing — for example, the Luminous Mysteries of the Rosary were unheard of when the first edition of this book was published. So, if you have a favorite sacramental that was not in this book, or if you have questions regarding a sacramental you may have found, you are welcome to write to us in care of Our Sunday Visitor.

This sharing of additional information on sacramentals keeps us from error as well. With the addition of new sacramentals and the renewal of attention to some of the old ones, sometimes the manner of manufacture or repair can result in confusion. One reader questioned a Rosary belonging to his grandmother, which had two decades of five beads each and three decades with ten beads. However, this was a result of his thrifty ancestor's having broken her standard Rosary and lost part of the beads — not a new form of chaplet!

Another example is the existence of at least two chaplets honoring the Holy Wounds. The one proposed by Sister Mary Margaret Chambon uses the beads of a standard Rosary, while the Passionists' version uses special beads interspersed with medals of the wounds. And yet today, in many Catholic stores, you can buy a chaplet of the Holy Wounds that is actually made like the Passionist one, yet attributed to Sister Mary Margaret.

But even if the proliferation of sacramentals can be confusing at times, we as Catholics are still fortunate: we can use sacramentals to "throw a net of blessings" over every dimension of our lives. Their proper use can help us to restore all things in Christ, providing for us a special touch of faith and drawing us ever closer to Our Creator.

INDEX